Wild Democracy

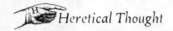 Heretical Thought

HERETICAL THOUGHT

Series editor: Ruth O'Brien,
The Graduate Center, City University of New York

Wild Democracy

Anarchy, Courage, and Ruling the Law

ANNE NORTON

OXFORD
UNIVERSITY PRESS

OXFORD
UNIVERSITY PRESS

Oxford University Press is a department of the University of Oxford. It furthers
the University's objective of excellence in research, scholarship, and education
by publishing worldwide. Oxford is a registered trade mark of Oxford University
Press in the UK and certain other countries.

Published in the United States of America by Oxford University Press
198 Madison Avenue, New York, NY 10016, United States of America.

© Oxford University Press 2023

Library of Congress Control Number: 2022919036

ISBN 978-0-19-764434-8

DOI: 10.1093/oso/9780197644348.001.0001

1 3 5 7 9 8 6 4 2

Printed by Sheridan Books, Inc., United States of America

Contents

Forward

There are times when a book has to be written with a precision that can be achieved only in a technical or scholarly language. This is not that time. This is not that book. I make no distinction between the writings of scholars or the writings of rebels, the writings of statesmen or the writings of dissidents. I go through terrain that is not enclosed, that remains a commons open to all. This is the democratic wild: unfenced, unconfined, untamed.

If we are to rule ourselves, this must be our terrain. We need to seek anarchy. We need to find courage. We need to rule the law.

Anarchy is the nursery and the refuge of the democratic. In anarchy, one is neither ruler nor ruled. Here people learn to rule themselves. Here there is, if only for a moment, in a small space, no one to order or to serve. Here people learn to provide for themselves. They learn to work together. Anarchy is not the rejection of politics, solidarity, or cooperation; it is the rejection of any ruler but oneself. Where no one orders and no one serves, people grow strong. They learn the courage to face what they must. They win the daring to do what they can.

Courage is the virtue of the democratic. People begin to rule when they find the courage to think things could be otherwise. They find the courage to speak freely. Courage fires their uprisings and revolutions. These fires can fail, but they can be made to burn again. Courage maintains the work of revolutions. Courage enables people to rule themselves in great things and in small ones. People who rule themselves are steadfast. They face constant uncertainty with equanimity. They learn when to change and when to endure. They learn to walk among their enemies unafraid.

Law is ours to judge, to break, to make, to uphold, and to bring down. If we are citizens, we are ruled by law, but we rule law as law's sovereign. If we are democrats, we are law's rulers. If we are courageous, anarchic, and free, we rule ourselves. People ruling themselves are people unleashed.

Democracy grows wild, sprouting in the cracks of a parking lot, stretching across the marshes to the sea. The democratic shows itself in expansive ambitions and small practices, under the constraints of law and order and in those anarchic spaces where people are neither rulers nor ruled. In this wild, anarchic to the root, rights too come out of the ground. They are born in our flesh, carried in our bodies from birth to death, grounded in the word and flesh of a human life.

There were dark times when I began this book. They grew darker. Now, as my writing draws to a close, I see the lights in the darkness. Perhaps they will blaze like a prairie fire. Perhaps we will need to stir the ashes once again.

THESES FOR DEMOCRATS

I

Anarchy, courage, democracy

1. Anarchy is the shadow and salvation of democracy. Authoritarianism is democracy's enemy.

People defend repression by declaring that to oppose it would lead to anarchy, a chaos so profound that a decent life cannot be lived within it. The fear of anarchy fills politics and philosophy. Yet for something that is so often threatened, anarchy is remarkably hard to find. Politicians and media commentators point to "anarchy," but the places they point to are not anarchic at all. Those supposedly anarchic situations have warlords and bosses. They are riven by feuds among the ambitious. They are chaotic, but this is not anarchy; there is not an absence of rule, there is too much.

If anarchy is hard to find, authoritarianism is difficult to escape. Long ago a prophet told a people who asked for a king:

> This will be the practice of the king who will rule over you. He will take your sons and appoint them as his charioteers and horsemen, and they will serve as outrunners for his chariots. He will appoint them as his chiefs of thousands, and of fifties; or they will have to plow his fields, reap his harvest, and make his weapons and the equipment for his chariots. He will take your daughters as perfumers, cooks, and bakers. He will seize your choice fields, vineyards, and olive groves, and give them to his courtiers. He will take a tenth part of your grain and vintage and give it to his eunuchs and courtiers. He will take your male and female slaves, and your choice young men, and your asses, and put them to work for him. He will take a tenth part of your flocks and you shall become his slaves. The day will come when you cry out because of the king whom you yourselves have chosen; and the Lord will not answer you on that day. (Nevi'im I Samuel 9:11)

Wild Democracy. Anne Norton, Oxford University Press. © Oxford University Press 2023.
DOI: 10.1093/oso/9780197644348.003.0001

We are still fools enough to tell children stories of good kings. Authoritarianism still holds an allure for the fearful.

Every historical epoch gives us its autocrats as evidence. There are the autocrats most often marked as evil: Caligula and Hitler, Ivan the Terrible and Vlad the Impaler, Stalin and Hitler, Idi Amin and Pol Pot. There are the autocrats foolish people praise: Alexander ("the Great"), Alfred ("the Great"), Richard ("the Lion-hearted"), Cæsar and Justinian, Peter ("the Great"), Catherine ("the Great"), and Napoléon. There are those who divide people: Luther, Cromwell, Mao, Nasser, and Perón. There are, moreover, always those ambitious for authority—unconstrained authority—in the present. Abraham Lincoln, who knew he carried such ambitions himself, thought that the more firmly established, the more accepted, democratic institutions were, the more ambitious men would be tempted to overcome them.

> Many great and good men sufficiently qualified for any task they should undertake, may ever be found, whose ambition would aspire to nothing beyond a seat in Congress, a gubernatorial or a presidential chair; but such belong not to the family of the lion, or the tribe of the eagle. What! think you these places would satisfy an Alexander, a Caesar, or a Napoleon?—Never! . . . Distinction will be his paramount object, and although he would as willingly, perhaps more so, acquire it by doing good as harm; yet, that opportunity being past, and nothing left to be done in the way of building up, he would set boldly to the task of pulling down.

It falls to the people to restrain those ambitious to be autocrats. They must "be united with each other, attached to the government and laws, and generally intelligent, to successfully frustrate his designs."[1] They must have souls great enough to see that the "family of the lion, or the tribe of the eagle" looks more like the family of the jackal and the tribe of the vulture (though those animals at least have the virtue of cleaning up after predators.) In order to do this work, the people must have the courage to oppose those they know are evil. They must have the pride, the dignity, and the sense of duty to stand against those who are called "great" and "lion-hearted."

Authoritarianism is not, however, confined to great men. We have learned, to our cost, that those most hungry for authority, most avid for power, can be very small indeed. The harm these do is twofold, for they do harm out of their ambition and harm from their stupidity.

Indeed, authoritarianism is not confined to men, great or small. The most astute critiques of modernity have recognized that the desire for an energetic and unhindered authority comes not only from those who want to rule but from those who want to be ruled. Conservative critics of liberalism note how readily people submit to systems or regimes that claim expertise or promise equality, prosperity, or protection. Weber famously saw the "iron cage" of bureaucracy imprisoning modern lives. People are hedged about by rules and regulations. We are expected to follow laws we don't know and might not understand if we did. We are embedded in systems that assess our wealth, tax obligations, debt, creditworthiness, health, probable longevity, political preferences, and a host of other things, by mystical numerology and without appeal. Critics on both the left and the right have long observed the tyranny of the "rule of experts."[2] Now we are faced with the faceless rule of algorithms.

Effective critiques of these impersonal, bureaucratic forms of totalitarianism have come from conservatives as well as democrats, socialists, and anarchists. Edmund Burke distrusted abstract principles and categories, trusting instead in tradition and custom, knowledge collected from many people over many generations. He saw that seemingly irrational customs often shelter wisdom and reason within them. He believed that conventions soften change and tame principle enough to fit it more easily into human lives. The Southern Agrarians, Wendell Berry, and others like them mourn the loss of a world closer to nature. They treasure the ties that come when generation after generation calls a place home. They have faith in the constraints that custom places on conduct.

These critics recognize popular wisdom. They have respect for the practices of ordinary people in the course of their lives. They are suspicious of those who rely on reason alone, knowing that human reason is limited by time and circumstance and distorted by interest, ambition, perspective, and desire. They recognize the coercive power of many schemes for the betterment of mankind.

Radical critics recognize that the drive of governments and governance, of states and the powers of the economic realm is toward centralization and the consolidation of power. Wendy Brown joins Sheldon Wolin in this: "[T]here is no such thing as a democratic state, since states abduct, institutionalize, and wield 'surplus power' generated by the people; democracy always lives elsewhere from the state, even in democracies."[3] If we are to be democrats, we must learn, we must practice, anarchy.

"Anarchy," Tocqueville wrote, "is not the greatest of the ills to be feared in democratic times, but the least."[4] Authoritarianism, not anarchy, is the danger that people should fear. The revolutionaries who hope to escape imperial rule, depose dictatorships, bring down monarchs and establish governments in which people rule themselves, find themselves confronting the ambitions of those who want to rule the newly or the not yet free. They will face defeat at the hands of the most ambitious among them. The revolution ends and the generals (or the colonels) take over. The revolution ends, and the leader called "the father of his country" comes to believe that it cannot continue without him. Few can refuse this temptation.

Authoritarianism is rooted in fear. Those who call for a strong hand, a firm authority, fear that things will change, that the present partial calm will not endure, that nothing is stable. They fear. Fear, as thinkers from Xenophon to Arendt have recognized, is at the heart of tyranny. The tyrant, Xenophon wrote in his dialogue "On Tyranny," is always afraid. The tyrant's fear grows, spreading until each person seems a threat: "The tyrants, all of them, proceed everywhere as through hostile territory. They themselves think it necessary to go armed and always to be surrounded by an armed bodyguard." They are never safe, Xenophon's tyrant argues, and least safe when they are at home, for "tyrants know that when they reach their own city they are then in the midst of the largest number of their enemies."[5] Every enemy the tyrant kills, every punishment the tyrant enacts creates more enemies, more reason for the tyrant to fear.

This is not, as Hannah Arendt saw, simply a pathology of dictatorship. Totalitarian regimes do the same. They see dissent in every act; they fear enemies everywhere. Everyone they kill, every punishment they exact creates more enemies, more reasons for fear. Their fear spurs them to find these enemies and prevent dissent. They resort to censorship, surveillance, and networks of informants who can, perhaps, prevent the attacks they fear, yet every piece of information they gather feeds that fear. Fear spreads, as Arendt describes, until each person fears everyone else. The apparatus of surveillance and punishment becomes total, enveloping every person within reach. Surveillance and informing become part of "a method of dealing with his neighbor which everyone, willingly or unwillingly, is forced to follow." No one is free; all are fearful. This is "a system of ubiquitous spying, where everybody may be a police agent and each individual feels himself under constant surveillance." In the end, because everyone is an enemy to everyone else, and the state has earned the enmity of all, victims are "chosen completely at random." Arendt argued that the "consistent arbitrariness" of totalitarianism "negates human freedom more efficiently than any tyranny ever could," for willingly or unwillingly, the subjects become the eyes and ears and hands of a tyrannical state.[6]

The tyrant's fear is a contagion. Fear is the enemy of democracy.

We have every reason to fear authoritarianism, whether it comes to us in the guise of a man or a state. We have little reason to fear anarchy, yet the fear of anarchy shadows democracy. Where the people rule, each person is understood to have standing and freedom. Each has the right to leave if they choose, rebel if they choose. Each person may participate, perhaps each person should, but no one can be compelled. Anarchy is not only a possibility; it is a necessity. Anyone can leave, and so it is possible that everyone might leave. Anyone can refuse, and so it is possible that everyone might refuse. That refusal, the right to say no to rule, is the guarantor of our freedom.

Anarchy is the shadow of democracy in a double sense. Fear of anarchy shadows democracy. Anarchy is not to be feared; it offers shade, a place to rest, a place to hide. The shade anarchy offers protects us. The people who are most free are often not those who govern, but those who refuse to be governed, not those who join in rule, but those who refuse to be ruled at all. In America, Patrick Henry argued, the common man did not want power, still less did he want national glory; he simply wanted to be let alone: "He enjoys the fruits of his labor, under his own fig tree, with his wife and children about him, in peace and security."[7] Jefferson famously wrote that the best government was "no government, as among our Indians," and if he misunderstood the governance of the indigenous he nevertheless saw in their lives his own desire to be governed lightly, or not at all. We should be, Whitman wrote, "men and women who think lightly of the laws."[8]

This is not an American desire. This is a human desire. James Scott's work on "how not to be governed" echoes a long tradition of people seeking an escape from power. Behind Scott one can see Eric Hobsbawm's brilliant writings on bandits and primitive rebels, and the work of that cadre of Marxist historians who brought forward the long history of rebellion and resistance in England and Scotland. Scott found the desire for an ungoverned life among Burmese peasants and mountain bandits. Hobsbawm found it in fifteenth-century England, nineteenth-century Mexico, and twentieth-century India. Christopher Hill found it in seventeenth-century England and wondered if it had fled to the Caribbean. Paul Gilroy, researching a diasporic modernity, found it crossing the Atlantic. Machiavelli wrote that while the privileged "want only to oppress, the people want only not to be oppressed." One can find the desire not to be governed in any people, at any time. The desire not to be ruled is a simple human desire. It is the first and last defense against domination.[9]

Most people, in most of their lives, want power to leave them alone. They believe that they should make their own decisions about how they live their lives, that they are the best judges of what is good for them. They know too that there are many decisions they are not able to make. The best of them—no, most of them—know what they do not know. They will have the wisdom to withdraw from decisions they are not competent to make.

If they have the wisdom to withdraw from decisions they cannot make wisely, they also have the wisdom to know the decisions only they can make. They know that they have skills and circumstances that are theirs alone. To live their lives as they think best, they need to have the freedom to cultivate their abilities, learn what they need, and act as they decide. Artists and writers are often firm in claiming that freedom. They know that strong, original, and creative work comes not only when one learns from others or is guided by others, but also when one refuses to learn, refuses to be guided. The wisdom of the community is great, but all communities need, especially in times of crisis, those who reject established knowledge and old wisdom. Politics, as much as art or learning, depends on people with independence of mind.

Any people who want to rule themselves must leave space for anarchy. People capable of ruling themselves will want the freedom to live their lives as they choose. They may choose to be ruled, lightly, and never without interruption. Anarchy is democracy's shadow in this sense as well. It gives people a space away both from ruling and from being ruled. For people living in freedom, anarchy is a familiar place. For free people facing the loss of that freedom, anarchy, not authoritarianism, should be the last ditch.

2. For anarchy we need the anarchic.

Poets, philosophers, and the people have long recognized that bandits, pirates, outlaws, and rogues are close to democracy. There are many reasons for this. For some, this is simply another way of casting the rule of the people as the madness of the crowd, the rule of the Great Unwashed, the rise of starved beasts who will fatten on the wealthy. For those who regard the rule of autocrats or elites as the natural order of things, democracy is simply a theft of power, and people who rule themselves are no more than criminals.

The popular imagination of bandit democrats sees it otherwise. Pirates and bandits are admired for what they refuse and what they choose, for the wrongs they flee and the wrongs they attempt to right. Those who steal from the rich and give to the poor are honored and admired. Those who rob the poor or con the elderly, who extort protection money or amass great wealth through dishonest means are scorned. Stories of honest bandits are shadowed by stories of the rich and disreputable. Wealth, these stories remind us, is not a sign of honor or merit. There are inequalities to be remedied. In honoring outlaws, people put the justice of the present order in question.

The bandit, the pirate, the outlaw, and the rogue are all outside law and custom. All defy order for its own sake. Some, like Robin Hood, are placed outside the law by unjust rulers. They are law's exiles. Their outlawry is a rebuke to the ruler's claim to justice. Some bandits are driven out by poverty. They are a rebuke to a country that cannot provide for its own. Other bandits, pirates, and looters defy the laws that govern property and possessions. Where law produces radical inequality, they refuse it. All refuse order for order's sake.

When pirates, bandits, and outlaws band together, like the Zapatistas, Phoolan Devi's band, or Robin Hood's Merry Men, they choose to rule themselves. They consent to rule and to be ruled. These remembered or imagined outlaws are, as Hobsbawm and Scott have argued, primitive rebels who are learning—if they have not yet mastered—"the art of not being governed."[10] They also point to a central question for all people: What is one's own? Bandits who "steal from the rich and give to the poor" demonstrate a democratic sensibility. In their rough redistribution of ill-gotten gains, they remove one of the most serious obstacles to people ruling themselves. Woody Guthrie put it this way in his ballad of the outlaw Pretty Boy Floyd:

> Many a starvin' farmer
> The same old story told
> How the outlaw paid their mortgage
> And saved their little homes
>
> . . . as through your life you travel,
> Yes, as through your life you roam,
> You won't never see an outlaw
> Drive a family from their home.[11]

Pirates too are on the way to the democratic. Pirates elected their captains for one voyage, agreed to serve under them, and retained the right to depose them when they chose. Pirates voted on missions and on the division of plunder. They also instituted social welfare programs, providing for those who were hurt or maimed or the families of those killed in battle. They included people of all races, all sexualities, "villains of all nations." Like Hobsbawm's bandits, the pirates often served, directly and indirectly, in rebellions against oppressive rule. They sailed into the unknown. They had the courage of people who consented to ruling and to being ruled, the longing not to rule at all.[12]

Outlaws deserve their name and the ambivalence attached to it. They are outside the law. Frontier outlaws are beyond law's reach; often they are political exiles or refugees whose rebellion precedes their outlawry. All outlaws, of necessity, live and work outside and often in defiance of the law. Their actions can show the limits, the fragility, or the injustice of the law. Bands of outlaws, like those of Pancho Villa, raise the possibility of other political orders, outside or against the state. Where the state is unjust, they can move easily into revolution. All outlaws put the commanding power of the law in question. They show the limits of the law's power. They show the distance between law and justice.

For Jacques Rancière, democracy belongs to the part that has no part, to the excluded. In *A Renegade History of the United States*, Thaddeus Russell "tells the story of "bad" Americans—drunkards, prostitutes, "shiftless" slaves and white slackers, criminals, juvenile delinquents, brazen homosexuals, and others who operated beneath American society—and shows how they shaped our world, created new pleasures, and expanded our freedoms."[13] This is, as Russell recognizes, an American (though not only an American) tradition. These people, the mad, the bad, the irrepressibly transgressive, mark the boundaries of sane, moral, and lawful a conduct, putting those boundaries in question. They expand dangers as well as possibilities: opening paths and setting traps. This might be, Russell declares, "history from the gutter up," but any look at American culture, at any moment, in any place, shows people ready to embrace these freedom-loving transgressors. The antiheros of every genre—videos, novels, comic books, history— testify to the importance of the rebel to the drive for freedom.

Russell departs from Rancière (or does he?) in seeing the excluded as alien to democracy. The democratic revolutions turned, he argued, from external to internal governance. People were called to discipline themselves. Russell has a keen eye for those forms of coercion that live in the mind and heart, governing conduct when government is silent— as well as those formal attempts, even (perhaps especially) by the partisans of political liberty—to regulate moral conduct. He provides a detailed account of the "renegades"and their contributions—witting and unwitting to freedom while recognizing that any world they would make "would be a living hell."[14] If we are to become democrats, we need to rule ourselves, but we do well to recognize the cost of the discipline

democracy demands of the people, and the ways in which it may de-
form us. We need to keep a space for anarchy not only in the world, but
in ourselves. Acts and practices that may seem, at first blush, to be distant from the political can be salutary political forces.

The rebels, the shiftless, and the transgressive who are suspicious of
power fuel the drive to freedom and the drive to greater justice. They
combat the excesses of those who want to govern too much. They
mock those who have the arrogance to tell others how to pray, how to
dress, what to eat, how to live. They open the possibility of other lives.
Drag queens and voguers changed how people saw and then how they
thought about sexuality, about race, about beauty, about who should be
welcomed when they appeared in the world. Once they were shocking
and outrageous. No more. Now they are ours.

These disobedient ones have served in other ways. Because they distrust power, they may protect others among the powerless. Because
they have the courage of their own judgments, they can stand fast
when rights and the just are under attack.

There is an old poem, written by a man who was a rebel himself,
about those who keep honor safe. Vachel Lindsay's willfully democratic and political poetry is out of step with my time but speaks to it
with a directness that pierces the heart:

> We slept thro' wars where Honor could not sleep
> We were faint-hearted, Honor was full-valiant
> We kept a silence Honor could not keep.
>
> Yet this late day we make a song to praise her.
> We codeless will yet vindicate her code.
> ... A battered, rascal guard will rally round her
> To keep her safe until the better years.[15]

The bandit, the outlaw, the rogue, the rascal, the battered, and the
shunned live at the very boundary of the country, in the nation but outside the state, of the people but outside the law.

When people believe the law has failed them, they may (they
should) turn to the people as a whole. They will have to ask, "Who are
my people?" They will look for guidance to the living and those yet to

be born, questioning the sins (and perhaps the achievements) of the past, reconsidering their hopes for the future. When the law fails them, they look to those the law has failed. They will look to those among the present people who live abandoned by the law, in defiance of the law, and to those the law could not reach. When the people falter, they may find their hopes sheltered in unexpected places. Honor finds a refuge where reputation is lost.

There is another appeal made here. The bandit, the outlaw, the renegade, and the antihero argue for the possibility of redemption. Flawed people, people who have done wrong, committed sins against god and man, done acts of cruelty and failed, over and over again, to be good, can still find their place. The antihero speaks to those who believe they have done wrong—that is to say, most of us, for there are few among us who have no regrets. These stories show a path. People see that they can overcome their past, their errors, their shortcomings. They can learn to rule themselves.

The outcast and the exile, the shunned and the rejected have a place among the people. In this respect, as in many others, the rule of the people seems to be well understood among the religious (though they too rarely defend it). People of faith have learned to look among outcasts and exiles for prophets and saints, for the presence of the divine. For Christians, it is the child born in a barn and killed as a criminal who becomes the Redeemer of Mankind. Jews remember that those who worked as slaves in Egypt were raised above Pharaoh and brought to the Promised Land. Islam has such figures at its center: the outcast Hagar and her child Ishmael, the Prophet forced out of Mecca. Hinduism shows us Krishna among the Gopis, Rama and Sita sent into exile. In every time, in every culture, there is the recognition that greatness, even divinity, is to be found among refugees and exiles, the abandoned and the rebellious.

The recognition that the rule of the people belongs to the bandit and the outlaw, the pirate and the rogue, is as strong in conservatives as liberals, in philosophers as in poets. Those who distrust the people are found more often on the right than on the left, but are present in both. They anchor their distrust of the democratic in suspicions of the rebellious and the transgressive. Jacques Derrida is understood—and, I believe, understood himself—as a man of the left. That did not mean that he was or wished to be a man of the people. For Derrida, democracy was so fragile that the people could not be trusted with it. That is a common—the most common—view of democracy among philosophers. Derrida, however, distinguished himself by concluding that democracy belonged to the future (*avenir*), but a future that was always out of reach. Democracy was *à venir*, a future that, although it is to come, never arrives.

Derrida recognized, nevertheless, that there are people who are close to democracy. Those were the rogue and the *shebab,* young Muslims in the street. Where the rogue is, he wrote, democracy is never far away.[16] For the people of the streets, for the people, democracy can never come soon enough. Democracy is *shaabi* in the Arabic that frightened Derrida; it belongs to the people, the masses, the crowd, the *shaab hurri*: to free people.

3. Democracy is shabby.

The Arabic word *shaabi* means "of the people," but democracy is also "shabby" in the English sense. Democracy is the regime of worn-out shoes and old clothes, of frayed collars and thrift shops. For Plato, and many after him, democracy was government of the poor. Democracy accepts and belongs to those for whom shabbiness is, in Pierre Bourdieu's apt phrase, "the choice of necessity." No one has to dress up for democracy. Democracy belongs not to special occasions but to the everyday. Democracy begins not in the halls of government but in the streets, in bars, and at kitchen tables. You come as you are to democratic debates. Politicians who want to signal (as they must) that they belong to the people take off their suit jackets and roll up their sleeves. During his 1952 run for the American presidency, Adlai Stevenson was mocked for having a hole in his shoe. He made it the symbol of his campaign. The worn-out shoe testified to his hard work and frugality; it marked his efforts to speak to as many people as he could. The shoe bore witness to his labor. His indifference to the worn shoe showed an indifference to the marks of wealth and status. That is at the heart of democratic practice. Every politician who eats a corn dog at a county fair or sits down at a diner in jeans testifies to the importance of appearing (at least for the moment) as an equal.

There is nothing new in this. The Scottish poet Robert Burns, who had proud disdain for show and a deep commitment to the rule of the people, contrasted their simple dress and manners with those of a wasteful, empty, and parasitic aristocracy:

> What though on hamely fare we dine,
> Wear hoddin grey, an' a that;
> Gie fools their silks, and knaves their wine;
> A Man's a Man for a' that.[17]

This democratic shabbiness is welcoming and welcome, but the name "democracy" is shabby in a more troubling sense. The name "democracy" has been used so often by autocrats, attached so shamelessly to dictatorships and totalitarian regimes, appropriated so carelessly by liberals, that it has ceased to mark places where the people rule.

Even where people affirm their faith in the consent of the governed, the institutions they call "democratic" are often not democratic at all. They reflect a profound distrust of the right and the ability of people to rule themselves. The rule of law, representative assemblies, and affirmations of rights (especially property rights) are not necessarily democratic. They are more often used to restrain the people than to enable them to rule.

Many of us are told we live in a democracy, but we see too few moments when the people rule. The name "democracy" is worn and shabby. We need to mend it.

4. Fear is the enemy of the free.

When Oliver Cromwell called himself the Lord Protector he taught people something about protection. Fear drives people to seek the protection of the strong. In times of fear, people turn to generals, dictators, strongmen, and *caudillos*. They believe that these, because they are strong, can offer safety from what they fear. They are wrong. Strongmen are not protectors; they are beasts of prey.

During Egypt's January 25th Revolution people acted fearlessly. They overcame their fear of a regime that had imprisoned and tortured people with regularity. Secularists discovered, as one told me with surprise, "We can work with the Muslim Brothers." The religious saw that secularists could be honorable, ethical people, who stood hand in hand with them and formed protective rings around them as they prayed. The Egyptian people took courage from one another. That courage did not last quite long enough. Before Mohamed Morsi's term was out, the same people who had found joy in a common struggle had turned against each other. They began to fear and fear destroyed them. They turned away from fearless work with rivals and enemies to the protection of a military dictator. Perhaps they will find the courage of Tahrir Square once again.

People flee to the protection of an autocrat when they have abandoned faith in their own power and that of their people. They have abandoned that sense of dignity and daring that belongs to those who have the courage to rule themselves. They become supplicants and sycophants. They will be forced to obey. They will find that they have more to fear from the leader than they had to fear from one another.

Those who are afraid are neither deluded nor (at least not always) dishonest. There are always reasons for fear. Perfect safety is a fiction, and a dangerous one.

In the late 1960s, as nuclear weapons transformed from doomsday bombs to ordinary weaponry in the minds of the people, Sheldon Wolin wrote of the perverse relation between our weapons and our fears. He saw that the increasing sophistication of our weapons—the ability to impose devastating destruction, to fire those world-destroying weapons from far away, to mark targets—did not make people feel more secure. Instead it made them increasingly anxious. Promised complete security, they became sensitive to every intimation of a possible attack. They felt not more secure but less.[18] Perhaps people recognized, consciously or unconsciously, that the weapons were a threat in themselves. There is always the possibility of accidents in their production, their storage, and their use. They provoke others to make weapons of their own. They can drive an arms race. The presence, even the possession of weapons of mass destruction, makes any incident a potential pretext for an apocalypse.

We are told that weapons make us strong. We find they make us vulnerable. We are told that increased security procedures make us safer.

They fill us with anxiety. We want to be free and brave, but we make ourselves docile and fearful. We want to protect the people, but we sow fears that divide them. We teach our people that they are prey.

The perverse effects of enhanced security are evident in other forms of security as well.

The enhanced security procedures that followed terrorist attacks in Europe, the United Kingdom, and the United States made us less safe and diminished our courage and our dignity. We were taught to walk through cattle chutes to X-ray machines and thank the people who pat us down for the privilege. We are told to enhance surveillance by serving as watchers ourselves. "If you see something, say something" might at its best remind us that ordinary people have the capacity for judgment, but it is more likely to make us see the people around us as potential terrorists. Worse, we may be tempted, we may have been instructed, to see some people as more dangerous than others. The Prevent program in the United Kingdom in the early twenty-first century required people to report Muslims in danger of radicalization. The process of being identified as a danger, reported to the state, and subjected to a program of deliberate reeducation is unlikely to diminish radicalization. At each point it reminds the targeted people that the state sees them as present dangers and potential enemies. At each point, it instructs them that the state is deploying its powers to separate, censor, and instruct them. At each point, it requires them to see themselves as apart from and feared by their own people.

Those who are targeted in such programs are not well served by them, but neither are those considered safe. They are taught to see themselves as prey, fearing every padded coat and backpack, shying away from any voice speaking, singing, or praying in another language. They are taught to see authorities not only as protection but as absolution. They cannot be wrong to report a neighbor, a friend, a child: they are doing as they are told. They are keeping us safe, while the category "us" grows ever smaller, ever narrower. They diminish the country they claim to preserve. They make their people more divided, more bigoted, more censorious, more fearful than they were.

Franklin Roosevelt was right to declare to a hungry, impoverished, and desperate people, "We have nothing to fear but fear itself." Without fear, with fear mastered, people can go on to do the work they need to do together. They can draw on the skills, the generosity, and the courage of their neighbors. They find that they have no one to depend on but themselves, and in that knowledge they find solidarity and fortitude.

Fear is not only a weapon of authoritarian rulers and intrusive states. Fear lives in neighborhoods. Fear lives in the mind. In the United States, white women were taught to fear Black men. They were taught that Black men presented a special danger to them, that they were more likely to be raped or robbed or attacked by Black men. Those women had already been robbed by white men. They lived under laws that gave their fathers, brothers, husbands, and guardians the right to control how and where and with whom they lived, how or if they earned money, and any funds they earned or inherited. They lived under laws and the greater power of customs that permitted their husbands to rape and beat them at will. They knew those men had power. They knew that power did not always serve them, had sometimes hurt them, always diminished them. Yet they were taught, from the time of their birth, to see those men as their protectors. Black men came to recognize that few things in the world were a greater threat than white women. A lie, a word, an ambiguous glance could outrage a bigot and inflame a lynch mob. White women, dependent on white men, could shift from friend to foe in an instant. White women could not be trusted.

Those laws, that teaching, drew a sharp line between Black men and white women. Each was taught to fear the other. Each was taught to see the other as a site of danger. Each was taught that rescue would come, if it came at all, from the powerful: from white men with standing and resources. This was the logic of lynching. It made solidarity between Black men and white women unimaginable for all but great souls.

Black women, indigenous women, Asian women, any woman marked as different, any woman alone was prey. Such women may have developed a sharper sense for footsteps in the dark, knowing that they had no security in a powerful protector. Some still put their faith in men: men of their own kind or more powerful men. There were times when their faith was justified. There are always men, always people, who act with justice and courage when law or custom teach them to do otherwise. Wiser women learned to rely on themselves.

You may think the time for those fears is past. I think you are wrong. There are other fears that operate in this way. When people need money, they may go to their friends. They may go to their parents, feeling shame. More often they go to the boss, to the bank, to a pawn shop or a loan shark. They go knowing that they may be denied, knowing that they are likely to be exploited. Wherever they go, their need makes them vulnerable. They go to those who are more powerful, and their appeal strengthens an already present hierarchy.

In each case, in every case, those who have reason to fear are better served by solidarity than by the protection of the powerful. If fear drives them, it should drive them to one another. Courage would serve them better than fear.

People who want to keep their freedom, their equality, their courage, and their capacity to rule themselves should refuse fear and teach themselves courage in its place. There are dangers in courage, to be sure, but those dangers threaten our bodies, not our souls. Living with freedom and dignity, great among equals, might require us to take a few risks.

5. If people are to rule themselves, they must have courage.

Courage is necessary for democrats. Revolutions require courage. If we are to rule ourselves, we must be brave enough to live with our enemies. We must be brave enough to go into the unknown. We must be brave enough to face what will come.

Perhaps this is not yet common knowledge, but it is surely the knowledge of the commons. When we look for people brave enough to demand to rule themselves, we see that courage. We see a man dancing around a water cannon in a back street in Egypt. We see people facing down tanks in Tahrir Square, Portland, Hong Kong, and Khartoum. We see a woman standing alone before armed police. We hear Mamie Till-Mobley insisting that her son's coffin be opened for her to see the mutilated body of her child. We hear her demand that it be shown to all. Courage calls forth courage. That call fires people to wrench open closed doors, to tear down fences, to go farther than they had dared to go before in pursuit of justice.

Aristocrats wore their courage like jewels. For them, courage was an ornament, a discreetly displayed excess of something everyone (that is, everyone who is anyone) was expected to have. Courage, for free people, is not a distinction; it is a necessity. People who choose to rule themselves need courage to make themselves a people, courage to debate among themselves and find their way forward ungoverned. They will need, if they choose, courage to form a government, courage to maintain that government when they are in the minority, courage to refuse it when they must.

We are a wild diversity of ever-changing people. No one is wholly visible to another. No one can be wholly known. In practice, democrats learn that they must be ruled by the will of people alien to their customs, their preferences, even their morals. They learn that some of their fellow citizens oppose their way of life, even their presence. They learn that some of these people work against them, work even for their expulsion or annihilation. They live with their enemies. They live with those they fear. For the most part, they do so fearlessly. All decent polities endeavor to protect the frail and the fearful. A democratic politics makes people brave.

Democratic ethics demand that one take things lightly, or, more precisely, that one act as if one did. The opponents of abortion need not keep silent. They may speak loudly. They may assemble; they may agitate. They may vote their conscience. They may believe, they may say as loudly as they can that the practice of abortion is routinized murder. But while they remain among people who believe otherwise they must discipline themselves. They will not lynch, they will not bomb, they will not silence others.

Those who argue that the decision to bear a child belongs to the woman whose body will hold it must also take that lightly. They know that opponents of abortion claim power over their bodies. They know that those who oppose the right to abortion claim to govern their bodies as intimately and as thoroughly as if they were slaves. They know that they are called murderers. They know that some opponents of abortion have bombed abortion clinics and murdered doctors. Yet they must find the courage to walk among their enemies unafraid.

The opponents of capital punishment seek injunctions, pardons, and commutations. They file briefs and hope to overturn judicial decisions. They lobby and they hope that their candidates will win election. They do not stage prison escapes or sabotage the machinery of execution.

So with us all. This is not out of respect for the law. This is out of respect for the people. Until we win the people over, we forebear. This is the discipline democracy requires. This is one form of the courage that belongs to democrats, to free people living a common life.

We are all required to act as if the things that matter most to us matter very little. This bears a family resemblance to the ethic upon which civil servants and officers of the court pride themselves. There is no distinction between persons. All come as equals before the law. All are met without fear or favor. Regimes change, the laws change, but these servants and officers know that they serve the people, not the regime.

The civil servant must act as if there were no distinction between parties, between patrons and rivals, friends and enemies, strangers and friends in the most fundamental things. They are required—we are all required—to pretend indifference to our passions and attachments in matters of rights. We are permitted to have, but not to act upon, our passionate attachments. I may love with an all-consuming passion, but I can give my love no greater claim to rights than I would give a stranger. The stranger, the enemy, has the same rights to speak, to assemble, to rule, to life, liberty, and the pursuit of happiness. Free people would not expect it to be otherwise.

This is not what the philosopher Richard Rorty used to call "taking things lightly," though it may—and should—appear to be. This is an iron discipline. We school ourselves to ignore slights, insults, and danger. We learn to hold our passionate convictions within us. They fuel our conduct, but they do not rule it.

We have become so accustomed to civil discussions of policy that we rarely recognize how much is at stake, how much courage is demanded of ordinary people in a common democratic life. The woman whose husband was shot by a mass shooter is expected to listen with grace and civility to those who advocate unrestrained access to guns. The man whose unborn child is aborted against his will is expected to show the same grace and civility to those who have licensed, defended, or participated in abortion. There are many issues before us, today and every day, which make these demands.

The costs these debates exact are not easily seen. They are clear enough to the woman in chemotherapy whose hair falls on the page as she writes her congressman on healthcare funding. It may be harder to see the costs for the man in his seventies who still owes money on his student loans, or the people who bear the weight of shame and failure because they make too little money. (Of all things, this is the least shameful and the most shaming.) Virtually every issue makes grave demands on someone. Some issues make demands on us all. Every day, all around us, people face these demands with equanimity. They know the costs of a policy that will harm them. They know that they may be faced with the defeat of a cause they honor or the rejection of an ideal they strive for. They know that the people who threaten these things share their country, their state, their town. They have the courage to stand fast.

We live with our enemies. Each party longs for the end of its rival. Right and left, conservative and liberal, we know that the other party wishes for our defeat. We know they hope to keep us out of power, not only for this election but for all the elections they can foresee. Our differences, and our enmities, go far deeper. We know, we democrats, that there are those who would like to see us dead or exiled, who wish that we had never been or that we will be no more. A certain kind of conservative longs for the end, if not of history, at least of the possibility of socialists and socialism, anarchism, radical democracy, and change altogether. The socialist longs for the end of the capitalist, the leftist longs for conservatives without power. Many long for the disappearance of the alien and the queer. The Christian fundamentalist longs for the conversion of the Jew, and the Jew who sees that conversion as a death sees the Christian fundamentalist not as a redeemer but as an enemy.

We live with our enemies. Where speech is free, they announce their aims. They seek our annihilation. Perhaps we seek theirs as well. Perhaps not. Perhaps we are wise enough to see the value of certain of our enemies. Perhaps we are daring enough to take pride in their strength. Whether they fall before us or triumph over us, we walk among our enemies unafraid. This is the courage that belongs to people who rule themselves.

Courage is required not only to live with our enemies but to live with one another. Where the people rule, each person lives with uncertainty and change. The people are always changing. People die, people are born, people are shaped by the people around them. They learn and they change. People change, and the people changes with them. Democracies are driven and desiring; they are always changing. The democrat cannot be certain what the future will bring, cannot even be certain of the parameters of the present. A democratic life demands that people face the possibility of change with courage and discipline. Those changes may compass our annihilation. The practice of democracy is the practice of facing death.

In his *Philosophy of History*, Hegel gave us a fable. Mankind had its birth in the East, he wrote. Humanity had its golden youth in Greece, like the *kouroi*, beautiful and good, yet it was not yet fully formed. It was in Europe, in that small center of the world, that it reached its maturity. Here, humanity grew to wisdom and judgment, finding its fullest political expression in the state. The fable is wrong, perhaps corrupt, certainly too small to hold us.

This is a European fable. It is an error, but like many fabulous errors, there is an unexpected, subversive truth in it. The Sun moved resolutely Westward. Asia, with all its grace and antiquity, was left behind. Africa remained in darkness, "the land of childhood, which lying beyond the day of self-conscious history, is enveloped in the dark mantle of Night." Hegel's account of Africa owes much to European ignorance and the imaginaries of imperialism, but even in this hostile terrain there is something to be found. "The Negro," Hegel writes, "as already observed, exhibits the natural man in his completely wild and untamed state."[19] In this image racialized enslavement and colonial rule meet human freedom and are overcome. Hegel's African promises more for democrats than does his European. There was no place for the Antipodes at all. But if the sun moved westward, what of the Americas?

"America is therefore the land of the future, where, in the ages that lie before us, the burden of the World's History shall reveal itself." This is "a land of desire." The Americas, Hegel held, were the Eveningland, the land of the unknown, "and the dreams to which it may give rise."[20] The Americas posed a problem for Hegel. Was this, as the Egyptians held, the land of death? If it were, was that land the place of annihilation or epiphany, decay or resurrection? Perhaps the European in Hegel was loath to see the New World as the site of transfiguration. Perhaps the Christian in him could not easily set aside the promise of a life after death. Perhaps, as an honorable scholar, he took refuge in the honest answer. He knew what he did not know. The New World to the west of Europe was the realm of the future, the land of the unknown. This was the Eveningland.

The fable is wrong, even corrupt, but light shines through the flaws in it. Hegel was right to look to the Eveningland. That is the land all people come to, and it remains unknown. We all go into the West, as the ancient Egyptians said. We do not know what lies beyond that horizon. He was right to see the Americas as the land of the future, the land of the unknown. The New World is a place, as all new worlds are, of surprise and uncertainty. That uncertainty did not belong to the Americas alone, but it was in the Americas that Europe confronted the limits of its knowledge. Columbus, mistaking the islands of the Caribbean for the East Indies he sought, made the limits of European knowledge undeniable. He had found a New World, but he had proved the Old World to be smaller and less knowing. Perhaps, as Edward Said argued, Europe thought it had already mastered knowledge of the Orient. Measured against the mountain of Orientalist scholarship, knowledge of the Americas would seem tenuous, fragile, and fallible. Perhaps the failure to see the indigenous as fully human confronted the European with an empty land. Perhaps, in the effort to fill that land with Europe, the Europeans encountered the alien in themselves. Perhaps they feared that the Americas were the place Europe went to die. In that welter of discovery and conquest, daring and greed, we can see that mistakes can be productive, that errors open the way to unimagined knowledge. Errors are a source not only of shame and self-reproach but of power and pleasure. Error is a gate to discovery.

Like all good fables, Hegel's is true and untrue, a myth and a revelation. The willingness to go forward into the unknown is given to us in our humanity. Each day, each moment is uncertain. We do not know if we will keep on living; we cannot fully anticipate what any moment will bring. That willingness to go forward into the unknown calls forth acts of courage. We honor those who go to sea not knowing what land, if any, lies ahead. We honor those who go into space, into unmapped deserts and the deepest trenches of the ocean. Facing the unknown is what we were born to. Those impelled by that drive answer a high calling of humanity.

We are, perhaps unknowingly, accustomed to the demands of death. We are the people of the Eveningland.[21] We look toward our own deaths and we are not afraid. We are Vikings. We sail off into the unknown.

Democracy is the practice of a little death, of many small annihilations. Democracy requires that at some moment one will cease to be. You will be ruled. You will be overruled. The people will decide against what you will. The people will decide against you. Your voice will be silenced, your hopes defeated, your will lost. In every election, in each debate, in reports of public opinion, in reading bumper stickers and yard signs you are brought face to face not only with the possibility of defeat but with the prospect of your annihilation. The will of the people will wash over your vision, your aims, your will, your voice like a great sea. You will be lost in it. All that you love and honor will be lost.

In the face of this devastation, more profound than death and encountered long before it, you learn courage. You learn to stand for your ideals when they are mocked or rejected. You learn to speak when speech is dangerous. You learn to act when success is far away and even hope is gone. You learn to make your own judgments about right and wrong. You learn to doubt the wisdom of those whose opinions are more popular. You learn to doubt your own. You are forced to a life of choice and refusal, reflection and will. You learn to be thoughtful in the midst of doubt, brave in the face of enemies, courageous in facing the always present possibility of loss.

And then, perhaps you rise.

We are taken up and moved with the people as by waves on a sea. We may will what the people will and move willingly. We may resist, and the sea will flow over us like water over rocks. We may be moved, changed in place and time unwillingly. Yet that sea, however great, may also be changed in its course. We can hold fast. We can go forward on that sea. We can learn to sail.

6. Democrats take risks.

People who can rule themselves excel at taking risks. The decision to set aside the comfort of kings or lord protectors or of leaving the decisions to the expert few is itself a great risk. People who rule themselves go willingly into an uncertain future. The decision to become a people—not the armed revolution that is so often necessary to affirm it, not the institutions and governments the people may establish— is the moment a people is born. They speak themselves into being. In the long reach of time, this choice has often meant accepting the need for revolution. People accept revolution with all the danger it involves. They risk all, "their lives, their fortune, and their sacred honor." They may lose their lives or the lives of those they love. They may be maimed. They may kill or maim others. They may take sin upon themselves. They may fail. They may end impoverished. They may be remembered only as traitors. They take the risk. They choose to go together, to work together, though they know that their aims may diverge. They know they are working not only with their friends but with those who may have been, or may prove to be, their enemies. They take the risk.

People who rule themselves take this risk not only at the moment of the founding but for the entire time of their existence. They may, they will, seek to fence risk out with laws and constitutions, with customs and practices. They may, they will, cultivate a respect for those laws and constitutions, for precedent, for their forebears, for the past. But they have eaten of the Tree of Knowledge. They know they can rebel.

Day after day, they are confronted by risk. There are the ordinary risks that nature, perhaps Nature's God, and certainly other human beings, pose to any people. There will be earthquakes and hurricanes, cyclones and tsunamis. There will be forest fires. There will be floods. The people, not the monarch, not the autocrat, not even the state they establish, will be expected to deal with catastrophes. They know that they must demand that the state respond. They know they are to judge that response. They know they can respond faster than any state. People can reach further than states or state officials, respond more quickly and more thoughtfully. They must anticipate other disasters. They expect themselves to learn.

So it is with the threat of war. People who rule themselves must meet the threat of war not as states but as people. When they declare war, when they marshal their defenses, they do so not only as rulers but as the ruled. They will make the decision and they will bear the costs. The burden must fall not on the few but upon all.

All the threats—natural disasters, economic catastrophes, war and the threat of war—are present to democrats, as they are to all people. The difference is that democrats are obliged to judge, consider, and respond. They cannot assign that responsibility to others. They are called—each separately and in common—to judgment and to action.

For people who are ruled, the great risks of war and famine, disease, disaster, and pogroms are something to fear. Perhaps the powerful and wealthy can protect themselves. Perhaps states, churches, temples, and mosques will protect the weak. Perhaps not. For people who rule themselves, these threats, these risks, these dangers are problems to be solved, for all, together.

There are other risks. These are risks we choose. When people are free, their minds and hands are unbound. They will explore, invent, take up great projects. Not all these ventures will end well. Explorers will be lost; inventions will have dangerous consequences. Bridges will collapse; new drugs will have unlooked-for side effects. Projects will fail. They are worth the risk.

Democrats become good at taking risks: adept at assessing them, clever at mitigating them, quick to respond to them, and, above all, unafraid. Courage gives them daring; judgment gives them caution; practice gives them power.

The greatest risk is the risk we pose to one another. This is the great risk of a common life. As the unflinching Thomas Hobbes recognized, "anyone can kill anyone else." We are always dangerous to one another. Ruling ourselves requires us to become adept at both friendship and enmity. We learn to defeat our enemies when we can, work with them when we cannot. We learn the joy and duties of friendship. We learn that there will be moments of enmity in friendship. We learn that there can be moments of friendship between enemies. We face the risks of a common life not blindly but with our eyes open. We have courage enough. We can work together and win through to a common life. We can learn when to work together, when to resist, when to rebel.

II
Free people keep something wild in them

7. Rebellion is not only a right: it is a duty.

There is a passage in the American Declaration of Independence that lays out the grounds for establishing governments and, then, the grounds for rebellion. Part of that passage reads, "when a long train of abuses and usurpations, pursuing invariably the same object evinces a design to reduce them under absolute Despotism, it is their right, it is their duty, to throw off such Government, and to provide new Guards for their future security." Rebellion is not just their right. Rebellion is their duty.

Rebellion is too often thought of as the passionate unleashing of anger, in which the ordinary restraints that govern conduct—laws and morals alike—are thrown to the winds. In the Declaration we see people in the midst of a rebellion, conscious not of their passions but of their duty. They know how hard it is for people to rebel, how long they resist, and how much they will suffer before they take that course.

That time of endurance is also a time of thought. People consider the evil that has been done to them, of course, but they give longer, harder thought to the costs their people will bear if they rebel. Rebellion is difficult and dangerous. The costs of rebellion will be borne not just by the rebel but by the rebel's family and friends. The chances of victory are small. Even if victory is won, there is no guarantee that things will be better than they were. People come to rebellion and revolution slowly, reluctantly. They do not come full of passion alone. They come after long thought. They do not come full of rage. They come stoically, with courage and commitment to a cause they know may fail. They do not come to satisfy an appetite for revenge. They come to fulfill a duty.

Wild Democracy. Anne Norton, Oxford University Press. © Oxford University Press 2023.
DOI: 10.1093/oso/9780197644348.003.0002

The idea that one might have a duty to rebel may seem shocking or perverse. It should not. Those who believe that governments should be ruled by the people should recognize that any failure to meet that standard imposes a duty. It is the people's duty to correct a government that they, after long endurance and reflection, determine to be irreparable. It is their duty to rebel against a government whose evils they cannot overcome. That duty requires judgment and self-discipline. That duty belongs to us all.

We should rebel more often.

8. Empire is the enemy of the democratic.

When Patrick Henry argued against the ratification of the 1787 American Constitution, he spoke, he said, as "a conservative for liberty." He was an old revolutionary, and there were things he missed in that document. We see (and perhaps he did as well) the stain of slavery on the Constitution. "I will not, cannot justify it," he declared. He saw (we do as well) the absence of an acknowledgment of the rights of the people. There was no Bill of Rights. Henry saw something else as well. He saw an arrogation of the sovereignty of the people. "Who gave them the right to say 'We, the People'?" Henry asked. He saw the ambition of Hamilton, Jay, and Madison, the imperialist, the capitalist, and the colonizer.[1] The Federalist Constitution, Henry argued, was not a document "to secure these rights" but one that aimed at the creation of "a splendid Government" at the price of liberty. If their government were to be established, he argued, "it will be because we like a great splendid one. Some way or other we must be a great and mighty empire; we must have an army, and a navy and a number of things." The desire for empire, for splendor, for glory, was antithetical to the love of freedom. The family, sitting under their fig tree, wanted neither to oppress nor to be oppressed, neither to be feared nor to fear. They had succeeded in that aim. "We are not feared by foreigners: we do not make nations tremble: Would this, Sir, constitute happiness or secure liberty?"[2]

The partisans of empire had an intimate relation to fear. They were afraid of foreign wars and domestic insurrections and, of course, of anarchy. They saw fear as an ally. The ambition for glory was allied to an economy of fear. Hamilton had argued that the ambitions of European empires could be forestalled only if the United States were to become an empire themselves. The newly free of the New World should fear the ambitions of the Old. Fear was our surest defense against the ambitions of others. Fear would prompt Americans to seek their security in a stronger, more energetic, more authoritarian government, less protective of their rights. The Federalists aimed, Henry recognized, "to terrify us into an adoption of this new system."[3] Fear was the friend of empire, the ally of ambition, and the enemy of liberty.

The logic of the protection racket is at work here. Charles Tilly dissected it to devastating effect in an article titled "War-making and State-making as Organized Crime." "Apologists for particular governments and for government in general commonly argue," Tilly wrote, "that they offer protection from local and external violence. They claim that the prices they charge barely cover the costs of protection. They call people who complain about the price of protection 'anarchists,' 'subversives,' or both at once."[4] History suggests, however, that the threat of violence was often due to actions of the state itself. Worse, the greater the threat, the more power the state would need. The more power the state gathered, the greater the threat it would present, not merely to external enemies but to local critics.

Henry recognized another link in this set of chains. The "great and splendid" state offered not only protection but glory. There are few monuments to the exile who has escaped persecution, the immigrant who abandons home for hope. There are few epic poems on the steel-worker, the dairy farmer, the administrative assistant, or the waiter. The small state, protecting the rights of its people, rids itself of titles and aristocratic display. The glory of empires does not belong to them. That is their true and honorable greatness.

The desire for glory is intimately allied to fear. Fear makes one long for the strong hand of the Protector and the power of an Empire. These offer not only protection. They offer glory. Individuals are taught to take pride not in lives lived ethically but in lives lived in grandeur: large houses, expensive cars, yachts, jets, and ever-growing ciphers recording astronomical personal wealth. There is no honor in this. There should be shame.

Instead shame falls on those who have no reason for shame. Those who are not wealthy are taught, day by day, that they should want these possessions. They are taught that they would be better if they had them, that they are less than those who do have them. They are seduced into shame. Lacking glory themselves, they may embrace the glory of a race or nation. As their fear lost them their liberty, their shame costs them their judgment and their honor.

The United States did not succeed in warding off the allure of glory or the glamour of evil. There is, as Henry feared, a standing army, despite constitutional efforts to prevent it.[5] The need for military appropriations to be approved by Congress every two years is a ragged remnant, the bleached bones of the Constitution's initial bravery. The long history of wars of conquest against the indigenous tribes and a growing ambition to rival the empires of Europe have been justified in all the languages of fear and ambition. Americans are not yet free of it.

The fearful passion for imperial glory has not gone uncontested. Washington's Farewell Address warned against military adventurism and condemned "overgrown military establishments which, under any form of government, are inauspicious to liberty, and which are to be regarded as particularly hostile to republican liberty."[6] Washington was admirably immune to glory, rebuffing Hamilton's monarchical ambitions, refusing a third term, and avoiding the gold braid and ribbons of military authority that have corrupted so many revolutionary leaders in the Old World and the New. He did not succeed, however, in preventing the hunger for imperial glory in others.

We have forgotten many of the wars we fought. The expansion of the United States across the continent was accompanied by Indian wars and the forced removal of many tribes. Looking back, we honor Hin-mah-too-yah-lat-kekt, Chief Joseph, not the generals to whom he surrendered. We have forgotten their names. We remember his courage, his care for his people, and the hard choices he made to secure them. We know, we Americans, that the Nimiipuu, the Nez Percé, were wronged. We know they acted honorably and with courage and judgment. We have come to honor them far more than we honor the troops the United States set against them. The same could be said of Thatháŋka Íyotake (Sitting Bull); Shi-ka-She (Cochise); Goyaałé (Geronimo); and the host of tribal leaders we honor and remember.

The Indian wars (fought from before 1776 into the twentieth century) are now a source of shame and regret. Yet we are a settler colony. We have much to learn, much to mourn, much to repent, much to repair, much to overcome.[7]

Theirs was not the only blood shed in pursuit of glory.

The Mexican War gave us the porous, ever-shifting borderlands that Trump and others have sought to divide. It would be hard for anyone raised in the West—perhaps in any part of the United States—to imagine an America without the words, religion, buildings, foods, music, clothing, and legends of Mexico. The Mormon Wars, more thoroughly forgotten, followed the assassination of Joseph Smith. Smith's disciples were chased from one town to another, pursued by lynchings, harried ever farther west. Once Mormons were outlaws; now they are senators. The Church of Latter Day Saints is now an ordinary part of the fabric of American life.

The pursuit of glory in the American move westward brought us riches, but they came from the generous hands of those we defeated. The glory generals won has turned to shame and ashes. The indigenous people they fought gave us models of freedom and courage. They have given us works of extraordinary craft and power and ways of seeing beauty and finding guidance in the natural world. In the shadow of plutocracy and climate change, the Lakota and their allies have stood fast in defense of the idea and practice of the commons.[8] They have testified that the desire for profit must give way to the welfare of the land and the people. They rightly argue that treaties must be honored. They testify to the sacred.

The turn of the nineteenth century saw the United States embroiled in foreign wars. Now, when long wars in distant places are more familiar to us, we may look with more suspicion on the passion for glory. We have learned that with these we have to bear not only the deaths of our own soldiers but the deaths of innocents; we have to bear not only the costs of glory but the shame that is its underside.

At the turn of the nineteenth century, the passion for glory was at its height. Americans entered the Philippines as allies of the Filipino rebels against Spanish colonialism. From 1898 to 1946 we served as Spain's successor in colonial rule. There were those, like Theodore Roosevelt, who dreamed of empire and hoped for a people hungry for glory. "If we are to be a really great people we must play a great part in the world," he declared. He could conceive of greatness only as war. He despised, he said, "the man of timid peace" and those "who cant about liberty and the consent of the governed." Americans, he hoped, would be "stern men with empire in their eyes" and "mothers of many healthy children."[9] In the debates over the American role in the Philippines, senators like Henry Cabot Lodge called for the United States to "step forward boldly and take its place at the head of nations." This was prompted by a naked desire for power and profit, justified by racial arrogance and religious bigotry.

Conquest, declared Senator Albert Beveridge, was "the mission of our race, trustee under God of the civilization of the world," for "Almighty God" has "marked us as His chosen people, henceforth to lead in the regeneration of the world." Indeed, God had gone farther, determining with divine omniscience that as "most future wars will be conflicts for commerce," the nation's future should be "permanently anchored at a spot selected by the strategy of Providence" to command the China trade, for "that power that rules the Pacific is the power that rules the world." The language of piety veiled blasphemy. Beveridge saw God as the servant of merchants. The "American Republic" was treated with no greater respect. The "world-redeeming work of our imperial race" required nothing less than the abandonment of the Constitution and the Declaration of Independence.[10]

Lodge made that explicit. He argued that that the destruction of the western tribes had made it clear. In driving the Cherokee off their lands, in the devastation of tribal peoples, "all questions about the consent of the governed went down into nothingness as they deserved to go."[11] He shared Roosevelt's contempt for those "who cant about liberty and the consent of the governed." For Lodge, for Beveridge, for Roosevelt and all those who shared in the lust for glory, democracy and republicanism were myths for children. The self-evident truths of the Declaration were fairy tales that an older and wiser nation—an empire—would surely reject.

We have forgotten many of those who kept faith with the Declaration. While Lodge, Beveridge, and Roosevelt boasted of the virtues of the "Teuton" and the "Anglo-Saxon," Senator George Hoar bore witness to "the God who made of one blood all the nations of the earth." The imperialists spoke of themselves as God's Chosen People. They saw empire as the "world-redeeming work of our imperial race." For Hoar, imperial ambition was a temptation to evil. He condemned "the wretched glitter and glare of empire which Satan is setting before us" and cried out in the Senate, "Get thee behind me, Satan!"[12] Not until the civil rights movement would people of faith speak so powerfully in pursuit of justice.

William Jennings Bryan opposed American imperialism explicitly, consistently, and with a great movement accompanying him. Like Hoar, Bryan saw colonialism as a temptation and a betrayal. The imperial enterprise was a repudiation of

> the principles upon which the Nation rests; it can employ force instead of reason; it can substitute might for right; it can conquer weaker people; it can exploit their lands, appropriate their property, and kill their people, but it cannot repeal the moral law, or escape the punishment decreed for the violation of human rights.

For these religious democrats, the betrayal of democratic principles was a sin, and as Bryan declared, "the wages of sin is death." There was another path to greatness, another conception of honor:

> Because our Declaration of Independence was promulgated others have been promulgated. Because the patriots of 1776 fought for liberty others have fought for it. Because our constitution was adopted other constitutions have been adopted.
>
> The growth of the principle of self-government, planted on American soil, has been the overshadowing political fact of the nineteenth century. It has made this nation conspicuous among the nations. . . . I would not exchange the glory of this Republic for the glory of all the Empires that have risen and fallen since time began.[13]

The steadfast opposition of Bryan and the People's Party speaks powerfully against the contemporary confusion of populism and nationalism. Bryan spoke for the consent of the governed not only in the United States but in all the world. He spoke against empire. His opponents spoke of Providential destiny and the nation. Bryan saw moral duty and the rights of all people. Bryan, Hoar, and their allies lost. The United States did not extricate itself from war and colonial rule in the Philippines for forty-seven years. We are still enthralled by empire. Empire is a betrayal of democracy.

This was, this is an American story of temptation and corruption and of courage and struggle against imperialism. There are other stories, other histories, for this is not only an American struggle. The French revolutionaries fell prey to glory in Napoléon. The proud nation of the Revolution and the Commune fell into empire, with colonies across the world. Nation after nation has fallen prey to revolutionaries who, when the work of revolution seemed to be accomplished, lost their respect for the people and their commitment to justice and claimed the powers of a monarch. Long before and after these, predatory rulers have sought glory by preying on the people.

Glory lies in ruling ourselves alone.

9. The democratic citizen is both sovereign and subject.

Rousseau's famous definition of the citizen as both subject and sovereign echoes Aristotle's description of democracy as ruling and being ruled in turn only to go beyond it. Rousseau saw how extraordinary the achievement of democratic citizenship is. Democracy was not simply a particular governmental design; it was a disposition and a discipline. The citizen must have the daring, the vision, the courage, and the arrogance of the ruler. And the citizen must rule that arrogance with an unrelenting discipline. The citizen must be willing to submit to the law, to accept the judgments of other citizens, to be ruled. The citizen must be a subject: deferential to the ruler even when the ruler errs, willing to serve, willing to sacrifice. The citizen must stand above the law: making law, forging the standards that law is measured against, changing law, rebelling when rebellion is required. Citizens rule others. They rule themselves.

The citizen as subject is necessary to any people who wish to rule themselves. Their ability to rule themselves is dependent on their ability to accept that they will not only rule but be ruled. Their ability to accept rule with dignity and grace and without fear is admirable. Their ability to accept rule without violence is necessary. Once, while watching a presidential election, my friend went to bed before the results were clear. When I asked how she could do that, she said, "I know there won't be tanks in the street in the morning." The commitment to accept being ruled without immediately taking up arms testifies to the trust a people must have in one another. Yet it also testifies to their courage, to face an uncertain future with equanimity. We can no longer be sure about the tanks. We must stay awake through all the watches of the night.

People who rule themselves accept the idea that they may lose, that their ideas will sometimes be cast aside in favor of others they reject. Though they can—and usually will—hold to their positions and principles, they accept that they will be ruled, at least for a time, in ways they do not approve and would not choose. They will wait and watch and judge the outcome. They will dissent, protest, organize, educate. They may change their minds. They may rebel. More often, they hold fast, work, and wait. The discipline of equality is not something they demand only from the powerful. They demand it of themselves.

The citizen is also, and most importantly, sovereign. It is not the recognition of other states, still less the recognition of international organizations, that makes a state. It is the people. The consent of the governed is the only legitimate ground for state authority. The sovereign people stand before, behind, beneath, and above the state. The power to make a people before that people makes a state lies in each person's hands.

Sovereignty belongs to the citizen not only as part of the people but as one person. If one is to rule as well as to be ruled, one must learn sovereignty. The citizen is required not only to submit to rule but to rule: to hold power and use it well. Those moments when the people come together are few and fugitive, yet the rule of the people is active and omnipresent. The people, as Tocqueville recognized, "hover above the entire life of the state, just as God does above the world, as the cause and end of all things." Though that present appears distant and invisible, it is within reach. Citizens are required not merely to rule *for* but to rule *as* the people. They have a duty to seek the common good. They also have a duty to act for it. They have a duty to rule. They are called to judge. They are called to make law. They are called to enforce the law.

They are called to defy it. Sovereignty does not belong to the exception. Sovereignty is a commonplace.

Some of the work of ruling comes formally, in the work of juries, town halls, and elections. The greater part (in every sense) comes outside, below, and beyond laws and institutions. Burke's wisdom was to recognize that people constitute themselves in the crafting of custom and convention. They decide what they are to be, in common and in practice. This is, as Burke saw, a long slow process in the life of a people, but people do that work in uncounted decisions that are usually the work of a moment. Some of those moments change the course of the people like a rock in a stream.

We honor individual acts of authority. We saw that strength and power in Greta Thunberg, sitting outside her high school with a hand-lettered sign. She held fast, and the world shifted. Acts that shift worlds are not always noticed. The people, the democrats who walk through the world as the eyes and hands and voice of sovereignty rule the commonplace unnoticed. The one who sees a wrong, who says no to a small injustice, who raises a hand to hold back force, who acts for the common good or the rights of one, embodies sovereignty and makes it a force in the world.

Subjects belong to monarchs, citizens to nations and to states. In a democracy, the distinction between citizen and person should be slight and suspect. Citizens should value the rights given to them by law far less than those they hold within themselves. As the Declaration of Independence (and not only the Declaration) has affirmed, the rights that belong to all people are inalienable.

They cannot be taken. They cannot be bought and sold. They cannot be given away.

The rights of citizens and subjects are far more fragile. The rights of subjects ultimately depend on the will of the monarch. Where the autocratic character of monarchy is tempered, as in the United Kingdom, by deference to an unwritten constitution, the subject's vulnerability may be lessened by law, long-established practice and convention. There, the rights of citizens are dependent on law and the state. They are not rights at all: they are gifts, privileges granted by the state and the law, as monarchs grant them to their subjects. What law grants, law may take away. What the state protects it may attack. When law or the state is seen as the source of rights, citizens are encouraged to defer to law and the state. They are told that they owe their rights not to "Nature and Nature's God" or to their own humanity but to a bureaucratic dictum. They are not their own masters. Still less are they the masters of the state. They have nowhere to stand against unjust laws or an abusive state.

Hannah Arendt, like too many intellectuals, believed that rights were the gift of law and the state. She had known persecution, exile, and statelessness. She recognized the need for rights, yet she could not bring herself to accept that rights exist before, beyond, above, and outside the law. She argued, therefore, for "the right to have rights." This demand is as contrived as it sounds. The demand leaves the question of what rights might be granted or denied to a state or an international organization of states. Whether one has or does not have rights is left to the judgment of lawyers and officials. The argument that human rights are the work of a consensus of international organizations, the gift of international law, rests the claim to rights—even the "right to have rights"—upon this all too fragile foundation. This view makes lawyers and legal scholars, states and organizations the arbiters of claims to rights. Those who give can take away. The right to have rights is no right at all.

Subjects and citizens can be exiled. They can be forced to become refugees. Their belonging to states and nations can be given and taken away like a passport. Yet they still carry within them their inalienable rights: the rights that belong to all human beings. Subject, citizen, exile, or refugee, people carry their rights within them. When they are forced back upon themselves, their rights remain. When they move, whether from home to work or into exile, they carry their rights with them. They cannot lose their rights, for those rights are inalienable. Their rights are as much a part of them as their hands or their heart. Their rights are held in their bodies. They are right incarnate.

10. Free people keep something wild in them.

Nietzsche wrote of himself:

> I hate to follow and I hate to lead
> Obey? Oh no! and govern? No indeed.[14]

Nietzsche is rarely thought to have a disposition toward democracy, but I (and many with me) think that what some have seen as aristocratic is far more descriptive of free people. People who rule themselves disdain servitude and avoid leadership.

There is nothing surprising in the desire of free people to avoid obedience. They pride themselves on their freedom. They see obedience in its simplest form (obedience to a command) as a threat—and an insult—to their freedom. They train themselves from birth to judge: to judge all commands, to question all authority. Nor should we be surprised that they prefer not to lead. They do not long to dominate. They have no desire to live among those who wish to be ruled. They recognize that dominion diminishes the leader as well as the led. The people they respect do not require their leadership. They would rather avoid any connection with people they do not respect.

Free people are like the Cat That Walked by Himself. "The wildest of all the wild animals was the Cat. He walked by himself, and all places were alike to him." Though free people make contracts and become accustomed to domesticity, they do it on their own terms and for their own purposes. A free person is always able, and often inclined, to go "out to the Wet Wild Woods or up the Wet Wild Trees or on the Wet Wild Roofs, waving his wild tail and walking by his wild lone."[15] Free people never forget how to walk by their wild lone. There needs to be something wild in us.

Machiavelli saw this. He wrote that there is no sure way of holding cities accustomed to liberty except by demolishing them:

> And whoever becomes master of a city accustomed to living in freedom and does not destroy it may expect to be destroyed by it; because this city can always have refuge, during a rebellion, in the name of liberty and its traditional institutions, neither of which, either with the passing of time or the acquiring of benefits, are ever forgotten.

Free people keep something wild and ungovernable in them. Those who have learned to rule themselves do not submit to conquest, to repression, or to the bribery of a soft life. Those who have learned the hard discipline required to rule and be ruled according to their laws and their own will, do not submit easily to others: "The memory of their ancient liberty will not and cannot allow them to rest."[16]

Free people shun both obedience and authority. Yet when they choose they can be very good at both.

Free people obey freely. When they choose to come together as a people, they do so willfully. They make their people, their country, their nature, even their state their own. They are transformed by this. Rousseau saw that this decision made the consenting person "an intelligent being, and a man."[17] People become, in one moment, both more than themselves and more themselves. They acquire a being—as an American or an Indian or a Palestinian—that is larger in time and space than the limits of a single life. Their interest suddenly extends to all those they now see as their own. They have a presence in the past with their dead compatriots, and a presence in the future with those who are yet to be. This belonging, this presence in time past and time future is the work of their will, their conviction, their love. The allegiance that overcomes their solitude is more profound because it is the gift of their solitude.

Knowing that they are part of a people does not end that solitude or overcome the differences that belong to each person. On the contrary, it throws their personal characters into high relief. They look around at their countrymen and see how very alien they are. They discover they are not like all others. They don't listen to the same music, like the same paintings, or eat the same food. They have different aims, different ideals. They compete for jobs. They may not share the same gods, the same goals, the same hopes for their people. They come to take pride in certain of their differences. They come to treasure others. Small differences mark out families and neighborhoods. For those who belong freely to one people, the differences among them become sites of greater intimacy and pleasure. They take them to heart.

Led by these passions for the places and people they take as their own, they follow passionately. They take pride in their obedience to laws they make themselves. They may take pride in obedience to laws they reject, while they struggle to change them. That is pride in their self-discipline, pride in their capacity to rule themselves. They will show that discipline even in disobedience.

Consider Socrates. Socrates is rarely thought to be a democrat, but in some respects he had a democratic sensibility. He works with Meno and Alcibiades, the slave and the aristocrat. One cannot quite say of him, as Whitman said of himself, "Kanuck, Tuckahoe, Congressman, Cuff, I give them the same, I receive them the same," but his wanderings through Athens have a democratic promiscuity.[18] He stood apart from the city as critic and gadfly, but he loved the law of Athens with passion and fidelity. The Socrates of the Apology and the Crito shows no respect for those of his fellow citizens who brought him to trial. He mocks them. He points out their errors and refutes their arguments. When asked what sentence he should receive, he proposes free meals for life. He walks among his enemies without fear. Though he disdains his accusers, he accepts the Athenians as his judges and he submits to Athenian law.

Socrates's death is an Athenian death: decided by Athenians according to Athenian law, accepted by an Athenian. His obedience is the work of a democratic discipline. Athens is his city, and he will not leave it. A wealthy foreigner offers him escape and exile. He remains in Athens. The laws of Athens are his laws. He made them. He fought for them, he reminds his judges. He defended them against the dictators who for a time took the place of the people. He accepts those laws and he will die by them. It is a more powerful testimony to Athens than any death at war could be. It is a more commanding discipline than force or law alone could impose. It is not in his submission to law that Socrates shows his democratic disposition. It is in his submission to the people, the city, and the law that he chose as his own.

Work as part of a free people, ruling and being ruled, sharpens both allegiance and independence. People are reminded, in all the work of ruling and being ruled, that they are not only like but unlike their compatriots. They belong to each other, but they differ profoundly: on issues, in their interests, in their principles, and in their ideals. They learn that likeness in one respect does not foreclose difference in another. They learn that difference is possible for people who have much in common. They become more sharply conscious of their own individuality, of their ties to their friends and neighbors. They join them in common projects, pleasures, and pursuits. When they join, they follow with passionate enthusiasm. Yet they remain conscious of themselves as individual people, unlike each other and of infinite value. In their legends and their common practices, they honor individual eccentricity.

Often (if not always) in legends of heroes, a person who is solitary, a loner or an outcast, is called to a mission for the people. In the words of scripture and reggae:

> The stone that the builder refuse
> Will always be the head cornerstone.[19]

There is a proud competence in those who walk by their wild lone. They know their own minds. They know their needs and how to provide for them. They are famously good at living simply and at providing not only for themselves but for others. They are critical in their judgments. They are hard to defeat. They live alone, constantly encountering obstacles and dangers, and therefore developing strategies to survive and prosper. They work with others freely: by choice, and in the recognition of common human needs.

III

Rights are born in the body

11. Rights are grounded in the body.

In many languages, the word for rights is also the word for law. Not in mine. Rights are the name my people give to the democratic demand. It is easier to speak of rights when the name does not call up a debt to law. Rights are before, above, and beyond the law. Rights are demands all people make, demands that call from the flesh. Rights make demands on us. Rights do not merely impose obligations; they command us. These democratic demands call us to witness, to recognize, to shelter and to nourish, to cultivate, to do justice, and to rebel.

Rights are written in the flesh. They follow from the human condition. They are grounded in embodiment. They are demanded by body and mind as each strives toward the fullness of the human, toward the fullness of each particular human.

The right to life is the simplest right, but from this right many others follow. If you have the right to protect yourself and preserve your life, you have a right to what is necessary for that. You have a right to food. As St. Thomas Aquinas affirmed in the *Summa Theologica*, it is no sin to steal food if food is needed: "It is not theft, properly speaking, to take secretly and use another's property in a case of extreme need: because that which he takes for the support of his life becomes his own property by reason of that need."[1] Indeed, the saint argued, it is no sin to steal for others who need food. For the same reason, the right to preserve yourself gives you a right to clothing and shelter: to what you need to protect yourself from the elements. The idea that healthcare is a human right is not an imaginative expansion of rights: it is simple common sense. Healthcare is needed by all who have bodies, which is to say, everybody. You have a right to care for your health, for without that you cannot preserve your life. Food, shelter, and healthcare must

Wild Democracy. Anne Norton, Oxford University Press. © Oxford University Press 2023.
DOI: 10.1093/oso/9780197644348.003.0003

be secured to all because these are necessary to secure the rights of all people to preserve their lives.

There is a mind sheltered in the body. That mind, and the soul and spirit with which it dwells, rely on the body. These too require preservation. They need the protection of the body that shelters them, but they need more. The mind requires its own food: education, tools, training, and resources. Securing the preservation of life, liberty, and the pursuit of happiness requires us to secure the ability of all people to learn.

If you have a right to liberty, you have a right to move away from oppression and exploitation. You have the right to leave. You have the right to migrate: to flee persecution, to flee war and violent criminality, to find work and preserve your life. You have a right to protect that liberty which is essential to you. Without it, you are nothing but an object in the world, the tool, problem or prey of others. The right to liberty enables you to become human: to protect your life, your ability to think, worship, honor, and live as you choose.

Does this imply that other bodies bear rights? Yes, it does. The recognition that people hold their rights in their bodies, that their rights are born and carried in their flesh, drives us to the recognition that other bodies have claims that cannot be set aside. The idea that the dog, the cat, the elephant, the sage grouse, and the industrially produced chicken have rights and claims on us is both familiar and unfamiliar. Ordinary people have the profound sense that animals expect something from us and that they are right to do so. We understand that we have a duty to all in the natural world. Their rights are entangled with our own. We recognize, too, that we should defer to the freedoms and claims of cats (for example) differently than we defer to those of lions, human beings, or dogs.

The rights of other bodies—of grass and trees, rivers and oceans—are also familiar and unfamiliar. People recognize that it is wrong to despoil, to waste, to dirty what has been clean. We recognize that such acts are unjust and that they do practical harm to things in the world. New Zealand's courts have given a legal form to the rights indigenous people ascribed to specific rivers and mountains. The indigenous understanding of these rivers and mountains as beings that have rights has made its way into once alien judicial institutions. New Zealanders have become more indigenous, more Maori, in their understanding of the world. They have become wiser and more honorable. Their acts call us to reflect on what rights we need to respect in the world of mountains, rivers, oceans, trees and grasslands, deserts and marshes. What does the material world demand of the democratic?

Some of the most thoughtful people in the West think of these questions as duties of care or stewardship. That sense of obligation serves people well, but it is not sufficient. The rights of things in the world around us depend not on our virtue but on the character of those other beings. Care and stewardship of other bodies, of our world and all that lives within it, are not acts of virtue but commands we disobey at our peril.

Those who believe that people are created by God in the image of God believe that God breathes rights into the body with the soul. In this understanding, deference to people's rights is the worship of God. The faithful see the rights of man as a reflection of the substance and so the glory of God. To respect those rights is to acknowledge the presence of the divine in each person made in the image of God.

We are not all faithful. Not all of us believe that we can speak for God or know the divine. Rights belong to the people of doubt and wonder as well as to the people of faith. There is no need for faith to ground the rights born in our flesh. Rights are born in the thinking mind and the fragile flesh. All our rights lie between precarity and power. Whether or not they are given by God, our rights follow from the needs and promise of the embodied.

The faithful, atheists, and those who claim no certain knowledge of the divine can all recognize the grounding of rights in the body. A person cannot be a person without life, liberty, and the pursuit of happiness. Without life, there is no person, no being, no body, nobody at all. Without liberty, no one can move in the world, no one can speak or act or live as a human being. The body that can speak and read and write has a right to speech. Without this, it cannot be what it can and should be. People are driven to see, and then to make, the new. They are driven outward, toward that which lies beyond their sight. These are the drives and capacities of every body. The denial of any of these fundamental rights forecloses the fullness of human life.

Whether they are given by nature or by nature's god, the rights grounded in our bodies carry commands with them. Every right is a demand, a duty, a command, an obligation, and a calling. Whether these demands are voiced or made silently in the presence of the body, they command. The defense of those rights, in oneself and others, is a duty. We are commanded to respect rights in ourselves and others, to be sure, but we have a greater duty. Rights not only protect us; they call upon us to act.

12. People have the right to life, to liberty, and to the pursuit of happiness.

All rights live in the right to a life. I chose the form that belongs to my people. Their language echoes Rainsborough's declaration that "the poorest he that is in England has a right to live as the greatest he."[2]

Rainsborough's statement is compelling in its simplicity. He gives it in plain language. Anyone, the poorest man or woman in the country, could hear and understand him. This is a revolutionary claim. Rainsborough sees that the democratic demand for the rights every body has by nature leads directly to the right people have to rule themselves.

The claim leads farther than we—even we who believe in natural rights—often recognize. Rainsborough is claiming not just life, bare life, but a life, the whole of a human life, the life that each of us has to live. What is this? This is the democratic demand: a demand that every person be able to live a full life. This is an argument not only for bread but for roses, not for bare life but for an education, the tools of a trade, for all that is necessary to make a human life.

The right to liberty is the right to shape a self in the world and to shape that world. People who rule themselves do as they think best, alone and together. The right to liberty entails the right to move freely in the world. To come and to go, to stay or to emigrate. Liberty also embraces all the political rights: the right to consent to government and to withdraw that consent, to judge and to act on that judgment, to speak freely, to assemble. People with the right to rule themselves are called to rule themselves. People who rule themselves bow before freedom of conscience. They are commanded not only to honor that in others but to act on it themselves.

The right to the pursuit of happiness affirms, as Rainsborough did, the fullness of the democratic demand. It is not enough to be fed and sheltered and left ignorant. It is not enough to protect the body and leave the life of the mind to chance. The democratic demand is not for bare life but for a whole life. Each person holds within them the demand for what that life requires. Each is called to fulfill that promise.

13. People have the right to assemble.

A life is at once a life apart and a life together. Democrats need to preserve those anarchic spaces where people are ungoverned and so can remain ungovernable. A full life is a life with others. That begins in the right to assemble. People have the right to work together to make space for themselves, in families, among their friends, in towns, wherever they please. They come together to shape the world as they think best. They gather to rule themselves willingly. They also gather to govern, reproach, challenge, and overthrow the governments they create, powers that rise to dominate them, threats to their freedom. The right to assemble, to appear together in all the fragility and power of the body, secures both their common good and their freedom to live apart.

In the United States, but not only in the United States, the right to assemble has been eroded. We are told that we can assemble only with the permission of the government and under the eye of the police. We can assemble only at certain places and at certain times. When we assemble we are fenced in and herded like cattle through the pre-appointed route of a permitted march. There are penalties for those the police determine are disturbing the peace or not observing the limits of their license to demonstrate. This is not exercising the right to assemble. This is permitting the state to take it away.

In the wake of the March on Washington, Malik el Shabazz, Malcolm X, recognized the limits of this iconic and redemptive assembly: "They controlled it so tight—they told those Negroes what time to hit town, how to come, where to stop, what signs to carry, what song to sing, what speech they could make, and what speech they couldn't make; and then told them to get out of town by sundown."[3]

It is easy and convenient to accept the restrictions on marches and demonstrations (which is to say, on our right to assemble). There is an implicit contract, quite often breached, that if the marchers and demonstrators stay in their place, the police will protect them. In any case, people know the route in advance, and they can plan, if not for an escape in time of danger (that may be blocked by the fences and inhibited by the presence of the police) at least for their trip home if things remain orderly, and for an escape if they do not. None of this, however, needs to be honored. Officials can suggest, and people can follow these suggestions if they choose. Accepting the limits imposed by the state may make revolutionary change possible. Yet it is a price, a burden, and a constraint that we should recognize and resist when resistance is necessary.

The right to assemble is a right. No license is necessary. No permit, no permission is required. When people accede to licenses and permits, it should be their choice alone and ought not to be done too often. Governments, and the people themselves, must learn again that the right to assemble is a right and not a privilege. Corporations, banks, and factories must learn that rights reach farther than the state.

Assemblies of free people can be displays of great recklessness and courage. The world has watched the people of Hong Kong rally in defense of their remaining liberties. They are the people Machiavelli described, who, having lived in freedom under their own laws, remember their ancient liberties even when they are lost. Sometimes the will to rule themselves seems to come not from a remembered history but from nowhere. We watch the people of Thailand struggle toward a democracy they have never known. The rebellious people may have little or no freedom to remember, but they drive toward justice all the same.

We watched the people of Tahrir Square rise up. People all over the world who had never been to Egypt or known an Egyptian sent one another videos showing the courage of the Egyptian people. There is a video of an Egyptian in London, Waseem Wagdi, that I watched in that time (and often since). He is a middle-aged man in a camel's hair sports jacket and a scarf, with a composed, educated manner and fluent English. He speaks calmly and analytically to the reporter at first, then with rising passion: "It is something, I had hoped, against all hope, would happen in my lifetime." He had hoped that his children would see freedom, but the people in Egypt, "the heroes in Egypt are not waiting. They are bringing all of our dreams through today." The reporter asks him what he would say to the Egyptian people. He responds, "I must say it in Arabic first," and turns to face the camera directly. Then with tears running down his face he bears witness to their courage and says, "I kiss the dirt under your feet." The people were, he says, "cleansing themselves of all remnants of fear."[4] They had the courage to rule themselves. He knew that freedom depended on courage. He honored that courage in the people who would not wait, the people fired by what King called "the fierce urgency of now."

You who read this will know that these revolutions were put down. They were, as revolutions often are, undermined and betrayed. They were overcome by military power, by the power of the wealthy, and by the fears people had of one another. Perhaps we will not live to see them succeed. Perhaps, in our sight or beyond it, they will find their way through.

Not all uprisings or assemblies are just or honorable or democratic. Not all assemblies are wise. Not all respect the rights held in the body. All people have the right to assemble. They do not have the right to assemble uncontested. Their assembly voices a demand. That demand may be just or unjust. The demand calls to us for judgment.

On January 6, 2020, a group of people assembled at the U.S. Capitol. Conscious of their power, filled with anger, and persuaded that the presidential election had been stolen, they broke through the police barriers and poured into the Capital. They wore bison headdresses and face paint, camo and flannel jackets. There were men and women, old and young. They said that they were right to come, right to break down the barriers to Congress and enter the Capitol because "[t]his is the people's house."

They had the right to assemble, to confront their representatives, to voice their anger and their demands. They were right to say, "This is the people's house." Their assembly, their chaotic entry, their costumes, and even the suspect liberties they took show that belief in the power of the people over their government endures. We should not condemn them for this. Nevertheless, the insurrection of January 6 was undemocratic, the work of authoritarianism and deception.

People can be mistaken; people can be deceived; people can be misled. Too many of the people assembled on January 6 were in thrall to the absurd conspiracy theories of QAnon; too many had listened too long to the dishonesty broadcast by Fox. Too many were made vulnerable by justified anger and reasonable fear. They were led badly. They were not judging; they were following.

They were also armed. Too many came not to voice their demands but to compel by force. There were those who crushed a Capitol policeman and beat others with flagpoles, baseball bats, and pipes. They inflicted broken bones and brain injuries. They threatened members of Congress, their staffs, people simply working at jobs in the Capitol, people visiting.

They sought, by their own testimony, to impose their will on the country. The use of violence, the indifference to the views of others, marked their struggle as authoritarianism in the making.

They sought not to expand but to limit rights and freedoms. They listened to authoritarians; they followed an authoritarian; they acted to impose their will by force.

The right to assemble carries with it the command to assemble when assembly is needed. This requires both judgment and courage. Out of revolutionary assemblies come repeated images of individuals standing unarmed before heavily armed soldiers and police. These images of individuals standing alone before power are not the opposite of the people assembled. They stand for the people. The rights that the assembly calls up belong to the whole people. They are therefore present in each of the people. They cannot be rooted out. It is for this reason, and because of their transcendent courage, that people facing guns and dogs, fire hoses, tear gas, guns and bombs, uncertain of any victory, still say, still sing, "We shall overcome, someday."

14. People have the right to speak and to be silent.

One of the rights sought by those who face the naked power of the state is the right to remain silent. Those who intend to rule themselves know that they must defend their bodies to keep their souls free. The closed body, safe from coercion, protected from dependence on others, shelters the open mind.

Lawyers and scholars have debated whether the right to privacy is a right at all. They are wrong to doubt it. Privacy is a right so profound and fundamental that it has become invisible. Without the right to privacy we lie naked before the eyes of whatever state or corporate power can place us under surveillance. We are in their power. Without the right to keep our bodies to ourselves we are no better than slaves the master can violate at will. Without the right to keep our bodies whole and healthy and in the forms we choose, we are dependent and, again, enslaved.

Those who can reach into your body have you at their mercy. This is the case whether it is the government, a corporation, a religious organization, or a private person.

The right to remain within yourself is also the right to remain silent. This is one of the prized rights of the Anglo-American political tradition. It was claimed by those who were asked to take oaths of loyalty to the ruler and the established church. It is claimed by those on trial who argue that they cannot be compelled to testify against themselves. Though it is honored in the Anglo-American constitutions, it is not confined there. This right belongs to all.

The right to remain silent affirms the right of every person to speak where and when they choose. The right to freedom of speech is allied to the right to freedom of conscience.

Freedom of speech is also intimately related to freedom of the press. The concentration of media in a few hands means that a few control what can be read or heard, what can be written in the papers or on billboards, what can be heard on the radio or seen on TV, even (perhaps especially) what can be seen or heard or read online. When only those who have wealth can speak or make themselves heard, freedom of speech is not fully established. When those who have wealth or power determine what can be said or heard, speech is not free.

If we cannot yet meet as equals in the public sphere, still less can we meet as equals at work. When we meet each other at home, we can question, challenge, and reason with each other. At work we know that we must be silent. It is now taken for granted in many, perhaps in most circles that freedom of speech is a right restricted to the political sphere. If freedom of speech is a natural right, grounded in our common embodied condition, carried in our bodies, it is carried into the workplace as well.

The right to speak freely applies not only to states or corporations or to control of the media. It applies to all places where some can speak and others are forced to be silent, where some have a voice and others remain unheard. Consider heckling. Heckling appears to be the voice of a mob silencing the voice of reason, an exercise of brute power: mindless and dictatorial. Do not be too ready to make this judgment. More often, the speaker is famous or powerful, invited to speak because they have already been heard or read many times. Those who heckle are those who have much less voice. They are unlikely to have the chance to question or challenge such a speaker. They meet on unequal ground. Even it out a bit: let people heckle. Do not be eager to condemn those who take the rare chance they have to be heard. If a British prime minister can face a little heckling, speaker, so can you.

Freedom of speech is not a license to speak without criticism, disagreement, or rejection. Those who listen are free to criticize, to argue, to answer, to tell the speaker they have said enough. Free people speak what and when they choose. We can bring passion as well as reason to what we say. In academic papers, in debates on television or online, in lectures, books, articles, and writings of all sorts, those who have a voice can use it. We can say what we choose, but we cannot silence our critics. We are responsible for what we say, and we must answer to others for it.

Freedom of speech does not require us to listen to all with equal deference and attention. That would be often foolish and occasionally dishonorable. People judge. They decide if the person speaking or writing has knowledge or practical wisdom. They decide if their wisdom is suited to the question at hand. They decide if the person is honest and likely to tell them the truth. They decide if the person deserves their respect. They decide if the person has been heard enough. They decide if the person needs not to be heard but to listen. In many cases, they should lend an ear and a voice to those who question and those who heckle.

In a time when there are those who are truly silenced—by the state, by the media, by corporations, by bosses, and by the people around them—it is unseemly for the privileged and the powerful to claim that they are silenced. It is dishonorable for them to demand a hearing on false pretenses. Honorable people will recognize their power and seek out those who are less often heard. That will not be easy. People are held within circles of family, friendship, work, religion, and acquaintance. While inequality persists, approaches to those less wealthy or powerful than themselves will be awkward, limited by distrust, anger, deference, or despair. Those without power find that approaches to the privileged are forestalled at every step. Inequality is the enemy of freedom.

Freedom of speech is not merely the right to speak without being silenced by censorship. It is the right to speak freely: to say what you choose, not a script dictated to you by another. There are still efforts to make people speak a script written by another: to denounce terrorism, to confess their sexuality, to refuse this or that. There are still efforts to make people speak against their will. These violate freedom of speech as profoundly as silencing does. They are the softer face of torture.

Torture is the effort of one person, often though not always in the service of a state, to make another speak against their will. Those who have studied (and those who have experienced) torture have learned that the tortured do not speak the truth. They speak as they are compelled to speak. The speech that is wrung from them through suffering is speech to end suffering, speech that signals submission. It may or may not disclose a hidden truth; it is no more and no less than the triumph of the torturer's will. Torture is the triumph of force over consent. Free people cannot use, cannot license, torture.

Let the silent speak if they choose. Let those who speak say what they will. Listen and judge.

15. Assembly nurtures the democratic. Assembly preserves the anarchic.

Democracy begins when people seize power for themselves. The process of making their government to suit themselves begins when they come together, acting together, binding their aims in a common cause.

Those who watch and study and, above all, those who police demonstrations look for leaders and organizers. The people who assemble rarely do. They look to each other. They may listen to speakers; more often they do not. They turn from speakers and talk to each other. They are many, yet in that crowd they retain their individuality. They come and go as they please. They chant or refuse to chant. Sometimes they sing. They choose to be loud or silent, joyful or somber. They choose to stand fast or to run, to fight or to refuse the fight. Assemblies remind us that solidarity is possible in anarchy, that an anarchic disposition and anarchic commitments do not foreclose the possibility of acting with others.

The anthropologist Victor Turner wrote that assemblies can loosen all the restraints of law and custom. People feel free and act on it. They are unbound. In their freedom they can affirm or refuse their government, their laws, their customs, and their people. They know that they make and unmake governments and people. They can refuse what has been for what could be. Turner saw this embedded in the coming-of-age rituals of many peoples. It was, he argued, part of "the ritual process."[5] Accepting new people into the group or tribe—or nation—alters the boundaries of the people. Acceptance changes not only those who are newly included but those who change with their changing people. That change, Turner argued, was the occasion for joy.

16. People have the right to a place in the world. People have the right to stay or to leave, to come or to go.

The rights to speak, to have a voice, to assemble, to rule are undergirded by a simpler right. The right to life entails a right to presence in the world. This, the simplest of all rights, is difficult to defend. The Cherokee, Jews sent into exile or sent to their death, the Roma, the Palestinians, the Rohingya pushed off their land, all are denied a place in their worlds. When people are sent to exile or to internment camps or deportation facilities, when their land is seized or they are massacred en masse the wrong is clear. They have been denied their rights. Those rights should be secured.

We know that when some people struggle to find a place in the world, they may displace others. The tragic history of Israel couples sin and redemption. All settler colonial states saw the indigenous lose their land to give shelter and sustenance not only to the wealthy and powerful but far more often to the poor and disenfranchised. Settler colonialism effected a double displacement: the poor and outlawed at home, the indigenous abroad.

There are other, more mundane ways in which people struggle to find a place in the world. The queer person in a straight community may be loved and sheltered or shunned and mocked. The religious believer living among casual secularists may feel lost and long for a place to worship with others. There are always people out of place. Some take pleasure in their solitude. Some take pride in their eccentricity. Some are valued by those around them—whether for their differences or despite them. Sometimes, in recognizing the value of those who are out of place, the community grows larger, greater in size and soul than it was.

This is not always a question of justice or virtue. Those who are harried and bullied are wronged, and it reflects badly on their community—and on each person within it. But there are also people who are simply out of place. There is no injustice done by those who cannot in good conscience worship as the religious among them wish. There is no fault in those who long for a life of prayer and piety with others. There is no evil in the small, intimate, provincial town that lacks the theater, the opera, the wild diversity that a would-be cosmopolitan longs for. We should not assume that people are born where they should be.

This simple principle should be obvious. There are, however, many who have written so lovingly of the virtues of community that they forget the trials of those who find themselves out of place. They cannot see the promise of flight, the courage of the emigrant and fugitive.

Simone Weil envisioned community as the nursery of the moral. Uprootedness is "the disease of uprootedness," "by far the most dangerous malady to which human societies are exposed." Over and over again she refers to uprootedness as a destructive "disease": "A human being has roots by virtue of his real, active and natural participation in the life of a community which preserves in living shape certain particular treasures of the past and certain particular expectations for the future." One heritage, one form of life alone can form an ethical person. People within communities should not be permitted to venture outside them in thought. "Outside influences" should be bound by the community, and people should "receive such contributions only from its hands."[6] Though she sees the defects of her own time and place, and of the Romans, the Hebrews, the Americans, and a host of others, she does not appear to recognize that the power of communities to shape people can be distorting, imprisoning, and corrupting. Uprootedness can be liberating and enlightening.

Too much turns on the metaphor of roots. That image sees belonging as bound to a place, disturbed by movement. That is not how people are made. People are made to stay and to go, to dig into the earth, to build from it and walk through it. People can leave the earth to sail or to fly—metaphorically as well as actually. Weil recognizes that "[r]isk is an essential need of the soul," yet she is limited by her fear of loss: "The destruction of the past is perhaps the greatest of all crimes."[7]

You have the right to a place in the world. You have the right to move. The right to be in the world depends in practice on the right to leave one place for another. Frederick Douglass, who knew the need to move, wrote of a "right to migration."[8] A slave who escaped his masters—and the law—he found his voice grew stronger as he moved steadily northward. There are many kinds of people on the move. Douglass was an escaped slave, a refugee, an American intellectual in Ireland and Britain, an American ambassador. There are refugees fleeing war, seeking to preserve their lives and the lives of those they call their own. There are the refugees made by natural disasters: floods and earthquakes, hurricanes and tornados. There are refugees made by our irresponsibility before nature: drought, dust bowls, floods, and wildfires. There are migrants who flee hunger. All these (and more) have a right to go out into the world because they have the right to life.

There are also people pressed by needs as imperative as, though perhaps less visible than, escaping wars and earthquakes. Local communities are often praised for their closeness, for the trust and kinship of the people within them. They are honored by many for their ability to maintain themselves over time, to develop their own ways. These communities, however warm and nurturing to some, may be stifling to others. People who do not feel at home there have the right to leave.

Perhaps they will find homes elsewhere. Perhaps they will always walk like Kipling's cat, by their wild lone.

A community too may decide that is does not belong. Perhaps colonial rule has become indefensible to them. Perhaps they have been persecuted. Perhaps they have simply grown apart from those they once regarded as their own. They should not be compelled to stay.

All people have the right to leave: to leave homes, communities, practices, and pasts behind.

If there is no place to go, the right to leave is empty. I will not pretend that I can decide for you, or that I can decide in principle, or indeed that we can decide in principle all that we owe or what we can justly deny to migrants and refugees. Rogers Smith has argued that we owe more to immigrants and refugees we have burdened in the past: the people who have fought our wars, the people we made war against.[9] This is a compelling criterion for judgment. There are simpler duties.

People carry their rights in their bodies. Those who breach the borders, who appear petitioning at the gate, who wash up on the shore, carry their rights with them. The rights that belong to all belong to them. They have a right to all that is necessary to maintain life, a right to fundamental freedoms. Though those rights may burden us, we cannot disregard them and maintain our honor. The migrant and the refugee have the right to pursue their happiness. They may have more rights among more generous people. Our practice in these and other matters should always exceed our principles. We should give more than we think is due. That is magnanimity, the virtue proper to people who rule themselves.

Thomas Paine, who seeded revolutions as he moved, wrote, "[R]eceive the fugitive, and prepare in time an asylum for mankind."[10] Open the gates to those who want to come. Open them to those who want to leave.

17. Rights are born in us. They are above, beyond, and before the law.

Rights belong to us: they are not the gift of law. They are not given by the state or by any transnational institution. There are civil rights, of course. The right to travel under a particular passport. The right to vote in a particular electoral system, to stand for election, to hold an office. The right to drive a car or have a dog. These are civil rights, given by a civil order. Some are important; some are not. They may be given by a particular people who have already ordered their government in the form they chose, by states whose procedures determine who will and will not be granted civil rights, even by a state controlled by an autocrat who confers civil standing and civil rights as he or she chooses.

Whether civil rights are, in practice, rights or privileges depends on the actions of the people or the state that claims to grant them. Privileges are granted; rights are demanded. Civil rights are privileges the state extends through law or dictate. Rights are ours, and their recognition is not something to plead for but something to demand. The civil rights movement, despite its name, demanded not privileges but rights. Their demand was not that rights be granted but that already present rights be recognized. The rights they demanded were twofold. They demanded recognition of the rights that belong by nature to all people: to life, liberty, and the pursuit of happiness. They also demanded the rights of their people: to vote, to stand for election, to hold office. They sought their freedom, as people and as a people, as living human beings and as Americans.

Our natural rights, grounded in the body, are fundamental and inalienable. They are not the gift of law.

18. Rights are inalienable.

Rights cannot be made alien to us. They are born into the living person, held in the warm flesh of the living body, and each of us holds rights like a soul. Are they transcendent rights? Perhaps. On earth, we know no soul separated from the flesh, and it is on earth that we struggle to rule ourselves.

Rights cannot be alienated. They cannot be bought or sold, traded or disavowed.

The slave on a plantation, picking cotton in Mississippi, cutting cane in Louisiana or Cuba; the miner in West Virginia or Witwatersrand had the rights that belong to any and to all people, long before those rights were acknowledged, much less honored as decency demands.

Rights are inalienable. To demand, to seize, to exercise those rights requires extraordinary courage. That courage is visible in revolutions, to be sure, but it is ordinary courage that enables people to live freely and rule themselves. The courage that stands against tanks is futile if it cannot be transformed into the common courage that enables a divided people to listen, to work with one another in ruling themselves, to speak freely, to walk among their enemies unafraid.

The duty to recognize rights, to secure them, to enforce and defend them does not fall to the police, to judges, to governments. That duty is ours. Our rights are grounded in our bodies. Our duty is there as well. We bear our responsibility in our bodies.

19. Rights are held in common.

We hold our rights in common. Rights are not a gift of law, defined and parceled out by those in power. Rights are a commons.

The commons differs from collective property. The commons cannot be owned at all. Holdings in common cannot be alienated. They cannot be sold or traded. They cannot be given a monetary value. So it is with rights. They cannot be alienated, sold, or traded. They cannot be valued in monetary terms. As with a common field, rights must belong to all equally.

The commons can generate private property, as a fisherman in Wisconsin takes fish from a river or a hiker in Sweden picks berries in a field. These may diminish the commons slightly, though often they help the commons to prosper. Rights held in common are simultaneously one's own and belonging to all. Rights are part of our common wealth in the fullest sense. The right of one person to preserve life, to stay healthy, makes all the commons safer and healthier. The right of one person to pursue happiness, to cultivate talents, to seek an education, to learn, increases the common store of learning and wisdom. The wisdom brought to the commons in this way increases the common store of material things as well. We learn to cultivate common wealth, to preserve the environment, to take in a way that generates common—and private—resources.

The commons generates rights and powers. As we cultivate the rights we hold in common, knowledge of rights grows and spreads like fire. Speaking freely, speaking openly, speaking without fear or favor teaches. We hear unexpected, unknown things. We are criticized, rebuked. We learn. We recognize forms of injustice we did not see. We grow wiser and more daring. We become more just. As we assemble we find ourselves in the company of unexpected allies. We experience unexpected kindnesses: a bottle of water, a shield. We learn what fraternity and solidarity look like, feel like. We see how a great body of people can move as one. In smaller assemblies we can see the courage of the few against the many. The right of people to think, to worship as they choose, not merely to possess but to practice freedom of conscience opens new understandings of the divine to us.

Rights are strengthened when they are held in common. They lose their strength when they are restricted. Rights held by only a few are not rights but privileges and, like all privileges, they are insecure. Rights held by all, secured by all, are fully realized in the world. The rights of the individual and the rights of the community are one. Because people's rights are grounded in their bodies they belong to all. Any failure to respect rights in another person diminishes one's own rights. There is no distinction here between public and private, individual and community. The protection of individual rights, securing each person in their rights, serves the whole.

Indeed it is only through securing the rights of individual people that our common rights can be secured. If you want to keep your rights, you must defend all.

Rights are thus one place, one commons where the distinction between private and public, individualism and community becomes misleading and meaningless. So too does the distinction between rights and duties.

Rights and duties are not opposites; they are related as concave is to convex. When the Declaration speaks of the right to rebellion, that right is cast as both a right and a duty: "it is their right, it is their duty, to rebel." That is true of all rights. They command. The right to speak freely becomes the command to speak freely and the duty to listen. The right to assemble becomes the duty to assemble, the command to assemble. Rights animate the people who hold them. They shape those people in themselves and in relation to one another. People who know their rights walk proudly, act bravely. They know no life is worth more than their life. They are commanded to protect their own rights, and that command impels them to protect the rights of all.

The commons is a field open to all. All take rights from it and, in doing so, increase the rights of all, as fire spreads when it is shared.[11] In making common rights their own, in using their rights to shape the world, individuals increase the commonwealth of rights. They strengthen themselves. They strengthen the people. They repair the world.

20. Rights are above, below, and beyond the law. Rights undergird the law. Rights elevate the law.

This is an old lesson, continually challenged. Law can block the exercise of rights. Law can hedge rights about with restrictions and limits. There is, however, nothing in the law that can take rights away from the people. Rights are inalienable.

Rights are the grounding and the mission of law. Rights are above, beneath, beyond, and before the law. Governments are made and laws established, in the words of the Declaration, to secure these rights. When they fail to do so, they lose their legitimacy. Laws must defer to rights if they are to be legitimate themselves. Rights are before the law. Just laws are made to ensure that rights can be made secure and put into practice. Rights are beneath the law, supporting it. Rights are above the law, governing it. Rights are beyond the law, giving law a mission to accomplish, a standard to achieve, an ideal to reach. Rights restrain the law.

Rights also drive law forward. Knowledge of the rights people hold drives them to secure those rights, drives them to establish governments. Knowledge of their rights drives people to put them into practice: to cultivate themselves and their people. Laws are one of their tools.

Rights are not fences; rights are a ground. They ground government. They are ground to be cultivated.

IV
Free people rule the law

21. Rule law. Do not simply be ruled by it.

"The Rule of Law, Not Men" was one of the battle cries of the English Civil War. It has an honored place in the history of republicanism and revolution. That declaration announced the end of monarchy, of all autocracy and tyranny. The word of one would no longer be enough to rule. Arbitrary rule, in which a favored few or a favored view would be treated differently, to rise and fall at the whim of the ruler, would be set aside. Those who longed for the rule of law saw a system in which no one was above the law and all people would be treated equally. They saw a system in which law endured and could be known to all. They saw an enduring order. Yet the rule of law is not and cannot be a good in itself.

There is no virtue in the rule of law when the laws that rule are unjust.

There is nothing rare or mysterious about laws that do evil. That icon of evil, the Third Reich, was a *Rechtsstaat*, a constitutional state, a state under the rule of law. The genocide of the Jews, the seizure of their goods, the ethnic cleansing of the Roma, the imprisonment of dissenters and those called deviants were all done under the law, with all the propriety and paperwork that law demands. The Rule of Law was the Rule of Evil then.

At their best, legal decisions can make a change of public sentiment visible, give it voice, and guide its development. Yet a legal decision can as easily (and I fear more often) stand in the way of justice and freedom. The Supreme Court of the United States has demonstrated, on too many occasions, its ability to affirm law against justice.

The *Dred Scott* decision sent Mr. Scott, who had been, by law, a free man in the state of Illinois and the territory of Louisiana, and a free man by right in all the world, back into slavery in the state of

Wild Democracy. Anne Norton, Oxford University Press. © Oxford University Press 2023.
DOI: 10.1093/oso/9780197644348.003.0004

Missouri. The Court not only denied Mr. Scott his freedom in the state of Missouri; it denied him and all descendants of Africans their freedom anywhere in the United States. In doing so it made freedom dependent on laws of ownership and residence. It made freedom the gift of the master and the masters' law. Slaves could not demand or affirm the freedom that was theirs by right. In denying Dred Scott his freedom, the Court denied Dred Scott his humanity. He was, Taney's opinion declared, a member of "a subordinate and inferior class of beings, who had been subjugated by the dominant race, and, whether emancipated or not, yet remained subject to their authority, and had no rights or privileges but such as those who held the power and the Government might choose to grant them."[1] Here the law served to seal the slavery not only of one man but of many. Law served injustice, law served evil, here.

Buck v. Bell, in which Oliver Wendell Holmes famously declared, "[T]hree generations of imbeciles is enough," purported to defend the confinement and care of those who were dangerous or unable to care for themselves and allow them to be sterilized for the common good. According to a contemporary website:

> Carrie Buck was a feeble minded woman who was committed to a state mental institution. Her condition had been present in her family for the last three generations. A Virginia law allowed for the sexual sterilization of inmates of institutions to promote the "health of the patient and the welfare of society."[2]

These, we are told, are the "facts of the case." In law, the "facts of the case" are not what an ordinary person would understand the facts of the case to be. They are what the judge determines them to be.[3] Here, the facts of the case—in the ordinary sense—were that Carrie Buck was not feeble-minded at all. She had had the misfortune to be raped by a wealthy and privileged man whose family found it convenient to have her put away.

When the Supreme Court reviewed the case, they did not inquire into the facts of the case but simply into whether the lower courts had followed the law. Law can be very far indeed from justice. Law is often, if not always, seen as a good in itself, subject to its own rules, and assessed not by the standard of justice but by its internal coherence and consistency.

Buck v. Bell legitimized eugenic sterilization. The decision came at a time when eugenics was widely popular, with contests for "Fitter Families" and "Better Babies." The fitter families and better babies were white and blond, what enthusiasts for eugenics might call "Aryan." Eugenics fit very well indeed with the Jim Crow laws and segregationist practices of the United States in the late nineteenth and early twentieth centuries. Like segregation, it extended beyond the Jim Crow South. Nor was it limited to conservatives. On the contrary, the conviction that experts, rather than the people themselves, should decide who should reproduce and who should not, suited the belief of many Progressives in the rule of experts. Here too the rule of law served injustice.

Fred Korematsu resisted the forced relocation and internment of people of Japanese ancestry in the United States during World War II. The U.S. Supreme Court affirmed his internment, arguing not that it was right but that it was lawful. Law served injustice here, but there was a voice for justice. In his dissenting opinion, Justice Frank Murphy argued that law must bow to right: "I dissent, therefore, from this legalization of racism. Racial discrimination in any form and in any degree has no justifiable part whatever in our democratic way of life. It is unattractive in any setting, but it is utterly revolting among a free people."[4] Murphy's dissent marked the divide between legality and legitimacy, liberalism and democracy, unjust law and the requirements of a free people.

The rule of law secured slavery in the United States. After slavery was abolished, Jim Crow laws kept the newly free chained. Law has subordinated women to men, workers to employers. Law favors the rich over the poor. A fine that is nothing to a rich man can impoverish a poor one. Worse, the practice of increasing the most trivial fines with time—parking meter violations for example—can lead in some states to imprisonment for failure to pay, regardless of the poverty of the defendant. In such cases, people are imprisoned not for their violations but for their poverty. The rich have the money to sue and to defend themselves in court. Few others do. The provision of pro bono lawyers, as every lawyer knows, does not correct this inequity. How many have died or faced imprisonment because the lawyers they were assigned were overworked, or given too little time or training? The rich employ the law to avoid paying taxes. The wealthy who employ these shifts are contemptible to be sure, but how are we to judge a law that in its very bones favors the rich over the poor?

There was—there is—no justice, no right in being ruled by such laws. If the law is not just, the rule of law is nothing to honor and cannot justly command obedience. "The law," James Baldwin insisted, "is meant to be my servant and not my master"[5]

There are also laws that are mistaken, antiquated, or simply silly. Should they be obeyed? Not necessarily. People who rule themselves must learn not to submit to the rule of law, but to judge the law. The state, even the liberal state can be as exacting a master as any king, and law the state's most effective tool.

I have put American laws before you, but this is not solely an American problem. There are, I suspect, more unjust laws than just ones. All are called to judge their laws. All must ask whether the laws that rule them secure the rights that belong to all human beings. They must ask whether the laws protect people and advance their welfare. They must ask whether the laws are just. When the laws fail, they must be changed. When the laws do harm, they must be broken. People who rule themselves rule their laws.

This is not a matter the people can leave to lawyers. No lawyer, no judge, no court, even those named "Supreme" or "Constitutional," can justly claim the final word on the legitimacy—and still less on the justice—of the law. Doctrines of judicial supremacy depend on the notion that law is the province of experts alone. When law is made by experts, by judges or lawyers, it is no longer the means that enables people to rule themselves. It becomes a prison and the means for placing people in servitude and slavery. Behind this elevation of law is fear of the people. The people are Sovereign, and they determine all questions that belong to the sovereign. They rule themselves. The law therefore must bow to them. The people shall judge.[6]

Law, like government, can secure rights, but it is not in itself a force for freedom. Law is a force for order. Order can be a protection or a prison. At its best, order gives us peace and the ability to plan. At its worst, law imprisons. Order forecloses opportunities, precludes change, and prevents the achievement of justice. Even the most benign orders can be stifling.

Law can help forge a better future, one in which rights are more secure, freedom greater, and people more able to pursue their own happiness, but it does not, in itself, drive toward the future. In states governed by precedent and common law, law anchors itself in the past. Common law is the work of convention in time. At its best, the common law captures the accumulated wisdom of generations of practice. At its worst, it preserves unjust practices, hardens them, and secures the yoke on the necks of the oppressed. In either case, the common law is conservative in its forms, methods, and effects. Above all, the notion of precedent as authoritative makes the conventional past the limit of law. All law, all judgment must be justified according to its adherence to the past.

The past, however, has rarely been just. The full text of Baldwin's quote runs:

> This is why those pious calls to "respect the law," always to be heard from prominent citizens each time the ghetto explodes, are so obscene. The law is meant to be my servant and not my master, still less my torturer and my murderer. To respect the law, in the context in which the American Negro finds himself, is simply to surrender his self-respect.

The rule of law must be understood not as a rule we accept but as a rule we exercise. The people are not simply subjects to be ruled by law. The people are sovereign, and they rule the law.

Any appeal to the principle of rule of law should be answered by the questions "What law? Which laws?" There is no honor, no morality, and no political virtue in the rule of unjust law. Many appalling crimes have taken place under the color of law. Every former colony will recall the inequities of imperial rule. Americans will remember more recent injustices: the effort to give cover of law to Guantanamo, black sites, and the deaths of George Floyd, Breonna Taylor, and many more. The rule of bad law deserves no reverence. It calls for action.

Rule of law should not, however, be abandoned as an ideal. We should listen for what is said in that phrase. We are bound not only to be ruled by law but to rule it. The rule of law should describe not only the rule of law over all people equally but our rule of the laws we make, the laws we are called to obey. Any people that began in revolution, or prides itself on the revolutions that freed it from arbitrary rule, should honor the decision to rule law rather than merely be ruled by it.

The rule of law by the people is a far more demanding discipline than simple submission. People are required to judge. They have to think. They have to consider what the law does—not merely in intention but in effect. They have to consider whether the operation of a damaging law might be repaired by interpretation. There are many people, particularly lawyers, who believe that the interpretation of laws is a matter for experts, that lawyers and judges should interpret the law and the people should remain passive. If the laws are the people's laws, they have the right and the duty to interpret them. This is true for all law, from the smallest regulation to constitutional laws. People may— they should—turn to others for help in this task. They should question, debate, think, defer to judgment they judge better than their own, but the right to interpret belongs to them. There are times when the most powerful interpretations belong not to the rule of experts but to the expertise of rule.

Langston Hughes's poem "Freedom's Plow" provides an example of how the texts that define a people are to be read. Hughes quotes the words of the Declaration of Independence, and then goes on:

A long time ago, but not too long, a man said
"ALL MEN ARE CREATED EQUAL,
. . . ENDOWED BY THEIR CREATOR WITH CERTAIN
INALIENABLE RIGHTS, AMONG THESE LIFE, LIBERTY AND
THE PURSUIT OF HAPPINESS"
His name was Jefferson. There were slaves then.
But in their hearts the slaves believed him too
And silently took for granted
That what he said was also meant for them.[7]

The slaves' reading was closest to the letter of the text and still closer to the spirit of that text. Their reading has an authority the founders' reading lacked.

We have come to recognize that a piece of writing can contain more meaning, more wisdom than its author knew or intended. When a piece of writing becomes the North Star of a people, its capacity for transcendence becomes still greater. So familiar is the text of the Declaration that women who read "all men are created" need not pause over the words. We know that what they said was also meant for us, whether those who wrote it knew it or not.

Many of us have learned to read our presence in texts not meant for us. We have learned to see beyond the failings of those who wrote the words to the promise we can read in them. We have learned that sometimes people need to steal the words of the rich and give them to the poor. Hughes offers us more than this, however. He raises the possibility that the meaning of the laws and ideals that govern us should not be judged simply by the intention of the author or by the judgments of experts but also by those on whom burdens fall most heavily or those who are most capable of seeing the promise the laws hold. For these reasons, and for many more, we should reject the idea that we should be governed by the "original meaning" of any text.

Words can become greater than they were. Laws can grow in what they offer, in the possibilities seen in them by the people. Laws can also have consequences—intended or not—that diminish the people who make them. Prisons were developed as a way of making punishment kinder, of enabling people to reflect on their errors and improve. They became places that increased the brutality of those who were imprisoned and those who imprisoned them. Laws have increased suffering they were intended to diminish. We have learned this. Now we must work to find better ways.[8]

Those who have found laws unworthy, inadequate, or simply wrong have to act. If they are among people of good conscience, the greater part of the laws is good, and there is no immediate need, they can act within the law, evade the law, and work to change the remnant of laws that are unjust. That work may be hard. In most cases, they neither can nor should act alone. They will have to explain to others the problems they have found in the law, to seek out solutions, and to organize to put those into effect. The work is demanding, often frustrating, and rarely easy. It is work for the thoughtful and the long-sighted. It is work for people strong enough to rule themselves.

There are laws no decent person can obey. They will not obey them.

22. Justice, like democracy, goes beyond the law.

Praise of anarchy, outlaws, rebels, and rogues may trouble those who believe in the Rule of Law, who prize order and precedent, who bow too deeply to tradition. People who rule themselves are concerned not only with obedience to the law, or even ruling the law. They are able to set law aside. The demands of justice surpass the demands of law. The protection of rights has a commanding power greater than the law. Law does not set aside the rights people have by nature. Rights surpass the force of law. People who rule themselves do more than obey the law. They rule it; they make it their own.

This is no revolutionary novelty. This is an old wisdom. Aristotle observed in the *Politics* that law does not always accord with justice. Justice may require more or less than the law lays out. Plato offered that lesson in the Euthyphro. Practical experience persuaded the British of the same thing. If law were all that was at issue, it would be unnecessary, even undesirable, to have a jury of one's peers. The verdict would be a matter of applied expertise. The judge, an expert in the law, would be sufficient. But knowledge of the law is not enough. The jury provides the means to give the community a voice in the justice of the verdict and the sentence. When people judge, in formal trials or in their ordinary lives, they ask not only "Is it legal?" but "Is it just?"

There is a space between law and justice, between law and rights, between law and the people. That space will not vanish. It is the work of time as well as politics. In this terrain, this legal no man's land, the people shall judge.

They judge whether the law is just. They judge whether the law is theirs. There are many people, every day, who look upon the laws they know and find them unjust. They must judge if it is their duty to rebel, to organize against the law, or to decide that this is one of those moments in which they can accept injustice done in their name.

Law belongs to those who make it. When a law becomes alien to a people, they should repeal it.[9] That law is no longer theirs, and they need not obey it. Perhaps once pious people, they have become less persuaded of the truths of their faith. Perhaps they have become more religious and believe they can work to approach the divine. Perhaps people who once thought they were from a single race or tribe have learned to welcome refugees and immigrants. People may realize that episodes in their past are more or less honorable than they had supposed. People change, they learn, they grow. Regret for past wrongs can be written into laws that look to the future.

In making their laws more just, they change who they are as a people. Their laws come closer to justice, and so do they.

Across the world, from the Amazon to the Antipodes, North to South, people have recognized wrongs done to indigenous people. The wrongs are many. Parents were stripped of their children; children were sent to boarding schools and stripped in turn of their languages and cultures, were buried in unmarked graves. Lands once held by people in common were seized by conquest, crime, guile—and law. Indigenous beliefs about an obligation to the land, to beings of and on the land, to spirits held within it were once mocked and ignored. Law made these wrongs possible. Law licensed and drove injustice.

People have come to regret the harm they did to the indigenous. Those regrets are not remorse alone. New Zealand has recognized Mount Taranaki and the river Whanganui as beings holding rights. In doing so, the people of New Zealand are doing more than amending wrongs done to the land and people who first made their home in it. They have taken the view of the indigenous people as the view common to all New Zealanders. They have learned. They have, thoughtfully, made themselves different than they were, in their laws as well as their learning. They have learned that colonialism wronged the Maori. That, perhaps, was the easiest lesson. They are learning a harder and more valuable one. They are learning what the land was and is to the Maori. The recognition of wrongs done testifies to their work to make themselves more just, more learned, more responsible. The will to make themselves more Maori, not only to learn from but to learn within Maori concepts, ideas, and understandings, makes New Zealanders an altered and transcendent people.

There are more mundane changes. People change around the world, and around the people the world changes. People who work to rule themselves are committed to sailing in that open, unmapped sea, changing course when conditions require it. They will find, from time to time, that their laws no longer serve the people they are or the people they wish to be. They will find that the future presents them with problems they did not anticipate. Weaponry changes. When navies sailed and states fought pitched battles from wooden ships, oak was a requirement of national security. States outlawed the cutting of large oak trees. Rich and poor bore the burdens of cultivating oak for the Navy. That has long been unnecessary, and the laws have been changed. Printing, publishing, social media all changed how people communicate. Each required new laws. Each made other laws unnecessary.

Ruling the law requires constant vigilance. Justice requires judgment. Justice requires us to make exceptions. Justice requires mercy. Justice requires ethics. When we see a law broken we decide if we will enforce it or look the other way. We decide if the law is just. We decide if justice requires an exception to a just law. We decide if justice will be done by demanding that the law be obeyed or that it be set aside.

People who rule themselves discover that law is not enough for them. Law does too little as well as too much. Grifters and greedy businessmen, caught in the evasion of taxes, in acts of naked nepotism or immoral acquisition, often reply defensively "It was legal" when challenged about their conduct. When someone's defense of their conduct is only "It was legal," they are likely to be acting unjustly. Obedience to law is not enough for ethics, morality, or simple human decency.

People who rule themselves are licensed to go beyond the law in rebellion, in disobedience, in mercy. They have the right, they have the duty, to rebel against unjust governments. They are required to be not only lawful but ethical. They are required to go beyond the law in their demands on themselves.

23. People should judge. Democracy depends upon judgment. Democracy hones judgment.

Judgment is at the center of democratic life. This is one of the most daunting and unrecognized demands made on people who rule themselves. In a democracy, among a free people one is always judging and judged, and that twice over. Each democrat is called to judge as part of the whole. Each is subject to the judgment of the whole. Each free person judges and is judged by the others.

Legislating is not the only role the people take in a democracy. They judge and they execute. They are called to see the laws they made put into action. They are executives. Judgment, of and beyond the law, is the work of the people, who are sovereign. Before, beneath, beyond government is the possibility of revolution. In their sovereignty, the people affirm or change their laws and decide the need for revolution. The people's judgment is made formal and institutional in the jury and in the work of election. People decide who is innocent and who is guilty. They decide whether the laws themselves are just, whether they should be upheld or set aside. The right of the people to judge not only the case but the law is acknowledged explicitly in states where jury nullification is recognized.

Judgment is demanded often in the ordinary workings of a common life. One is called to decide whom to vote for, what (if any) party to join, what verdict to give on a jury, when to press for the making or the repeal of laws, which laws to obey and which to ignore.

One is also called, every day and in times of the greatest crises, to decide who and what is to be tolerated. Generations ago Marcuse declared, "Tolerance is extended to policies, conditions, and modes of behavior which should not be tolerated because they are impeding, if not destroying, the chances of creating an existence without fear and misery." Many would agree that "what is proclaimed and practiced as tolerance today, is in many of its most effective manifestations serving the cause of oppression."[10] We are, however, divided over which policies serve repression and which liberation, which policies ought and ought not to be tolerated. This is, with varying intensity, nothing more or less than democratic politics. We have different interests. We are differently situated. We have borne different burdens and enjoyed different privileges. We are moved by different fears and hopes. We work for different ends. In confronting the fact that we do not want what all others want, we demonstrate our capacity for unity in difference, our common courage, and our ability to rule ourselves.

This should be, as George Washington recognized, our pride. In his letter to the Hebrew Congregation of Newport he wrote, "It is now no more that toleration is spoken of, as if it was by the indulgence of one class of people, that another enjoyed the exercise of their inherent natural rights."[11]

People who rule themselves are called to judge every day. They are called to judge in the formal institutions and ad hoc practices that enable them to govern themselves. They judge—and they are conscious of judging—in all their dealings with one another. They judge in acting as sovereign and in accepting subjection. They judge when they learn to rule themselves in the small matters of everyday life. Practices once seen as evil can be recognized as unimportant differences. If someone eats pork and someone else does not, what of it? If someone is tattooed, what of it? We learn when to judge and when to withhold judgment. If someone goes to church on Sunday rather than the mosque on Friday or the synagogue on Saturday, what of it? Let conscience guide them. The capacity for democratic judgment guides people away from toleration and toward a recognition of natural rights. This enabled Washington to say—and to take pride in saying—that the government of the United States "gives to bigotry no sanction, to persecution no assistance."[12]

We also learn to our sorrow that practices, acts, and laws we thought were acceptable or even good are wrong. Clearing forests for farmland once seemed a work of honorable labor. Plastics were a splendid invention, useful from the kitchen to the hospital, saving resources. Spanking was a sensible way to correct a child. Driving the indigenous off the land made the land able to feed many more. In coming to terms with unrecognized evil and unintended consequences people learn. They become wiser, more conscious of their fallibility, more careful in their judgments, more just and more generous than they were.

People who rule themselves hone their judgment. They are more to be trusted than those who are merely shaped by custom or educated in law.

Change is accomplished not only by individuals changing their own minds, learning and reasoning. Change comes to communities as well. Burke recognized and commended change that moved in geologic time: the slow erosion of a mountain, the slow building of a coral reef. Burke's favored forms of change were almost invisible. They proceeded through small and temporary deviations. No single change was obvious or disruptive. Each seemed to preserve a long chain of precedent and ancestry. At any moment, a person might say "We do as we have always done." Order was preserved. So too was a sense of belonging to a people that stretched into the past. Any thoughtful person—libertarian, socialist, liberal, or conservative—can recognize the power of popular practice. Change is often accomplished gradually, through the small, combined efforts of people making prudent decisions day by day.

This is, most often, how societies change. The role of the individuals within them proceeds according to a different tempo. The building of social consensus and convention is slow, gradual, incremental. Yet it is impelled by immediate and often urgent demands on individuals. Those decisions, though they may be impelled by long reflection, are made in a moment. You decide whether you will punch that Nazi. You decide to join or restrain a protest as it forms. You decide to speak or remain silent. The demand for these decisions clearly comes thick and fast in times of crisis, but it comes just as thick and fast, though more discreetly, in the conduct of daily life. For a people, judgment may be slow and incremental. For individual people, judgments are fast and decisive.

Mindful of this, we should consider how Carl Schmitt's "Sovereign is he who decides on the exception" might be subverted and redeemed in the conduct of a democratic life.[13] Schmitt's statement is taken, as its author intended, as declaring that in the end decisions are always made by one man: not by law, not by custom, but by the will of that man. Sovereign rule was an imitation of an incarnate divinity. If one recognizes how decisions are made in practice, the image of the single willful ruler melts into air. Customs, conventions, and constitutions are shaped by individual decisions. The acts of individuals become economic forces. Change through the commons, like change in individuals, can be fast or slow.

The will to judge, the insistence on judging, is essential to democratic practice. The democrat must be willing to praise and blame, to permit or deny, in order to perform the most fundamental functions of democracy: to legislate, to execute, to judge. Judgment requires thought, work, and courage. The one who judges must be willing to decide, to make a decision now. One cannot always defer to another person or another time. This willingness to set deference aside marks the sovereignty of the democrat, the willingness to rule as well as to be ruled. The willingness to rule requires courage.

Judgment drives the judge outward. Ruling drives the ruler outward. Judges and rulers must consider the questions, problems, even crises that do not concern them. They must listen to, learn of, imagine the positions of others. In these practices, the one who judges, the one who rules confronts a chaos of the known, the partially known, the unknown, the suspected, the feared, the unheard of. The one who judges, the one who rules learns aspects of the lives of others. The one who judges, the one who rules confronts the chaos of an outside that is always outside, always other, never fully one's own. The one who judges, the one who rules confronts—and must answer—the demand to act in the face of the unknown and unknowable. Among free people, all judge, all rule.

24. The people are wise.

The claim that the people are wise is at once the most doubted and most accepted claim for democracy. It belongs to old documents and to the virtual. It has an honorable and bastard pedigree. The ancients placed democracies among the ignorant cities, yet they also recognized that only the wisest know that they do not know. Ignorance is the beginning (and sometimes the end) of wisdom. Conservatives praise the wisdom of custom and tradition, of settled people whose ancestral ways reflect a long learning. This is one form of the wisdom of the many. Another has become common in our time. The wisdom of the many is harnessed in wikis.

There is another form of the wisdom of the people that approaches the divine. Aristotle argued for democratic wisdom in the *Politics*. He wrote that "the many, of whom none individually is an excellent man, nevertheless when joined together can be better—not as individuals, but all together." Combined, their varied virtues and capacities can surpass the wisdom of a single man.[14] Al-Farabi echoed and expanded this argument in his aphorisms.

Aphorism 57 opens the possibility that the virtues and capacities necessary for governance might not exist in a single person, as those who searched for a "philosopher king" wished. Instead they might exist "dispersed among a group. . . . So this group all together takes the place of the imagined king."[15] Al-Farabi, moreover, believed that wisdom was primarily the result of education and habits that are in large part owed to custom: "It is not possible for a human being to be endowed by nature from the outset possessing virtue or vice."[16] Moral and intellectual virtue are potentials. To be realized, they must be cultivated, both by the people concerned and by those around them. The people make themselves, and they may make themselves wise.

In Al-Farabi's view, wisdom was always work done in common. The potential was there in each individual, but people could become wise only if that potential was cultivated. The growth of wisdom was not due to parents or to teachers alone. It depended upon the institutions, customs, and practices of the city.

There are many now who argue that the people collectively decide as well as or better than experts. This claim underlies the structure of Wikipedia and other wikis. Wikipedia showed one way democratic wisdom might be formed. The first Wikipedia entries were often undistinguished, often wrong. Yet anyone was able to edit and correct them. Rapidly—far more rapidly than most scholars expected—the errors diminished. This was due primarily not to the work of scholars and experts but the combined work of people who knew something— often something small—about the subject. Errors fell, one by one, to the work of the many.

The crafting of artificial intelligence also depends on the laborious efforts of many individuals. For a machine to classify reliably, it must be taught to see as people see: "A.I. is learning from humans. Lots and lots of humans."[17] A multitude of humans. These humans are, moreover, rarely experts. The people training artificial intelligence systems to recognize hazardous growths in human systems are not doctors. They need not even be trained in medicine. They can be trained to recognize one small thing, and their collective identifications of that thing create a model that surpasses both their individual judgments and the judgment of experts. This work is done not only by the multitude rather than experts; it is also done by the relatively poor.[18]

We have learned that the greatest wisdom of the people is to know what we do not know. This knowledge is protection against arrogance.

It is also a spur to work. Discovery, invention, philosophy, learning, all come from the knowledge that we do not know and the desire to overcome our lack.

Despite ignorance people must act, must decide. People are fallible: what then?

"The people," William Jennings Bryan declared, "have the right to make their own mistakes."[19] Bryan was a prophet and a statesman, followed by multitudes, praised by poets, and feared by elites. He became a reviled figure, caricatured as ignorant and fanatical. Popular judgment surpassed that of the elites. We should honor Bryan more than we do. Bryan opposed imperialism. He opposed eugenics. He is often castigated for his role in the Scopes trial, but only because history fails us. The textbook Clarence Darrow defended was not a defense of the theory of evolution; it was a textbook on eugenics.[20] Bryan was a tireless, intrepid advocate for the people against the dominion of the wealthy and the enforcement of hierarchy.

Bryan was also clear in his understanding of legitimacy. Hélène Landemore dared to make the harder argument: that democratic multitudes can decide correctly. She set aside the question of right. Bryan dismissed the question of correctness in favor of the question of right. His answer echoes Locke: "The people shall judge." They have the right. Yet when one considers how people learn, Bryan and Landemore are not far apart. People learn by making mistakes. Theories advance when a flaw is found. Contradictions and gaps in a text point the way to a fuller understanding. The inexplicable invites investigation. The people not only have the right to make mistakes; they have the need to make mistakes, for it is in confronting our mistakes that we make ourselves wiser and better than we were.

25. Democracies depend on truth.

People who rule themselves depend, like all rulers, not on their wisdom and virtue alone but also on good information. We are called upon to judge, and to judge justly we need to know the facts. We are called to make, to enforce, and to submit to the law. Each of these requires knowledge. Knowledge, however, is not the only form of truth we need.

We need people to speak the truth as they see it. Perhaps this is necessary for the trust that some see as essential to democracy. I think we can live with our enemies and that we need not trust them too far, but I still think we need them to speak the truth as they see it. We need to hear that truth, certainly, but we also need the courage it takes to speak it. Ancient philosophy saw speaking truth fearlessly as an attribute of wisdom. We need that wisdom. Religious scriptures see speaking truth to power as prophetic. We need the courage to chasten and correct our rulers. When we rule, we need those who have the courage to restrain and rebuke us. Those who rule themselves, if they are to touch the divine and give it voice, must speak the truth. There are hazards enough moving into the unknown. We must bring what light we can.[21]

26. Truth prospers when the people rule.

Democracy, it is said—most particularly by liberals and philosophers—is dependent on truth, but truth is independent of democracy. Democracy does indeed depend on truth and, more importantly, on truth being open to all, but it is also true that truth depends on the rule of the people.

Revolutions have been marked, in matters great and small, by an opening to knowledge. The people of Paris who opened the Bastille and rummaged through the drawers of the Tuileries were not simply bent on humiliating those who had claimed to be their betters. They were opening secret places to the gaze of the people. They were looking into power in its most desperate and its most ordinary places. They sought truth, recognizing that truth serves democracy.

Truth, however, cannot prosper without the democratic. There have always been those—the wealthy, the privileged, and those arrogantly convinced of their intellectual superiority—who claim that an enlightened despotism serves truth and its adherents better than democracy. They have learned, to their cost, that tyrants make poor patrons for those who struggle toward truth. The list of those killed for truth-telling far surpasses the list of those protected by their privileged patrons. Nevertheless the myth persists, preserved by fear of the people and a foolish faith in the protection of the privileged. The martyrdom of Socrates by the Athenian democracy made him the patron saint of this mythology. In this account, Socrates was sacrificed to the hostility of an ignorant *demos*. There is much to admire (and something to condemn) in the story of Socrates before the Athenians, but this reading of the myth is untrue.

Truth thrives on democracy. Democracy makes learning accessible. To be a democrat one must have access to information, to knowledge, to debate, to what wisdom one can acquire. Democracy makes information, knowledge, and wisdom accessible to all who reach for it. More people are engaged in learning. As more people are brought into schools, to discussion, to debate, more information becomes available. More is learned by more people. If they are democrats, they learn to judge. Knowledge is tested against diverse experiences, assessed from different perspectives, subjected to more challenges. These challenges speed the acquisition of information, the spread of knowledge, the attainment of wisdom. Each moment in the growth of knowledge, of publishing, of the media brings new hazards and makes new demands, and people who rule themselves are prepared to meet them.

Truth, like democracy, is not a stable, certain thing. Truth, like democracy, is something we struggle toward. The struggle for truth and the struggle for democracy require the same virtues. They require courage. People who want to learn have to take risks. There are explorers, volcanologists, scientists who fly into hurricanes and chase tornados. There are medical researchers who give themselves diseases or try untested treatments on themselves. There are astronauts and divers, test pilots and spelunkers. There are war reporters. There are also those quieter but no less daring people who ask "strange, wicked, questionable questions," who brave laughter, ridicule, and occasionally accusations of madness to unsettle old conventions, try out new theories, and find their way to a truer understanding of the present or the past, or our practices and principles.

Anyone who looks for truth does well to remain mindful of their fallibility. The challenge, for those who strive toward truth, is to make it clear to the people that the search for truth does not end, that all seeming certainties may be uncertain, that those who claim certainty are rarely to be trusted.

There is a simpler reason why truth depends on democracy. All undemocratic regimes depend on lies. Aristocratic and monarchical regimes depend on the belief that monarchs and aristocrats are superior. There are generally other lies attached to these. People are taught that aristocrats are more well-bred, more cultured, with an ingrained sense of elegance or duty. They are taught that their place in the social order is determined by nature or the deity, that their subordination is just. Authoritarian regimes depend on lies. Dictators claim, as Hafez al-Assad once did, that they are "the Great Pharmacist," or the Great Whatever and lay claim to a host of achievements that an honest glance could debunk. "Kim [Jong Un] could drive a car and hit a light bulb with a rifle at 100 yards, all by the age of 3." An official biography claimed "he had perfect pitch, that he could ride the wildest horses at age six, and [at age nine] had twice beaten a visiting European powerboat-racing champion." He was following in the footsteps of his father, "who wrote six full operas in two years, 'all of which are better than any in the history of music'" according to his official biography, in addition to the 1,500 books he wrote in college.[22]

Hierarchies of race and sex, the aristocracies of a corrupt modernity, depend on lies: that one race or sex or class is superior to another, that one race or sex or class is entitled to deference, that one race or sex or class has the right to command. Capitalism lies constantly, about the worth of things and people, about the making and unmaking of the world.

Faith may lead people to believe that they know the truth, or the only truth that matters, and that they not only may but must testify to that truth. That is their duty. Those who question the certainties of faith have a duty as well.

Democracies may err, democrats may lie and mislead themselves, but democracy is not founded on a lie and does not depend on lies for its survival.

Democrats and those who work toward truth cannot afford to lie. Not to the authorities, not to the people, not to themselves. New findings, however dangerous, have to be faced and contested. While they hold, they command our deference, but they are always doubted, always questioned, always subject to challenge. The desire for certainty is dangerous, the belief in certainty, destructive.

V

Democrats live with open hands

27. Democracies are places of wild diversity.

The idea that one can describe the institutions and forms of government in a democracy is fundamentally wrong-headed. Each democracy is distinct. When the people rule themselves, they do so in the
manner they decide. They may choose to fill offices by lot or by election, for a term or a task, or to have no offices at all. They may regard
representation as necessary or abhorrent. They will draw their boundaries in different ways on different dimensions: by territory, language,
religion, ethnicity, descent, or principles. Perhaps they will have no
boundaries at all.

We do not yet know what democratic peoples will become, but in
our time and, I suspect, for a long time to come, they will not be wholly
democratic. They will be, they must be, different from one another.
They will defer, perhaps wisely, to the customs of their people. They
will do things other people (and other peoples) regard as decadent,
puritanical, or silly. They will value things that others dismiss. These
differences, great and small, will set them apart from one another.

When we look at other democracies we will not see our own. We
will see other people building a common life together, another people
making themselves as they choose. Perhaps we will be astonished by
what they build. Perhaps we will want to make those things our own.
Perhaps we will regard them as shameful and degraded. Perhaps, over
time, we will change our judgments. Perhaps not.

Do not expect to see people becoming more and more alike in their
ways of life. People who are free do as they please. "Aren't they free?"
Plato's Socrates asks of democrats. "And isn't the city full of freedom
and free speech? And isn't there license in it to do whatever one
wants?"[1] Free people (as Plato did not write) do as they think best.

Wild Democracy. Anne Norton, Oxford University Press. © Oxford University Press 2023.
DOI: 10.1093/oso/9780197644348.003.0005

People who rule themselves build new worlds together. These cities, states, countries will not be the same. Freedom for individuals unleashes curiosity and invention, exploration and discovery. We have not yet seen democracy in its fullness. We have seen only shadows of democracy and only a few types of democratic institutions. We should expect to see many more as people become more skilled in governing themselves.

There will be differences in how people understand themselves as a people. Perhaps they will believe that they are united by their faith. Perhaps they will believe, as people have believed before, that they have a common descent from trees or dragons' teeth, that they belong to Canaan or Aztlán. Perhaps they will believe that they have a common gift: for living peacefully with one another, for exploration, for learning, for trade, for generosity, for careful work, for queuing and all that queuing symbolizes. The differences may be greater than we expect, greater than we want, greater than we know, but we should not be afraid. We should be curious.

The love of the new, of the different and the alien, has long been seen as an attribute of democrats. Democracy, Plato wrote, was "probably the fairest of the regimes" and the one most open and in love with difference. The democratic city was the sort of place that appealed to women, the young, and the masses (perhaps not the condemnation he intended). "Many perhaps . . . like boys and women looking at many-colored things, would judge this the fairest regime."[2]

Perhaps it was not democrats but those who distrusted democracy who treasured childish things.[3] The aristocrats preoccupied with ancestry, blazoning themselves about with heraldry and fancy dress, the absurd costumes of kings and cardinals and judges, the gilt adorning generals and autocrats, all of these catch the eye of the light-minded. Perhaps the ornaments of the wealthy and the powerful are baubles. Perhaps they are weapons. Perhaps they are a test.

When Al-Farabi took up the passage, Plato's slightly contemptuous acknowledgment of democracy's appeal became a paean to democracy.

Democratic cites belong, for Al-Farabi as for Plato, to the category of the ignorant cities, but the distinction between the ignorant and the enlightened is altered by the advent of monotheism. For Plato, the enlightened—those few, let us say in accord with tradition—that escape the cave seeing the light of the fire as a pale imitation, a fragment, of the sun. They come to enlightenment through their own will. Enlightenment is knowledge of the being of the things that are and the nonbeing of the things that are not. It is stable and enduring. Gods have little or no part in it. The divinity of truth is apart from them. Though the wisdom of the few enlightened ones has often been presented in mystical terms, it is in important respects technical knowledge. It is accessible only to an elite. It endures unchanging. It can be mastered, but it cannot be easily shared. Mastery sets the few apart and gives them the right to rule.

Al-Farabi's commitment to Islam altered his reading of the text. For the peoples of the book, who share a commitment to a single divinity and truth revealed in scripture, enlightenment is quite different. The will of God, not the work or the will of men, makes it accessible. It cannot be mastered, and it remains mysterious. Revelation masters even the messengers, who suffer for the message and are overcome by it. Enlightenment through revelation is stable and enduring, and it is fundamentally accessible to all.[4] But in the absence of a prophet or messiah, it is subject to the limits of memory and record, preserved only through the necessarily imperfect means of imitation.

In this world, the ignorant cities appear differently than they did to Greek philosophers. As Socrates was once recognized for the wisdom of knowing that he did not know, so the ignorant cities, mindful of their ignorance, may surpass the wisdom of those who have only the echo of prophecy in scripture, only the imitation of virtue in the *sunnah*.

Under this understanding, democratic cities are ignorant, but they are also free. They are the only cities able to come to virtue and to good governance through their own reason and reasoned will. They are the cities that may come closest to divinely inspired prophetic direction.

Plato wrote dismissively of democracy. Yet even in his hostile and contemptuous account, this place of pretty and desirable things emerges as a place of danger and promise. "Aren't they free?" Socrates asks of democrats. "And isn't the city full of freedom and free speech? And isn't there license in it to do whatever one wants?" These are indictments for Plato, the marks of an ungoverned, perhaps ungovernable people, led by their passions and appetites.

Al-Farabi's emendation of Plato's account has a different character. He writes:

> On the surface, it looks like an embroidered garment, full of colored figures and dyes. Everybody loves it and loves to reside in it, because there is no human wish or desire that this city does not satisfy. The nations emigrate to it, and reside there, and it grows beyond measure. People of every race multiply in it, and this by all kinds of copulation and marriages....
>
> Strangers cannot be distinguished from the residents. All kinds of wishes and ways of life are to be found in it.... The bigger, the more civilized, the more prevalent and the greater are the good and the evil it possesses.[5]

I have not found a more beautiful and precise description of the democratic city. Al-Farabi recognizes not only the danger but the promise of democracy. For him, as for Plato, diversity is characteristic of democracy. The gates of the democratic city are open to all; the city attracts all, whether they are welcome or not. Al-Farabi suggests that whatever the conditions of their arrival, these wildly diverse people will join one another. They will trade together, make and sell and eat each other's food, taste each other's pleasures, and make new children of every color and kind. Democracy does not overcome difference. Democracy attracts and proliferates difference. Democracy breeds diversity.

It is diversity, Plato and Al-Farabi thought, that attracts people of every race and kind to democracy. Muslims might consider how Al-Farabi's description of democracy echoes the Qu'ran: "Oh mankind, indeed We have created you from male and female and made you peoples and tribes that you may know one another" (49:13) and "[O]f his signs is the creation of the heavens and the earth and the diversity of your languages and your colors. Indeed in that are signs for those of knowledge" (30:22). All should see, in this Qu'ranic verse, and in Al-Farabi's description of democracy, the power and beauty of cities where the people rule.

This runs directly counter to the view, common in our time, that democracy depends on trust and trust upon homogeneity. I hold to the old wisdom. Democracy calls to all people. Homogeneity is contingent, relative, and fleeting. The Swedes or Norwegians or Danes who may appear so like one another to an American see Jutlanders and Sami. They mark ethnic and racial differences we cannot see. They see differences of class and faith, differences that mark out farmers from fishermen and herdsmen. They recall violent conflicts between regions and interests. They remember that these differences have led to battles in the past. They remember the years when they took horses and children from the Roma. When they look at the United States or Canada, Mexico or Brazil—indeed, any part of the New World—they may well see themselves as homogeneous. Among themselves, they see diversity.

Differences come and go. Once Americans knew ethnic slurs to diminish Hungarians, Swedes, Finns, the Irish, Italians, all the recently arrived immigrants of the late nineteenth and early twentieth centuries. These slurs are largely forgotten. Where they are remembered, they have lost their sting. Where the sting remains, work needs to be done, for make no mistake: this is no predestined progress. On the contrary, once small and benign differences can come to be seen as great and threatening. Arabs, hardly noticed at all in the first half of the twentieth century, came to be seen as racial others in the opening of the twenty-first. A geopolitical realignment, the emergence of new foreign conflicts, a border skirmish, a local conflict over fishing rights or mushroom hunting can awaken old enmities or create new ones. Injustices people have not recognized or rectified stand in the way of people ruling themselves. It is our duty, our discipline, and our work to face difference with courage and greatness of soul. It is our reward to find not only pleasure but wisdom.

28. The democratic disposition is cosmopolitan.

The word "cosmopolitan" was coined by a man who ruled himself, a philosopher whose practices were democratic. Diogenes is remembered for carrying a lantern in the sunshine, saying he was looking for an honest man. In his own time he was distinguished not only by his wisdom and eccentricity but by his indifference to wealth and rank and status. He disrupted Plato's lectures, outraged public customs and conventions, and showed no deference even to the most powerful.

When Alexander came to see Diogenes, he is said to have offered him anything he wanted. Diogenes is said to have replied, "Move, you are blocking my sun."

Democracies, because they are founded in the consent of the governed, will be different from one another, reflecting the will of that particular people. Yet because democracies are founded on certain principles, because they are bound to recognize our inalienable rights, they are open to people of all kinds: "Everybody loves it and loves to reside in it." These cities, these nations pride themselves on the people they attract. Their citizens boast of the array of foods, goods, languages, and ideas that flourish there. New Yorkers, Londoners, Parisians see themselves as wholly unique, and yet they often claim that they hold the world within them. Cairo calls itself the *umm ad dunya*, the mother of the world.

There is, no doubt, an arrogance in this pride. Yet the pride democrats have in their worldliness has humility in it as well. The Declaration of Independence submits the claims of the newly made people "to the judgement of a candid world." There is no requirement for a particular process of civilization, cultural education, expertise, or ancestry. Anyone may judge, anyone in the world. The requirements of democratic justice should be visible to all.

The democratic disposition is cosmopolitan in its desires, in the reach of its offerings and its attractions, and in the humility and arrogance of its claims to universality. Democracy can accommodate anyone. Democracies must accommodate everyone, respecting the rights that belong to them as people. They must provide for everyone, ensuring the things that all people need to survive. They must listen to everyone, submit the conduct of the government to the judgment of all. Everyone must be given a hearing; no one may be silenced. Democracies—and democrats—are open to the views of all the world.

Democratic cosmopolitanism is at once humble and arrogant. No one, citizen or foreigner, is worth more than anyone else. Each has rights. Each has the right to sit in judgment on the state and its people. The pride taken in that cannot be faulted. There is, however, a dangerous temptation to arrogance for cosmopolitan democrats. The conviction that all people are equal in their rights and in their worth can lead too easily to the conviction that we know what is best for others.

If all people are like us, we know what they need. Our best defense against this arrogance lies in respect for the principle of the consent of the governed. "A decent respect for the opinions of mankind" should chasten us. Respect for the men and women we hope to help or defend obliges us to listen and defer to their views. Without that deference, we do not serve democracy. We betray the principle that people should rule themselves.

The democratic disposition is cosmopolitan. Democratic principles and loyalties must be as well. Subjects give their allegiance to a person; nationalists give their allegiance to a nation. Free people can do neither.

29.   How free people love their countries.

If the democratic disposition is cosmopolitan, if democracies open themselves to others, if free people value the rights they carry in their flesh above the nation and the law, is patriotism possible? Can free people love their countries? Can that love be honorable?

Some on the left believe, mistakenly in my view, that a love of country precludes a commitment to humanity. This is no more true than that a love for your cat or your dog precludes love for other cats and dogs, or that a love for your partner or your child precludes love for others. On the contrary, it is through the particular that we learn that depth of affection, respect, and commitment that makes love for others possible. Love for one's people, the desire to make a country to be proud of, pride in the work done so far, and love for the country yet to be built drives all toward humanity.

Conservatives believe that leftists do not love their countries. They are wrong, but there is a decided difference in how left and right face the patriotic. People on the left are commonly committed to a cosmopolitanism grounded in a respect for common rights, common needs, common capacities, yet they are very much aware of their countries as their own. They think it is as unseemly to praise your country as it is to praise yourself. People on the right do not seem to share this view. What the left regards as a polite and seemly reticence, they regard as a refusal of love. The right sees their reticence as shame.

There is no defense for flag-waving, chauvinistic patriotism among free—or even decent—people. Such people claim to honor their country, but they forgive every sin and forget every shortcoming. Their indifference to their country's faults speaks of their shamelessness and of the falsity of their patriotism. If the conduct of their people does not matter to them, those people are not their own. They claim to love their country, but the flag they wave could be any flag. They know their weakness, so they look for strength, but the leader they follow could be any leader. They lack judgment, so they choose unwisely. They are afraid, so they look for a master, and an enemy. As anarchy nurtures courage, self-reliance, and solidarity, this empty patriotism breeds authoritarianism, bigotry, and war-making. This is not love of one's country; this is the love of any country, any order, any power.

Perhaps people will come to love different countries differently. Perhaps they will not see themselves in nations at all. Free people will make themselves as they choose. They will build their democracies differently. They will become different peoples: in different places, with different customs.

Perhaps I can speak only for my own love of country.

There are those who love the land. Perhaps they love it because the land has fed them and sheltered them for time out of mind. Perhaps they love the land because it holds the bones of their ancestors. Perhaps they love it because it has shaped their ways. That love sinks into the soil. Perhaps it is merely love of beauty or love of one's own. This is understandable, but it is nothing to praise.

Love of the land is not love for America. The "purple mountains' majesty" that Americans sing about is not important. Some Americans will never see those mountains. I love the waves that break like a bear moving off the California coast, the round rocks like moons among the wild roses of Rhode Island, the baked reds and greens and blues of the mesas of New Mexico, the wheat fields filled with fireflies at twilight in the Midwest. Yet love of these is not love of country for my people. We could be Americans in other places. We are Americans in other places. In a country so large, we do not live in the same places at all.

We do not speak the same languages. We do not have the same religions, eat the same foods, play the same music. We do not have the same virtues. When Whitman made poetry of lists, he called to this

America, to the America of fragments and gathering. What we are has not yet come into the world.

Loving the America of the past and present is always mixed with grief. We do not have our country yet. We love the America we long to be. There are pieces of that steel in the past, pieces in the present. We know they are fragments. We know we are imperfect. We are beating that steel into shape. We are building. We are planting. We are feeding a fire that must spread across the prairie, seeding the grasses that will grow when the burning is done.

So it is, so it will be, with other free people. Love of country must be, in no small part, a refusal of what we are in the present for what we long to become. That love builds on earth out of the earth, with the minds and hands of the living. It bears the mark of those people, and they are free to love it as their own. A decent love knows that others do the same, and finds solidarity in this. An honorable love of country works for the fulfillment of democratic demands.

30. Democracy is generative. Democracy is excessive. Democrats live with open hands.

Those who doubt and distrust democracies, who prefer "energetic" (which is to say, arbitrary and autocratic) executives bemoan democratic slowness. Democracies, they say, deliberate endlessly, never deciding. They are indecisive. They talk, they chatter. They are inefficient, unable to make things happen. Yet democracies are also faulted for acting too fast: moved by passion and appetite, by resentment of the rich and lust for their goods. These criticisms, often made by the same person in the same text, are contradictory, yes, but in their contradictions there is recognition of a quality found among people who rule themselves. They are generative.

They make things happen. They create goods. They invent new things, new processes, new ideas. There is room, in a free country, for someone to run with an idea that others think is crazy. That idea may be bubblegum or Saran wrap. It may be harnessing electricity or transmitting information over wires and bouncing it off satellites. It may be the abolition of slavery, giving women the vote, or free healthcare for all. People in democracies talk, they debate, they chatter endlessly, and out of that comes invention. People who rule themselves proliferate things, ideas, rights. They make laws and regulations (perhaps too many). They are striving to remake the world.

They mull things over; they carry ideas like a child in the womb. They take the time to let policies mature, to explore ideas, to debate, to consider, to let the plan mature among them before it is brought into the world. The work of engendering may be slow and deliberate. The agreement, the making, the spread of a new commitment can be like lightning. They think fast. They make fast. They think on their feet.

Fast or slow, people who rule themselves overflow with plans, goods, ideas, inventions, actions. They create excess.

That excess is a source of pride. Free people always struggle for more: more freedom, more rights, more power, more inventions, more discoveries. They go farther in their imagination and ambitions. They do not believe that anything is closed to them. Their daring and their courage spur them on. Because each person is valued, all understand that they must be educated and their fundamental needs ensured. They are free to cultivate their abilities: free to invent, free to discover. Their achievements open opportunities to others. "Job creation" is not the province of the few whose accidental patronage is praised to the skies, but of the many, whose work overflows with generosity. People who rule themselves are excessive in their ambitions, in their daring, in their imagination of what they can become. That is how they grow.

Democracies, radical democracies, maintain within themselves the spaces of anarchy. They are always experimenting. They proliferate institutions, practices, and modes of resistance. Their capacity for solidarity enables them to work together, to assemble, to make committees, unions, cooperatives. Their anarchic spirit enables them to take these down again. Their capacity for solidarity enables them to build forms of governance. Their anarchic disposition drives them to change governnments, escape governance, try again. They experiment. They are not bound to what they have or to what has been. They build from the ruins of the past when they choose; they refuse the past when they choose. Their experimentation has two effects. First, they expand the available forms of governance. They provide their people with more places to work together and more ways in which to do it.

Second, the proliferation of sites of governance makes voice and exit easier. If they choose to leave one site of solidarity and power, they can more easily find or make another if they choose.

Generosity belongs not only to democracies but to democrats. The democratic ethic is an ethic of open hands: hands that hold the reins lightly, hands that grow and make, hands that reach out for the new and the unknown, hands that reach out to one another.

31. Democrats can tolerate the undemocratic.

"What are my parasites to me?" Nietzsche asked.[6] Perhaps this was aristocratic disdain for him; for us it can be the generosity of the democrat. Walt Whitman asked:

> Do I contradict myself?
> Very well then I contradict myself
> (I am large, I contain multitudes.)[7]

Democracies have a virtue once marked as aristocratic: they have magnanimity. We are the many; we contain multitudes. We embrace, as Al-Farabi recognized, peoples and practices of all kinds. Not all of those are democratic. Yet they are taken in, fed and sheltered, heard and considered. We are big enough. This practical generosity can be found in conservatives and radicals, in law and practice. It is an old virtue, and one cultivated throughout the world. The Arabs who say *ahlan wa sahlan* welcome the traveler as their own, giving food and shelter. When I was a child in Thailand, exploring the streets and the *klongs*, people would invite me into their houses and share their food. On a bus in Tunisia, the women shared food with each other. There is an old graveyard by my family's house. In that graveyard is an early nineteenth-century gravestone, recording the death of a woman who came to the house as a stranger, fell sick, was nursed, and died there. The epitaph records not their pride in caring for a stranger but their praise of a woman they barely knew.

Free people live with open hands. They accept refugees, for these people are entitled to the rights that belong to all people. They are to

be protected. They accept immigrants. They grant asylum to the persecuted, food and shelter to the refugee. They are proud that people want
to come to them, and they have faith that they can make a place for all.

People who rule themselves know, in their greatness of soul, that
they can often live untroubled by the presence of the undemocratic.
The wisdom that enables them to recognize that we are all dangerous
to one another and the courage that enables them to walk among their
enemies unafraid make it possible for them to live with even the most
profound dissenters. They have learned that they are not harmed if
there are a few people who believe in divine right, if they give a little
space to an enclave that adheres to an undemocratic set of practices or
scriptures, or to a tribe unwilling to live with others. They have learned
that isolation may be chosen, and that though aristocratic pretensions
must be governed, they need not be annihilated.

Perhaps there will always be those who think that they or theirs are
superior to all others. Perhaps in time all people will come to think
that, and in their pride come to the magnanimity that treats inferiors
with welcoming grace. Perhaps they will grow wiser.

32. All you need for democracy is humanity.

Those who doubt and distrust the ability of people to rule themselves
hedge democracy about with requirements, as if it were a country
club with peculiar criteria for admission. Democracy is only for the
wealthy, the educated, for men, for people of a certain race or tribe or
religion, for people who have a certain level of income or a certain culture. This may describe a country club in the segregated South or a
swim club outside Beirut, but it does not describe democracy. There
are no admission fees. There are no educational requirements. Those
who restrict membership to a particular tribe or race or religion make
democracy impossible if they cannot claim to have the consent of the
governed.

A more common and quite respected position argues that democracy is impossible without trust, and trust is possible only among "one's
own," that is, they say, among those of the same culture or ethnicity.
This is wrong many times over. People who can rule themselves are

brave enough to live with their enemies. They are attracted to difference, and people of all kinds are attracted to them. Moreover, it is not
so easy to determine who is alike and who is different, even when the
signs of those differences—as with race—are codified and detailed.
Difference and likeness are attributes that shift with context. We are
all alike in our mortality, in the inalienable rights that belong to our
embodied humanity. We are all different in the radical solitude of body
and mind, in how we shape ourselves and how we remake the world.

Insistence on the need for cultural (or ethnic) homogeneity for
social trust, and on the necessity of social trust for democracy, is
weakness at best and bigotry at worst. People who cannot learn to
live bravely and openly with those who are not like them are not
yet prepared to rule themselves. They are not yet fully prepared for
politics.

The complex of desire and courage that democracy calls forth in
democrats is never for one *demos*, one people, alone. The democrat
cannot easily tell strangers from residents. Democrats may look at
their fellow citizens as foreigners. They may know them as political
rivals, even as enemies. They learn to walk among them unafraid. They
are able then to face true enemies with courage and equanimity.

As political struggles and disputes school them, they learn to see
both enmity and friendship in their fellow citizens. They learn to see
the potential for citizenship in the stranger. If they are conscious of the
rights that belong to all people, a common humanity may teach them
to see all people as, in the most fundamental sense, their own. They
may look at foreigners as they look at citizens. They may look at them
as others, alien and intriguing, opening worlds of danger and promise.
They are prepared to walk out into the world impelled by curiosity and
desire, shielded with courage.

33. The strength of the poor is the strength of democracy.

Fear of democracy is often no more than fear of the poor. That is a fear
that justice may someday spare us. Until then, we should ask ourselves
why the poor should seem to be at the heart of democracy.

This fear—that is also a hope—is very old. Plato's writing links poverty to deprivation and strength, to appetite and self-restraint. Machiavelli's observation that the poor want only not to be oppressed has a more immediately political expression in the writings of peasant rebels. That desire was captured in a list of demands that the rebellious peasants of 1525—his contemporaries—made to their overlords. Article 7 of the *Twelve Articles of the Swabian Peasantry* declares, "We will not be oppressed anymore."[8]

The poor are people in their simplicity, with few possessions. They lead precarious lives, with few resources, lacking secure supplies of food, shelter, and protection. They are people who learn how to provide for themselves. They are people who learn to work with others. Plato and Lacan, Ibn Khaldun and Antonio Negri, have all recognized that power comes from lack and that poverty can give rise to strength.

Judith Butler's work on precarious life reflects on the ability of people to build solidarity from grief and mourning.[9] Grief, loss, and mourning are, Butler argues, entailed in our mortality. They belong to us all. This universal experience may illuminate other rights held in common. The experience of a precarious life—of poverty, danger, abjection—is an intensification of this universal experience. Thus it may not only make individuals and their relations of solidarity stronger; it may also position them to see the situation of mankind with greater sympathy and acuity.

Reflection on precarious life invites the recognition of a common vulnerability, a common experience of loss.

We can also see promise in our common precarity. In the Putney Debates, Col. Thomas Rainsborough famously declared:

> I think the poorest he that is in England has a life to live, as the greatest he; and therefore truly, sir, I think it's clear, that every man that is to live under a government ought first by his own consent put himself under that government; and I do think the poorest man in England is not at all bound in a strict sense to that government he has not had a voice to put himself under.[10]

Rainsborough shocked his superior officers. Gen. Henry Ireton responded that if he maintained this he must "fly for refuge to an absolute natural right, and you must deny all civil right."[11] Rainsborough did, and he was right to do so. The right to be governed only by governments that have our consent, to rule as well as to be ruled, belongs to all people, rich and poor. It belongs to us in our naked humanity.

Democratic cities, as Plato presents them, emerge from the violent power of the poor. The poor see the weakness of the rich and doubt their strength. Democracy "comes into being when the poor win."[12] Plato's dialogues present this triumph of the poor as the work of an unlovely envy. This view predominates in the canon. Rainsborough saw it differently. So did Ibn Khaldun.

For Ibn Khaldun power arises out of lack, on the territorial, cultural, and economic periphery, among those who are forced to rely on themselves. Hardship and deprivation produce people with qualities that enable them to win power and use it well. As individuals, they become self-reliant. They acquire fortitude. They are forced to be disciplined, strong, inventive, intelligent, and stoic in order to survive. Their private strengths and virtues are not, however, enough to preserve them. These self-reliant people also develop the strongest ties of solidarity.[13]

Ibn Khaldun's account of the emergence of power on the periphery is at once familiar and challenging. His conception of the frontier is familiar, capturing the combination of independence and cooperation that characterizes frontiersmen from the nineteenth-century American West to Jim Scott's Burma. Yet despite its familiarity, this account presents a challenge to enduring prejudices in Western political thought. Conservatives too often see the poor as lazy, lacking in talent or morality, undisciplined. Those who see the poor in this way will strip themselves of their own virtue, losing generosity and greatness of soul. They will also fail to see where the strength of the people comes from.

Hardship produces not dependence but fortitude. Much follows from this conception of power's origins. For democrats, it marks the "great unwashed," the "teeming masses," the *shaab* who are both "the poor" and "the people" as fit—perhaps especially fit—to hold power. It inverts the understanding that saw—that sees—power as the preserve of the privileged, to be extended to the subordinate only insofar as education and imitation assimilate them to their betters.

Butler saw the possibilities of a solidarity built from grief and mourning. Mindful of Ibn Khaldun, we can think differently of precarious life. We should not forget our common vulnerability or abandon the likeness seen in a common experience of loss. Yet we might also recognize with Ibn Khaldun, with our own memories of frontiersmen and pioneers, leaders and saints, that precarious conditions can forge strong and self-reliant individuals: people with fortitude. As these people draw together, binding themselves to one another, they go from strength to strength. Precarity produces not only recognition of a common vulnerability but the achievement of a common strength and fortitude. For Ibn Khaldun, precarious life is the forge of strength and the nursery of power.

Ibn Khaldun instructs us to look differently at poverty, hardship, deprivation. His theory grants great dignity to these. People formed under conditions of hardship, in a precarious life, are no longer suspect democratic subjects. They know what it is to be ruled, and they have learned to rule. They have been trained in a hard discipline. They have learned, singly and collectively, to rule themselves.

This reading should drive us to a reconsideration of the significance of double consciousness for democratic subjectivity. The experience of African Americans and other oppressed and subordinated people furnishes individual accounts of the process Ibn Khaldun describes at the level of tribe, nation, state, and empire.[14] Frederick Douglass describes how poverty made slaves ingenious. He remembers his grandmother's cabin, the shadowed paradise of his childhood, and the clever mechanism she used to draw water. The enslaved learned to make. They learned to think. Slaves, W. E. B. du Bois famously argued, needed a "double consciousness." Their vulnerability obliged them to see not only from their own position but from the masters' perspective as well.

So it is with the poor. Poverty requires thought. The ordinary requirements of life—finding food, finding shelter—require ingenuity. Anyone who has seen a poor person in the global south hammer a satellite dish from an oil drum, or seen the compact and clever ways a homeless person carries shelter in a bundle, has seen the evidence of this ingenuity. Anyone who has experienced poverty, even briefly, has learned how very clever one has to be to manage. The poor need to make the most of what they have and what they know: to forge alliances with friends and family and cultivate the few resources they have. The rich can simply spend some money. They do not need to think at all.

Plato wrote in the *Symposium* that desire was the child of poverty and resource. Ibn Khaldun's work makes that observation political. The poor join together because they must. The poor become resourceful because they must. They become powerful because they can. Their poverty taught them to be clever and enterprising. They learned that solidarity not only enabled them to survive; it made them stronger than their enemies.

Reading democracy in light of Ibn Khaldun, affirming the capacity of those who live under hardship to acquire self-reliance, practice solidarity, and acquire power, counters the exclusionary liberalism Uday Mehta identified.[15] The two Mills, and other enlightened liberals committed to the project of empire, saw the capacity for democracy as an achievement contingent on education, the cultivation of certain mores and specified cultural or civilizational contexts. For many more that capacity was dependent on financial as well as cultural capital. Ibn Khaldun's work reminds us that we need nothing for democracy but humanity.

Ibn Khaldun's account also counters the assumption that anarchy and individualism are opposed to solidarity and social action. Ibn Khaldun recognized that solidarity is not an alternative to individualism but its necessary accompaniment. They are related as concave is to convex. The conditions that make individualism necessary make solidarity desirable. According to this logic of origins, the more an individual is forced to self-reliance, the more that individual sees the virtues of solidarity. Solidarity grows not from the weakness of the dependent but from the recognition of limits in the strong. This recognition is not peculiar to Ibn Khaldun. It animates anarchism across time and space. Kropotkin's anarchism is famously allied to his recognition of the necessity—and the drive—to mutual aid. For Kropotkin, solidarity was natural, a consequence of the form of human and other embodied beings. David Graeber, citing the work of Joanna Overing, describes anarchic practices among the Piaroa.[16] The *acequias* of New Mexico are communal irrigation systems, run on the old anarchic system of the commons.

Ibn Khaldun's understanding of hardship casts further light on Plato's conception of the origins of democratic power. Plato wrote that the "lean, tanned poor man" standing in the ranks of the Athenian army looks to the soft, fat and wealthy and says, "Those men are ours. For they are nothing." This account is not wholly in accord with portrayal of the many as empowered only by their numbers. Here, in the shadows of the dialogue, we can read a reluctant and allusive acknowledgment of the strength of the impoverished individual and the individual democrat. If we read Plato differently, in light of Ibn Khaldun and with the experience of poverty, we can see the origins of democracy in the strength and fortitude of the poor and the disenfranchised. We can see democracy as the political fulfillment of a solidarity begun in the common bearing of hardship.

The democrats seen in this reading are stronger, fiercer, and braver than the fearful people of liberalism's social contract. Those who contract in Hobbes live in fear, make their contracts from fear, and fearfully consign themselves to the rule of an autocrat.[17] The women who make the Devil's bargain in Rousseau's *Discourse on Political Economy* seek dependence to ensure their safety. They fear, they seek a protector, and they make a dictator. Rawls too roots contract in anxieties about an unknown future.

Ibn Khaldun reminds us that the poor are not always fearful, that they are often capable of protecting themselves and others, and that this recognition was present in Greek democracy as well. "What," Socrates asks, "do the people of democracies call themselves? They call themselves rulers."[18]

Want teaches anarchic fortitude, the strength of those who walk by themselves. Want teaches self-reliance. Want teaches ingenuity. Want drives people to solidarity. Mutual aid is part of the ingenuity of want. Those who want work to fulfill their needs find that they can do more. They are driven from want to wanting, from need to ambition and desire. They have learned that together they can do great things. This is dangerous and daring knowledge. The desire for glory drives domination. The desire to secure the democratic demand for themselves and others, to turn democratic excess against democratic want, drives toward greatness.

VI
Taxes

34. Taxes are how people pay for the work they do together.

People love to inveigh against taxes. Their taxes are too high, there are too many taxes, too many governmental bodies. Taxes are imposed by a government that does not understand how hard it is to run a business, that doesn't see that the wealthy are wealth creators. Taxes are the government's hand in your pocket. In America, we are reminded that tax protests are the very foundation of the Republic. The Revolution began in resistance to the Stamp Act. The rebels who dumped British tea in Boston Harbor were resisting taxes. "No taxation without representation" was a war cry of the Revolution and remains the motto of a still disenfranchised Washington, D.C.

Libertarians charge that taxes are coercive. They steadily increase governmental power. They make bureaucratic authoritarianism possible. They are often a covert attempt to reshape people's behavior (the soda tax, or "sin taxes" on alcohol and tobacco). They are often a tool, openly used, for redistributing income: taking from the rich to give to the poor. Critics are correct to question the use of taxes to control behavior, especially when it serves to "nudge"—that is to say, to influence behavior covertly. They are right to cast a suspicious eye on the state, for states possess coercive power. There are elements of truth in these critical accounts of taxation, but there is something fundamental that is lost. It is astonishing that libertarians, who accept the tyranny of bosses, debt, usury, and other exactions of finance, should cavil at taxation. It is absurd that anarchists, taught as they should be by Kropotkin, should object to a practice of mutual aid. There can be unjust taxes to be sure, but there is nothing opposed to liberty, nothing hostile to anarchy, in the choice of people to work together.

Wild Democracy. Anne Norton, Oxford University Press. © Oxford University Press 2023.
DOI: 10.1093/oso/9780197644348.003.0006

Where people rule themselves, there is nothing coercive about taxation. Taxes are not an alien government sticking its hand in your pocket. Taxes are not an imposition. Taxes are how we pay for the work we choose to do together.[1] They testify to down-to-earth, common-sense commitments and to the dreams of the people. Ruling the nation is not simply a matter of inspiration or good ideas. There is practical work to be done. There are roads and bridges to be built. There are harbors to be cleared, canals to be dug, wildfires to be fought, oil spills to be cleared. If people want running water and sewer systems, they must repair or build them. In his paean to common democratic work, Langston Hughes writes:

> The eyes see materials there for building,
> See the difficulties too, and the obstacles.
> The hand seeks tools to cut the wood,
> To till the soil and harness the power of the waters.
> Then the hand seeks other hands to help—
> Thus the dream becomes not one man's dream alone,
> But a community dream.
> Not my dream alone, but *our* dream.
> Not my world alone,
> But *your world* and *my world*,
> Belonging to all the hands who build.[2]

We are the builders. We support ourselves. We take care of our own. Trying to evade this is shameful and petty. "A man would be ashamed to be told that he signed a petition, praying that he might pay less than his share of the public expense," Thomas Paine wrote, "or that those who had trusted the public might never receive their money; yet he does the same thing when he petitions against taxation, and the only difference, that by taking shelter under the name, he seems to conceal the meanness he would otherwise blush at."[3] They should feel shame, these critics of taxation.

There are those who say of people poorer or frailer than they, "They want to be given things," or, only slightly less grudgingly, "We give them...." They believe that money is taken from the hard-working and deserving and given to the lazy and profligate. They are usually wrong, but what if it were true? These are their people. Such people may pride themselves (however mistakenly) on their self-sufficiency, but they can never claim to love their country. They regard taxation as a transaction. They expect to be given something for it, and they are looking for a bargain. This is a small, greedy, mean-spirited mentality. These people have not even advanced to politics, much less self-rule. They do not know their own people. They have no pride. They lack the greatness of soul people need to rule themselves.

Magnanimous people glory not in what they take but in what they can give. If others take more than they do, so what? If others feed off them, they say with Nietzsche, "What are my parasites to me?" The honorable take pride in generosity. They glory in giving. They smile and say, "You are welcome." If they love their country they say, "You are my people and I will see you fed."

Those who begrudge their taxes, who have no desire to share their wealth, have no love of country. Their affection does not extend far enough. Those who love their country take all within it as their own. They steward their land, they build with beauty and efficiency. They aim to "walk in beauty."4 They are proud of their people and treasure them—even those they count as their enemies. They feel a responsibility for all within it, good and bad. They are ashamed to see any one of their people in need.

For the subjects of a monarch, national greatness may lie in conquest or empire, in the grandeur of the monarch's castles or the size of the Crown Jewels. For democrats, "the crown jewels" has become a colloquial term for something every man possesses. Military dictatorships and nations governed by force take pride in the size of the military. Military parades, aircraft carriers that might never leave the harbor, and uniforms with a great deal of brass are the currency of national greatness.

Economists teach us to see national greatness in the size of a nation's GDP or the wealth that millionaires and billionaires are able to amass. For those who value wealth alone, who measure greatness in renminbi, dollars, or euros, displays of private wealth may be a source of pride.

Democrats take pride only in their accomplishments and the welfare and accomplishments of their people. They are proud of what they build together. They are proud when everyone has food and shelter, when everyone learns and takes pride and pleasure in their work. They take pride not in the wealth of the few but in the prosperity of all.

It would be unjust to say to someone "Roads will serve us all, but since you need them for your business, you build them." It would be arrogant for someone to say "I am wealthy" (or "I am ambitious"). "So I will build your roads and provide your defense." No one should be trusted with that power. Who is that one person to decide for the people?[5] People who rule themselves are proud: proud of their independence, proud of their abilities. Are we too poor to build our own roads? Are we too poor to protect ourselves? No, we can do this for ourselves.

The idea that taxation is coercion has its origins in resistance to monarchies and dictatorships. The dictator who taxes you does indeed have his hand in your pocket. The elected official who builds himself a palace with public funds is a thief. When people rule themselves they are not taking from someone's pocket and putting it in someone else's. They are spending common funds on a common project. They are working together.

Paine, who fought for democracy on two continents, argued that though rebellious people had opposed the taxes their rulers laid on them, they would not end all taxation. On the contrary, Paine thought free people—people who ruled themselves—would simply tax themselves differently. They would be free of the expense of a monarchy: the pageantry that accompanies it; the expenses of a dynasty and its hangers-on. They would fight fewer wars and spend less on armies and navies and the machinery of combat. They would not, however, dispense with taxes altogether. They would tax themselves willingly.

For a people who rule themselves, under laws they make and willingly submit to, the greatest shame would be to neglect their duty to one another. For a free people who live together willingly, the sight of people who are homeless or unfed, who struggle to find work or get an education is shaming. When we see that, we see our failures.

Our duty extends beyond those who are ours by law and custom. There is a greeting in Arabic: *ahlan wa sahlan*. The late Farouk Mustafa used to translate this as "You are among your people and your keep is easy." The greeting comes to strangers as much as to one's own. To say this, to practice this, is the mark of a people who have ears to hear the democratic demand and eyes to see it, who live with great hearts and open hands.

When I was a child and we were about to move overseas, my mother took me aside. She explained to me that I would see beggars. This was, she told me, a sad and terrible thing, and I should prepare myself for it. I learned in that moment that for a country to have beggars was a cause of great shame. I did not know then that my country's beggars had been hidden from me. I have learned since to long for the day when I can say, "There are no beggars in my country."

VII

The problem with liberalism

35. Undemocratic governments are unjust, but not all democracies are just. Democracy is a necessary but not sufficient condition for justice.

Al-Farabi wrote that places where the people rule are open to the greatest evil and the greatest good. He wrote of the democratic city, "The bigger, the more civilized, the more prevalent and the greater are the good and the evil it possesses."[1] Democratic people are free to shape themselves and their common life together as they see fit. They will not always do that well. Langston Hughes writes:

> The people often hold
> Great thoughts in their deepest hearts
> And sometimes only blunderingly express them,
> Haltingly and stumbling say them,
> And faultily put them into practice.[2]

People struggle. They are sailing into the unmapped, unknown future. They may be (they will be) deceived and misled. Perhaps the people, as the Prophet Muhammad believed, will "never be agreed upon an error." Perhaps "the voice of the people is the voice of God."[3] Until that unity, people will struggle to make themselves. They will make mistakes. They will be tempted by glory and rendered powerless by fear. They will do wrong. They will have to govern as the Vikings sailed, steering out of the dangers they encounter in uncharted waters. Such mistakes can be costly, even devastating, to the people and to others.

It is necessary, therefore, that people take precautions against possible errors. There should be no loss, no error that would leave the people vulnerable. There should be no single place or person whose fall would end the people's rule or damage it beyond repair. When

Wild Democracy. Anne Norton, Oxford University Press. © Oxford University Press 2023.
DOI: 10.1093/oso/9780197644348.003.0007

power is spread across regions, when people employ different forms and practices in governing themselves, when each person watches out for the common good, threats are countered from the start.

Perhaps there can be a people that is democratic and evil. Every virtue has an attendant vice shadowing it.

Perhaps democrats will come to value their people, their particular people, more than all others and mistake a race, a religion, a tribe, or a set of customs as that which must be preserved at all costs. Perhaps the courage, the daring of democrats can become mere recklessness, a willingness to gamble with things—and, more important, people—that can lead to a lust for glory and dominion. Perhaps curiosity, openness, a passion for the new can expose the people to unexpected dangers.

In writing this, I can see how a democracy might turn to evil. When I write "people who rule themselves," I think it much less likely. The idea of a people, a *demos,* that can be defined in ethnic or tribal terms carries the possibility of bigotry and chauvinism within it. People who have learned to rule themselves need have no commitments to ethnic or tribal identities. They are not bound to a *demos* or a tribe. People who have learned to rule themselves have already become disciplined. They have learned to judge their laws, their government, and themselves. They have learned to wait, to stand fast, to rebel when duty requires it. That judgment, diffused throughout an entire people, makes errors less likely and makes it harder for evil to take hold. People are protected by the spaces of anarchy they keep in their country and in themselves.

There is no people known to me that can claim to truly rule themselves. We have made democracy shabby by taking our work for it as an achievement. We have only the seeds and seedlings of democratic practice. We rule ourselves only here and there, in practices that have not fully grown up among us.

We struggle to rule ourselves. Democracy is a commitment, a conviction, a principle, a star to steer by in the unmapped sea. It is not what we have or what we are. Perhaps it is, at its best, what we long to be. Those who want neither to rule nor to be ruled, when they need or wish to act together, have learned that it is possible to preserve their freedom by acting democratically. We are learning how to rule ourselves, in small ways and great ones. We are not dreaming; we are

working. There is work to be done and many obstacles to overcome—
not least those presented by the supposed friends of democracy.

36. Liberalism is a problem.

People speak of "liberal democracy" as if one word slid easily into the
other, as if there were no space between liberalism and democracy.
They speak as if there should be no space, as if democracy were acceptable only when accompanied—or corrected—by liberalism. Liberalism
would guarantee rights and establish the rule of law. Liberalism would
protect the rights of minorities and dissidents. Liberalism would protect democracy from demagoguery and tyranny. A liberal democracy
would have regular, transparent procedures.

The problem with liberalism is that it does both more and less than
it claims.

The most admirable of these liberal claims belongs not to liberalism
but to democracy. Liberals faced with democratic critiques of liberalism fall back on the claim that rights belong to liberalism. In this understanding (or lack of understanding), democracy is the brute power
of the people, indifferent to the rights of individuals and vulnerable to
the ambitions of demagogues. Liberalism is the name for the contracts,
constitutions, rules, and procedures that secure rights and limit the
people in their passions and appetites.

If rights were the gift of liberalism, liberalism would command our
allegiance. They are not. Rights follow from no contract, no covenant,
no law. They are not made by a particular set of procedures; they do
not depend for their existence on the ratification of a state or any legal
order. They are ours, born in our flesh and held from birth to death.
Rights belong to the people.

Rights are a democratic demand, not a liberal gift.

Liberalism, republicanism, and constitutionalism were once
presented as supplements to democracy in the simple sense: additions
and procedures—norms—that would protect the rights of minorities
and dissidents; protect democracy from demagoguery and the tyranny
of the majority. This line of thought gave us the Bill of Rights. It has

also given us a welter of procedures, a plethora of laws, and a maze of institutions, most designed to ensure that the people do not rule.

Liberalism comes from fear and gives fear power. Fear of the people—that is to say, fear of ourselves—is at the heart of liberalism. Liberals fear the masses. They are—we are—the "great unwashed," full of appetite and ignorance, lacking knowledge, lacking civility, lacking breeding. Liberals fear the anger of the people. They know that people's most fundamental rights are violated daily. They know that people are silenced and powerless. They know that people are hungry. They know people lack homes, education, access to the knowledge and tools they need. They know that even those who have these things and more are burdened by inequality and deprived of freedom. They know, perhaps they prefer, that people are taught to desire and to defer to wealth. This fear generates laws and political institutions that hold the masses—that is to say, the people—in check.[4] Holding the people in check leashes us all.

This fear generates bureaucracies, procedures, institutions, and practices—(perhaps worst of all) "best practices"—that extend and enhance the powers of states, corporations, and other forms of consolidated power.[5] Liberalism thus operates as a supplement not only in the commonplace sense but in the sense Jacques Derrida gave it. Liberalism adds only to replace.[6]

The replacement of democracy by the liberalism that pretends to supplement and secure it takes two forms. First, the apparatus of order and procedure, taken initially as the guarantor of rights and government by consent, comes to be seen as its substance. Second, that legal and bureaucratic apparatus that Max Weber aptly named the Iron Cage retains its generative power, extending its reach ever more thoroughly across the state and into people's lives.[7]

Liberalism retains and enhances fear. The more liberals strive for order and protection, the more intensively they govern. Concern for rights gives way to concern for safety. Fears of the unknown, of the other who might be friend or enemy, of the mass of the people in which one is always both a part and apart, cannot be eliminated. They belong to the human and, more markedly, to the democratic condition. They require us to show some courage.

In my own country, liberalism has made people more fearful and less democratic. Americans committed to liberalism are inclined to go to courts for recognition of rights. They are reluctant to try to persuade their fellow citizens. Perhaps this is because they hesitate to press their views on their fellow citizens. If so, they should consider their views more closely and be ready to change their minds if those they talk to persuade them. Perhaps they have contempt for others, thinking that they are too foolish, too bigoted, or too self-interested to listen to reason. That would be both tragic and shameful. Perhaps in choosing the courts as a field of battle, they feel they will have an advantage over their opponents. That too would be tragic and shameful. Perhaps they are afraid. Perhaps it is simply too much trouble.

Whatever the cause, too many liberals have come to fear open debate and discussion. Liberalism has inclined too many to believe that they cannot trust the judgment of their fellow citizens. Rather than seeking to persuade those who do not agree with them, they try to enforce their will through the courts. The faith in courts and expert opinion creates a desire for willful and immediate domination in citizens. Our disdain for each other can make us tyrannical.

Reliance on law and the courts for the enforcement of rights is undemocratic, disrespectful, lazy, and cowardly. The courts have a duty, as all branches of government—all people—do, to secure and protect the rights of each and all. Free people should not rely upon them alone, or even primarily. We are fools when we rejoice too much in this or that legal decision. Laws without the support of the people will not be well executed. They may not be enforced at all. When we acclaim legal judgments, we may erode the will to change the people. We assign the task of doing justice to a few people who may be neither good nor wise, who are subject to little oversight, and who are committed to seek not justice but legality. We become lazy. We mistake law for justice. We mistake liberalism for democracy.

Fear of the people endangers democracy. Derrida feared democratic elections so profoundly that he supported a military coup. He and other French intellectuals, panicked at the prospect of a possible election victory by the Front Islamique du Salut flew to the protection of authoritarian rule. They clothed ambitious Algerian generals in the guise of saviors of democracy. Those generals would cling to rule until their hands were withered with age. The French had no right to choose who would rule Algeria, yet they defended military rule there. Democracy, even liberal democracy, is still *à venir* in Algeria. Coups in Bolivia, in Egypt, in Turkey, in Chile, and in many more embattled places have presented themselves as necessary to save democracy. They attack what they pretend to save.

In Catalonia, movements of the Catalan people to separate from Spain were met with violence and the hard hand of an unrelenting state. In responding to the movement, Spanish officials showed a telling confusion of the democratic, the liberal, and the constitutional. The Catalan secessionist movement was "undemocratic," they argued, because it did not follow the rules, because it set aside the Constitution. They avoided the question of popular support for secession, that is to say, the consent of the governed. Their objections were legitimate procedural questions, but they did not touch the question of democracy. The proposed Catalan referendum of November 9, 2014, may have been unconstitutional. To be sure, it violated national norms. Yet neither of these means it was undemocratic. On the contrary. If the Spanish government was committed to the democratic rather than the liberal, it would have let that referendum proceed. Instead it took ever more undemocratic measures against Catalan independence. Catalan politicians were arrested, forced into exile, and later tried. People in the streets were attacked by police brought into the province from outside. Spain then witnessed the absurdity of Felipe Borbón, called King Felipe, declaring to an international congress of legal experts in Madrid, "It makes no sense, it's unacceptable to appeal to a so-called democracy that is above the law."[8] He may have had a receptive audience in lawyers. Nevertheless, the statement is fundamentally wrong. The rule of the people is always above the law. Without their consent, there is no law that can justly command. In a democracy, wherever the people rule, the law is not the final authority. The people make the state, the constitution (if there is one), and the laws. They remain the laws' master.

The undemocratic character of the Spanish state response is still more evident if one considers the possible outcomes of the projected referendum. The secessionists might have lost dramatically, though that appeared unlikely. They might have won dramatically, though that was far from certain. The referendum might have done no more (and no less) than confirm the presence of a large proportion of Catalans who wished to leave Spain. If those opposed to secession had won dramatically, Spanish national unity would have been confirmed. If the secessionists had won, or simply demonstrated their strength in Catalonia, Spain as a whole would have been obliged to acknowledge— and respond to—that alienation in order to secure the unity of Spain. The state did not wish to do so. The Spanish state could not wholly succeed in silencing the people (people have many ways of making their opinions known), but it could demonstrate the state's indifference to the people's vote and affirm that the unity of Spain rested on something other than popular consent in Catalonia.

The Spanish response to the Catalan independence movement was not simply opposition to the possibility of secession. Nor was it simply the elevation of procedure over substance. It was a firm and multifaceted affirmation of the state's fundamental indifference to the will of the people. In that sense, it was entirely appropriate to make a king the messenger of the state. Monarchists are not, however, the only ones who reject the rule of the people.

Liberals and liberal theorists are among those who have feared democracy the most profoundly and constrained it the most effectively. From Locke to the present, they have directed their energy at preventing people from ruling themselves. Their reasons? They fear the anger of the poor. They fear that those who have little will take from those who have more. This is the most common justification for limiting democracy, yet it is demonstrably untrue. The fearful fear instability. They fear, above all, the loss of privilege and power. For some privilege and power come from wealth, for others they are licensed by a claim to higher knowledge. They believe that their expertise, the rule of experts, would be better for people, if only they knew. All these fears have at their heart the old claim "I am worth more than you."

The late philosopher John Rawls, writing in *The Law of Peoples*, contrasted "liberal" and "decent hierarchical peoples" in the search for a just "Society of Peoples."[9] Rawls was twice mistaken. First, liberalism is not sufficient for justice. Second, the distinction between liberal and hierarchical peoples is deceptive. Those Rawls cast as "liberal democratic peoples" have not yet satisfied even the standard of liberalism, much less that of democracy. The great liberal revolutions of the seventeenth and eighteenth centuries set forth ideals still beyond our reach. The "liberal democratic peoples" that Rawls sees as the foundation for a just "Society of Peoples" look far more like "decent hierarchical peoples." They are marred by the remnants of historical injustice. They still hold—and still defend—structures of exploitation and inequality, not least, as many critics noted, hierarchies of sex and sexuality, race and ethnicity.

There are many hierarchies that live in those countries Rawls saw as liberal. They change their forms, they shift, but the hierarchies remain. Hierarchies of race and sex, the arbitrary raising of some bodies over others, the belief that wealth should command deference and exercise power, are neither just nor decent. Rawls was wrong in a third sense: there are no decent hierarchical peoples.

The limits of liberalism are shown at its foundations. Locke's formulation "life, liberty, and property" placed property at the heart of liberalism. There is both right and wrong in this. For Locke, property was not simply something to be bought or sold. Property, in the first instance, was the body and the rights held within it. Those rights enabled people to make things in the world their own by hunting, gathering, building, and making. This was, and remains, defensible. The construction of a "sacred right of property" by Locke, Rousseau, and generations of liberals moved rapidly from the person and the person's rights to possessions. Property lost its connection to the body and the rights sheltered within it and became another word for possessions. This was a degradation and set further degradations in motion. The defenders of slavery in the antebellum United States claimed that the sacred right of property enabled them to hold their slaves. The defenders of economic inequality in the present claim that the sacred right of property entitles the wealthy to power beyond the reach of others. The rich can buy speech and silence. They can buy influence. Perhaps they can buy elections. Power of this kind is antithetical to the democratic. No free people can accept it, for if they do, they will be ruled by wealth.

37. Populism is a democratic force.

"Populism" has been used to name a strange collection of parties and politicians throughout the world. Argentina's Juan Perón, America's

Huey Long and Donald Trump, Hungary's Victor Orban, Turkey's Recep Tayyip Erdoğan, Greece's Golden Dawn party, the French National Front and National Rally are all called "populists" by scholars and the media. These scholars and pundits see populism as marked by intense nationalism, hatred of foreigners, fear of immigration, and a distrust of elites. They see populism as the enemy of liberalism.

The people they deplore are not populists. That name was stolen. The theft is a symptom of greater crimes. There is a populist party: the People's Party of the nineteenth-century United States. None of these people belongs to it, none of the parties have any ties to it. The true Populist party is small now, but its positions remain strong in currents of the Democratic Party in the United States and throughout the Latin American left.[10] In many respects, populism remains the dominant current of political thought where it first originated, in the American Midwest. Populism emphasizes equality of worth; respect for those who labor in fields, in factories, on building sites and on the roads, in schools and hospitals; and sharing wealth among the people. This is in stark contradiction to elite European accounts of populism.[11]

American populists are not hostile to pluralism, they are at home with it. Their politics caught fire from those who grew up on the land and those who moved to it. They had absorbed waves of refugees from failed revolutions in Europe. Irish Rebels and English Chartists, Germans forced to flee after 1848, all found a home in the Midwest. Those who came and those who welcomed them found common ground not only in the belief but in the practices of equality. They did not distrust pluralism; they were pluralism. French, German, Italian, Polish, Swedish peasants from every corner of Europe came and sent their children to school together. They married across cultural and religious lines but kept much of those cultures alive in the kitchen, in clubs, churches, and synagogues. Pluralism was not a problem for them: they lived it. Those who were political refugees did not leave their politics behind. They believed Americans had the rule of the people at heart. They made themselves American in this. They brought Chartism from the United Kingdom to the United States. They brought Finnish miner radicalism to the mines of Minnesota and Wisconsin. There were immigrants farming, mining, keeping shops, brewing beer, making bread. They were soldiers. John Peter Altgeld was an immigrant, brought to the United States as an infant. He lied about his age to serve in the Union Army (with my immigrant ancestors). He became governor of Illinois. As governor, Altgeld advocated—and secured—stricter child labor and workplace safety laws. He pardoned three men unjustly convicted in the Haymarket riot. He made Illinois more just, more democratic, more equal. In the American Midwest, throughout America, immigrants strengthened both pluralism and populism.

The identification of populism with racism that has become popular in the late twentieth and early twenty-first centuries has its unseemly origin not in antiracism but in hostility to equality. Those who fear populism fear the depth and longevity of the populist insistence on redistribution and the populist ethic of equality. Were there racists among nineteenth-century American populists? No movement, not even abolition, was wholly free of that taint. There were, however, more efforts at cross-racial alliances in labor than in management, in farmers' alliances than in finance. There was unity to be forged across the racial divide in opposition to the power of wealth. The historic populist commitment to equality threatens racial as well as economic hierarchies now as it did then.

There is also a strong vein of populism in Latin America. Here, too, populism comes into being as resistance against the dominion of the wealthy. Here, too, populism has often, if not always, gone hand in hand with pluralism. Evo Morales of Bolivia, José Mujica of Uruguay, and Luiz Inácio Lula da Silva of Brazil, aong others, sought to expand the political to embrace the formerly disenfranchised: the indigenous, women, and (always) the poor. The rise of populism in South America fueled the rise of democracy there as Europe and the United States saw their democracies attacked.

The ability of European scholars to erase this history of the Americas in seizing the name "populist" testifies to the persistence of European imperial arrogance. Populism is what they say it is, though those they call populists did not take that name for themselves. Those who did take that name—parties throughout the Americas—receive little or no attention from European scholars. Imperial arrogance persists long after the empire is gone. Europe and those Umberto Eco called "Europeanized intellectuals" have proved indifferent to how parties and movements name themselves, and the policies and histories that accompany them. "Populism" becomes a code word for bigotry, and part of the history of people's struggles to rule themselves in the Americas is erased.

Populism belongs not to the Old World but the New. There are, however, two characteristics that unite at least some of those the Europeans call populists with the true populists of the New World. They distrust elites and they demand equality. Populism remains a democratic demand founded in the conviction that people have the right to rule themselves, and to live their lives.

Commentators were quick to label the Gilets Jaunes of France populists, but they were slower to hear their demands as an indictment of the growth of radical inequality. Where distrust or intolerance of immigrants could be found among the dissatisfied, the deprived and the *démunis*, it could distract attention from the core demands of the Gilets Jaunes. That intolerance was more fully and effectively manifest among elites, evident in Nicolas Sarkozy's expulsion of the Roma and his denigration of Islam; in the novels of Michel Houellebecq and the work of Alain Finkielkraut. Elites, it appears, are entitled to their hatreds; they are deplored only when they appear among the poor.

Popular demands for dignity, for respect, for the ability to live a decent life have a long history. They echo through ancient bread riots and slave rebellions to the uprisings of the present. Populism belongs to that history. The willful distortion of the name and history of populism has served the interests of the privileged. It is long past time that these democratic demands, those who make them, and the history they carry receive not only respect but fulfillment.

38. Institutions alone cannot ensure that the people rule.

Institutions are tools. There is no tool that can be used only for good. The courts can protect minorities or serve the powerful, defend rights or pervert them. The legislature can advance the rights and prosperity of all the people or serve the interests of the powerful, protect the environmental commons or serve the interests of polluting industries.

The executive can seek personal glory, wealth, and power or serve the common good. The executive can be the tribune of the people or a corrupt demagogue. The military can hold to their oath to defend the Constitution or become an institution that undermines democracy.

Institutions, like other tools, are breakable. They lose their sharpness; they rust and decay. They are shaped by one set of needs and conditions and may work quite differently in another. Institutions have to be built and maintained, but they must also be continually questioned, often corrected, and occasionally remade.

Americans are in such a moment as I write. The institutions and practices that Americans regarded as furnishing defenses against totalitarianism—and other forms of authoritarian domination—have failed us. We have had confidence that the free market, modern science, and technological innovation would protect democracy and prevent the concentration of power in the hands of a few. We have had confidence that guarantees of free speech and the power of a free press would advance the truth upon which democracies depend. But the concentration of media in a few hands made it the tool of oligarchs. The role of algorithms, artificial intelligence, and machine learning in social media installed invisible censors in a field too many saw as free and ungoverned. Our confidence was hardly rash; it was supported by a theoretical canon, by the disciplines of history and political science, and by the common sense—and experience—of many generations. But it is tragically misplaced in the present. These institutions have not only failed to defend us; they have become another form of totalitarianism.[12]

Reliance on the free market to spread wealth (and power with it) has concentrated power in private hands. The free press, under the conditions of a market free in name only, has become gatekeeper, censor, and agitator. Rather than serving as a vehicle for the expression (much less the contest) of diverse ideas, the media has come to define political views that lie outside a small range of opinion as inadmissible and absurd. Profit seekers in social media direct their readers to ever more extreme and violent opinions. The truly absurd is given an artificial but compelling centrality.

Science and technology, including the social sciences, which were once thought to be ungovernable and so the means for permitting individuals to escape governance, have instead become the means for confinement and regulation, not only of acts but of thought. The institutions that the Enlightenment presented as undoing private power have come instead to consolidate it. The institutions presented as the means for the liberation of the people have become the tools of a more effective domination.

There are other dangers to democracy now. Sheldon Wolin has asked, "What if democracy instead of being prone to license were to become fearful . . . submissive rather than unruly?"[13] Contemporary American citizens (how inappropriate the name seems!) *have* become fearful and submissive. That fearfulness, that anxiety about external threats once was a defense against tyranny. Now it is the means for licensing tyrannical authority and securing submission to it. It is easy to see, in the distances that open between 9/11, the security regime of the Bush years, and the present, how fear has produced a reliance on surveillance and a restriction of civil liberties and a more docile and complacent citizenry. It is easy to see citizens who have become submissive.

What is to be done? How are we to find our way back to the struggle toward democracy when the institutions we once relied on fail us? Those institutions are not sacrosanct: they can be changed. The work of democracy requires that people are always thinking about what will serve democracy best: what institutions will secure power in the hands of the people and enable people to use power well and wisely. There will come a time, many times, when people need to refuse institutions that no longer serve them well and craft others to take their place. That is democratic work.[14]

39. How free people might choose their leaders.

Many of those who present themselves as experts in the comparative study of democracy or democratic theory argue that democracy can be assessed by consulting certain metrics. Are there elections? Have offices changed hands? Has the party in power changed? They do not ask "Do the people rule themselves?" That is the only question that matters.

In what follows I set aside debates over representation as a diminution or even abandonment of democracy. I take the use of representation, for all its faults and dangers, as a defensible choice for free people.

Free and fair elections are one of the strongest tools for any democracy that relies on representation. At their best, they allow people to choose who will perform the tasks they assign. They can choose on whatever basis they think best. When they consider candidates, they judge. When they campaign, they act. When they go to the polls, they judge. They decide issues in referenda; they decide ballot questions. They change regulations; they make law. Each election demands consent to ruling and to being ruled, and offers the opportunity for judgment and dissent. Those who vote assume the duty of rule. Those who stand for election need the courage to step forward and be judged by their people. Those who win feel the power of rule and the burden of responsibility. Those who lose, face the future with courage and equanimity.

Elections call forth courage, but they are not perfect instruments. They can be designed to maintain injustice and inequality. They can be undermined by money, a flawed press, or more brutal means. At their best they are, as Weber argued, a monstrous amalgam of two opposing forms. They are lawful, rule-governed, and orderly. They entail assessments of the merits of the candidates and the needs of the moment. They are collective acts, in which the many decide and individuals judge for the whole. Yet they are also acts of grace. Each individual, in the silence of their own heart, decides who is to be elected. Grace calls to grace: the incalculable grace that may call from a candidate to the people, the grace the people confer with their choice.

Election is not, however, the only way for free people to choose leaders. One can rotate offices among the people. Leaders can be chosen by lot.

The idea of choosing representatives and officials by lot strikes terror into most people, myself included. For all our criticisms of public officials, we appear to believe that they are more likely to be qualified and dutiful and to have more integrity than someone chosen at random. Yet lot was one of the most common ways in which ancient democracies chose their leaders. Perhaps we should consider lot with cooler heads and more courage.

Whether or not we choose by lot, we should act as if we do. People who choose their leaders and representatives by lot should have confidence that their fellow citizens are well-educated, that they know our history, both good and bad. We must therefore work hard to ensure that all are educated. We also have an interest in seeing that they have the common good at heart. We who live with our enemies know that their conception of the common good may well be mistaken and certain to do us harm. We should cultivate courage in ourselves and limits in our government. We will need to face our enemies, and we should ensure that whatever harm they do will be limited in time.

There are other tools. There are, I suspect, other forms and methods and tools for ruling ourselves that we have lost or forgotten. There are others we may yet develop. We will be able to harness techniques of mass consultation. We will learn how to rule together. None of these tools will be perfect. All can be turned against the people. Each will have its uses.

Perhaps we will find that people need far less rule and no leaders at all.

40. The people, steering.

Written into the Old Norse word for "the rule of the people," *folkestœring*, is an affirmation not only of the right but of the ability of the people to take their country into unknown and dangerous places. The image of a single man holding the rudder of the ship of state did not fool those who knew sailing well. A ship was a ship. A people governing themselves was another matter. Ships, sailing, and steering capture many aspects of self-governance, but not all. Experience with sailing did not persuade the Vikings that executive power belonged to one alone.

Then again, perhaps it was sailing that taught the Vikings. Rudders, like stirrups, belong to a later historical moment. Perhaps the Vikings held an older knowledge. Long before rudders, those who went viking had learned that people rowing together can steer a ship, changing their course as they choose, if they work together. Perhaps that knowledge stayed with them. In any case, it is there for us.

Carl Schmitt's much-quoted claim "Sovereign is he who decides on the exception" need not detain us long. Exceptions are made every day, by those in power and those without it. When an exception is made in one's own favor or self-defense, it may be called an evasion. Evasions are one of the most important "weapons of the weak."[15] To secure their lives, their liberty, and their pursuit of happiness, those without power are constantly required to make exceptions. When those in power are unjust, their rule is arbitrary. Every act is an exception, for there is only one rule: the rule of the powerful. When those in power are just, they recognize that law does not always secure justice. Mercy and magnanimity make exceptions. These may be signs of greatness, but they do not determine sovereignty.

Sovereignty belongs to those who make and unmake governments, who rule others and themselves, who make and unmake peoples. They rule, they steer, together.

41. Without free and courageous people, there are no democratic governments.

This thesis is both true and false. It is false because people, in their moments of greatness, can overcome themselves. They may not be ready to rule themselves, but they may have the courage to assume that burden in the hope that they can rise to meet it. It is false because people are never wholly democratic. At their best, they work for democracy, work in democracy, work on democracy. They struggle to rule themselves, constantly facing the dangers in that rule and, worse, the forces that erode it. They find freedom, strength, and protection in the anarchic space that is both a part of and apart from the democratic.

This thesis is true because what elements of the democratic we have in the present, and the democracy we work for in the present and the future, are grounded in our capacities, our virtues, and our desires. They are made by our work.

Those who intend to rule themselves collectively must be able to rule themselves individually. Democracy demands the discipline to meet the unknown future and the known enemy with courage. People who rule themselves cultivate both solidarity and self-reliance. They depend on themselves and step forward to help their people. They sacrifice for the common good and regard it quite correctly as no sacrifice at all.

42. Decentralization protects the ability of people to rule themselves.

When Michel Foucault offered a theory of power that saw it not as concentrated at one central point but instead diffused throughout an order, many readers were filled with fear. They saw themselves constantly under the gaze of power, controlled at every point. Power surrounded them. They had nowhere to turn. Those people who already knew themselves hemmed in on every side found this analysis liberating, for it enabled them to see the structures they had only sensed around them. They could begin to find their way through, though they too were daunted by the extent and pervasiveness of power spread so broadly.

When people struggle to rule themselves, the more power is spread the safer they are likely to be.

When times are hard, decentralization is to institutions—and to rule—as guerrilla war is to conventional war. Attacked in one place, people can regroup in another. The emergence of a would-be authoritarian in one region need not threaten the whole. The failure of one practice or institution need not place all at risk. Nothing depends upon a single leader.

In more ordinary, peaceful, times, decentralization cultivates qualities that make the people's capacity to rule themselves more deft, more sure, more adaptable, more daring. They are more willing to experiment when failure is less threatening. If the experiment fails in one venue, others are safe. They watch people in other places do things differently and see what they might improve in their own.

The connection between local communities and the capacity of people to rule themselves runs deep in political thought and deeper still in the minds of people with a sense of place. Many institutions—the practices of African villages and the Haudenosaunee longhouse, the Russian *mir*, the Indian *panchayat*, the New England town

meeting—are praised for their democratic character and for their intimate, organic connection to the lived experience of the people.

Intimate communities and close ties are no longer confined to living
on the land. There are many of us who have our closest ties with people
who live far from us. People have become ever more adept at creating
community. Our local communities may be manifold. We may be
close, we may work together with the people who live near us. We share
common dangers and common hopes: fear of hurricanes, perhaps, or
hope for a good fishing season or fewer wildfires. We have to learn to
live together in the ordinary aspects of life: walking and driving and
riding bicycles, keeping sidewalks clear of snow. Yet these people,
nearest to us in space, may not be nearest to our hearts or minds.

There are intimate communities on the internet, bound together by
common experiences, common passions, common aims. Political life
takes place here as well. Alliances are formed, solidarities are earned,
strategies are crafted, and people learn from long discussions and
debates with one another.

People craft still other communities. These are far from the communities that grow in and from a place, far from the intense immate-
riality of the internet. These are old forms of community, cultivated in
writing and episodic meetings, in moments taken out of time. They are
common among scholars.

Those who write of the political value of community, who craft
institutions designed to create or cultivate community, who write of
democratic deliberation seem to consider only communities of place.
That is not how people live. That is not how politics is experienced.
People have been adept in creating communities in many forms. All
promise ways in which people can rule themselves. All run the risk
of becoming stifling or oppressive. Communities protect only when
they can be abandoned, only when other communities are found to
shelter the democratic, only when we leave enough ungoverned space
for anarchy.

Not all decentralizations are geographic. The same logic applies to
levels and methods of governance. What is used successfully in one
system can be adapted for use in another. It is not enough to petition the center: people who want to accomplish something need first
to consider multiple ways the problem could be resolved and decide

which would be easiest and most effective. They are asked to think strategically about power and to use their own judgment constantly. They learn multiple ways to exercise power, and they become more adept at each. They become better at steering.

In a wilder, more anarchic democracy, decentralization ceases to be a description of institutions and becomes an ordering principle and an ethic. There are elements of this in my country. Who holds power? The president? The president is bound by law. Congress can govern the president. The Supreme Court can govern the president. No branch has the final word, no branch—and certainly no person—has power that cannot be countered. Their power, moreover, flows outward and can be dammed or diverted. It depends on the judgment of all those officials and citizens who put law, regulations, executive actions, military commands into practice. Above all, the president, the Congress, the Supreme Court, the judges, soldiers, and sailors are sworn to the Constitution, and therefore to the people. This is only one dimension. There are states, counties, cities, and townships, each with its own institutions, practices, and ways of life. There are jurors who can decide cases and nullify law. There are citizens who have the right to vote, to sit on juries, who judge the laws and practices of power as they walk through the world, who make and unmake governments. There are people, empowered by no more and no less than the rights born in them. Sovereignty belongs to the people: to each as well as to all. In an anarchic democracy, power moves always and inexorably to the people.

Politics is not the same as government. The practices of a people ruling themselves are not confined in government buildings or limited to elections. Politics is practiced at home and on the street, in writing and in the broad, irregular spaces of the internet. All of these have uses and value. Any one of them may save us in hard times. Multiplying the planes and possibilities of politics advances and protects the democratic.

Think, for example, of people who discover that they have lead in their water. If their water supplier is a private company, regulated only by the market, they must appeal to the company. If the company fails them, they may have nowhere to go but the nearest unpolluted source—or back to the market for a water purification system. The same applies when the water is supplied publicly without oversight. Even now most people have far more resources than that. They can go to the supplier, to any public office that regulates water. They can call on their local or national officials. They can do this, usually, not just on one level or to one branch of government but many. They can appeal to the press and publicize their problem in the media. They can assemble and protest. The proliferation of levels and networks gives people access to more strategies, more ways of seeking help, of making injustice visible, and of solving their problems. Their task will not be easy. They will have obstacles to negotiate and defects in their institutions to overcome, but without the proliferation of approaches to political power their task can be made impossible.

When politics is confined within a narrow space, limited to a small set of actors or institutions, power is intensified and confined to the few. That is the case not only for governmental institutions but for privately owned political venues. Consider the media. Long ago people learned to doubt and distrust media that was under the control of the government. They quite sensibly questioned whether media controlled in this way would give space and voice to an opposition party, to rebels or dissenters. Those dangers are no less true of media concentrated in private hands. Private owners, families, corporations all have interests, all may choose to silence or diminish opposition. Silvio Berlusconi's control over Italian media distorted and corrupted Italian politics long before he held office. Rupert Murdoch distorted and directed politics on three continents. The tabloid press, intent on profits, has often shown itself indifferent to truth: willing, for the sake of money, influence, or the preferences of its owners, to field lies. Mark Zuckerberg's Facebook has famously sold its members' data without their knowledge or consent, enabled the manipulation of electorates, encouraged the intensification of partisanship and violence, and permitted the public circulation of lies by political candidates. In all these cases, the absence of alternative ways to communicate and other sources of information has limited the political possibilities and resources available to the people. Rather than the media providing information and giving clarity, they too often cause us to fumble in the dark with paths and obstacles hidden from us, directed into channels chosen by the powerful and profit-seeking.

People who recognize that power over the media is concentrated in a few hands look elsewhere for information: the internet, their friends. News, knowledge, and information are often fragmented. Conspiracy theories offer more. In the place of fragments they offer full explanations that cover all the aspects of a story and more. They offer detailed, rational explanations. They often have all the apparatus that a searching public has learned to look for: references, citations to books and articles, quotes from scholars and public figures. If the scholar is not competent or respected, if the public figure is a fraud, who's to know? Conspiracy theories describe (in detail) a world in which a few hold power. That, at least, accords with the readers' experience.

Multiplying the planes and possibilities of politics also depends on time. The ability to change an official, a rule, a regulation, a law, an institution increases the strategic possibilities of politics.

No tool serves only one hand. Laws, institutions, constitutions have changing effects as the political order changes around them. The ability to change, to sail where there is no firm, certain, and unchanging ground is necessary for those who would rule themselves. Their political structures must be changeable if they are to serve them well.

When a people choose how they will govern themselves, it is important that they leave space for anarchy. In choosing how to govern themselves, people need to consider not only how to govern but how governance is to be avoided. They need, in James Scott's phrase, "the art of not being governed."[16] They need to leave space for anarchy.

43. People can always recall their representatives, servants, and officials.

In *Insurgent Universalities*, Massimiliano Tomba revives the concept (and our hopes) for a revival of the practice of the imperative mandate. The imperative mandate, Tomba argues, is profoundly democratic. In it, people assert their right to recall their representatives at will. The imperative mandate, Tomba writes, was a medieval European institution that emerges again—revived, rediscovered, or simply discovered anew—among the sans-culottes and communards of the French Revolution, in soviets and workers' councils, and in the practices of the indigenous and the Zapatistas.[17] This may sound legalistic or archaic. It is not. I saw it in a set of handwritten electoral rules that came from a slum in India.[18]

In their work on electoral practices among the Indian poor, Tariq Thachil and Adam Auerbach found that slum dwellers were not passive fodder for party machines. On the contrary, they were political people, who sought to elect those who would advance their common interests. They sought knowledge about the candidates, they recruited, they organized, and they voted. They not only voted; they governed the voting processes that would give them local leaders. Thachil reproduces a handwritten set of electoral rules from one of these slums. There are ten rules. The ninth rule is "If the president is found guilty for doing any wrong an immediate meeting will be called and he shall be suspended or punished."

The imperative mandate, despite its rather elegant and esoteric name, is nothing more or less than the right of the people to remove any officer, any leader, at any time. It does not belong to a lost golden age. Those people in an Indian slum who wrote and acted upon this principle proved that it is not utopian but accessible.

One is not elected, or otherwise granted the power to represent, to speak for, or to speak as the people, to remain untouchable for a length of time. On the contrary, the right to represent or to act for the people, or some group of people, depends on that investiture being constantly renewed. What people give, they can withdraw.

The imperative mandate—the ability to recall a representative at any time—is democracy unleashed in time, the work of free people who refuse to keep the democratic to a schedule.

44. Executive energy belongs to the many as well as the one.

Many who write on constitutions argue that executive energy can be found only in the leader, never in the people. This belief was an article of faith for monarchs and autocrats. In the United States, Alexander Hamilton's effort to build a stronger presidency was fueled not only by personal ambition but by the vision of a single, willful man, free to act quickly and decisively. In recent decades, Schmitt's "Sovereign is he who decides on the exception" has become an article of faith for theorists on the left as well as the right. Scholars nominally committed to democracy or socialism argued for the necessity of a leader. George W. Bush claimed, "I am the decider." Were they deaf to the sound of those words echoing over the ruins?

The idea that concentration of power in a single executive produces swifter, more decisive action is fundamentally mistaken. It presumes that the decision, once made, goes into effect. There are few executives, even those who have dictatorial powers, who can singlehandedly accomplish what they have decided. They depend on others to put that decision into practice. The *patrón* orders; the *peon* obeys (or disobeys). The king commands, and liegemen and servants scurry off: to follow his orders well or badly, to remember or forget, to hurry or to drag their feet. Whether we acknowledge it or not, executive power is always diffuse.

The ruins of postwar Germany (but not only Germany) testify to the hazards of placing faith in a single leader. The ruins of Katrina and the World Trade Center testify to the ability of people to act with energy in times of emergency. When the planes struck the World Trade Center, the American president was far away, reading to schoolchildren. No warning had been issued, and whatever plans were in place were overcome by the extent, gravity, and shock of the attack. Long before any federal response came, the people of New York had begun the work. Firefighters, police, and ordinary people with special skills, or simply hands and a mind, gathered to rescue those they could. They were fast and they were effective. The city was their city; the people were their own.

In every large natural disaster, the people first on the scene are often neighbors. The person who takes you off your roof in a flood might be a firefighter, but they might also be a neighbor with a boat. In hurricanes, tornados, and earthquakes, people respond. They do not wait for the energetic executive. They begin the work themselves. After Hurricane Katrina, the energetic executive was slow to respond, and the response, when it came, was inadequate. The people of New Orleans lacked adequate resources, but they had energy; they knew their neighbors and their city. The people of Puerto Rico lacked the resources necessary to respond to Hurricanes Irma and Maria, but they showed the same energy, tenacity, and local knowledge in their responses.

Even when the attacks are expected and a central authority has plans in place, the responses to attacks and disasters often come from those who are there. Britain planned for the Blitz and had mobilized to respond to it, but in doing so the British relied on a system of neighborhood wardens to warn of air raids, get people to shelters, put out fires, and rescue people from the ruins. The instruction "Keep Calm and Carry On" became emblematic of the British. It captures an aspect of response that is often absent in discussions of executive energy. In natural disasters and the most unnatural of wars, success depends not only on decisive action but on qualities of composure, steadfastness, and resilience. The Palestinians, who have lived in crisis for generations, have learned to value their own steadfastness, for it is on that quality that their endurance depends.

Crises are addressed not only in the moment of decision or the long endurance of hardship but in carrying out the work the crisis makes necessary. The quick, spontaneous response, without leaders or instructions; the steadfast courage that maintains people in crisis; the ability to continue to build themselves—these are necessary if people are to rule themselves.

All attacks, all disasters, all crises are local. Though they may threaten everyone, everywhere, they will hit in a particular place and at a particular time. They will hit particular people. The fastest response will come from those who are present at the site. The crisis will require not action in the abstract but action in this place, this time, among these people. Those who share that place know it best. They will be able to act swiftly, where people new to the place must hesitate. They can make judgments newcomers may not be prepared to make. They can make those judgments quickly. It is the people, spread throughout the country, who can respond most quickly and most decisively.

They have another invaluable quality in a crisis: they are slow to leave. The people they rescue are their people. The place they struggle to repair is their place. They will be steadfast when another crisis draws away the attention of central authorities. The people, unlike a single energetic executive, can respond to more than one crisis at a time, act in more than one place at a time. They are faster, their reach is further, their knowledge more intimate, and their commitment more profound.

We cannot place our faith in the energy, intellect, judgment, or decisiveness of any single person. We depend, whether we acknowledge it or not, on the energy, intellect, judgment, and decisiveness of those who are present. We rely on them to respond to the crisis as it happens. We rely on them to act wisely, to maintain their composure, to be steadfast against the forces that attack them.

Perhaps those who pull people from the wreckage are the many hands of the sovereign people. Perhaps anarchy offers not only shade but the freedom to act in a crisis. Perhaps they recognize their own precarity, their own mortality in the damaged people they see before them. Perhaps they are simply people seeing a need and acting. In those moments they are people with the courage to rule themselves.

VIII
Force is the enemy of the free

45. Military power is a danger to democracy.

Armed force is a threat to any people. An invading army can enforce its will and, in the course of that, kill and maim. For this reason, people who rule themselves will need to protect themselves against armed force and military attacks. That is not enough. They need to do more.

A look at the history of revolutions will show, all too clearly, the hazard that military force poses to free people. Those countries that throw off imperial rule or a despot of their own will find it hard to avoid falling prey to military rule. Gratitude to the general who brought the victory and fear of the former ruler often persuade people to settle for an exchange of tyrants rather than ensuring that the people rule. Few leaders are clear-sighted enough to see the enduring damage done by military rule. Fewer still have the courage to trust the people they have led and hand over power. Those who do, make demigods of their people and themselves.

Even among people fortunate or brave enough to have avoided military rule, the military poses a continuous threat. Rule can always be imposed by force. The early United States tried to forestall this threat by forbidding, in the Constitution no less, the establishment of a standing army. The newly independent states were to rely instead on militias. That proscription lasted less than a generation, despite its presence in the Constitution. It has, however, proved more resilient in the principles of American soldiers.

All soldiers are taught that it is their duty to refuse an unconstitutional order or one that violates the code of military conduct. A dedicated commitment to the teaching of ethics in the service academies has given us officers who have the discipline that protects the democratic. They are sworn not to a person or a flag but to the Constitution. They are sworn to the people and to the text in which the people craft

Wild Democracy. Anne Norton, Oxford University Press. © Oxford University Press 2023.
DOI: 10.1093/oso/9780197644348.003.0008

a constitution for themselves. No one, not a sergeant, not a general, not the Commander in Chief, can require them to perform an unconstitutional act. They have a military code of conduct which requires them to refuse any order that violates that code. With rare exceptions, they have recognized that they are not a sword for their leaders but a shield for the people, and they have kept their honor. Nevertheless, the danger remains.

There are temptations for soldiers and temptations for civilians.

Military excellence is conventionally proven in wars. Ambitious soldiers hoping to excel may be a little too eager for conflict. Perhaps this comes to be balanced by a more intimate sense of the costs of war, but the lure of glory can be very great, and the criteria for promotion more compelling still.

Civilians and military alike may be tempted by the deceptive ease and finality of force.

Civilians may come to see the military as their servant or their surrogate and avoid the responsibilities that fall on all people who rule themselves. This is especially true where the decision to go to war is made not by the people as a whole but by their representatives. Those who make the decision to go to war must do so in the full knowledge that they are sending their children and their husbands and wives. They must make the sacrifices they ask of others. They should be willing to go themselves.

46. Free people go to war together or not at all.

People who rule themselves cannot fight wars as others do. Under kings and dictators, liberal or authoritarian regimes, wars are declared by the ruler or by the government and fought by some arm of the state. That may be a standing army, a volunteer force, a militia, or mercenaries hired by the state. When people rule themselves, they are both ruler and ruled. They make the decision to go to war, and they must bear its costs. The closer they are to democracy, the more costs they must assume. When the people rule, the people bear the costs of war. Those costs are many.

It is both just and prudent for the people—all the people—to bear the costs of war. It is just because those who make the decision to go to war should be the ones to bear war's burdens. That is rarely the case. The wealthy, the privileged, the powerful rarely fight the wars they propose. Those wars are likely to serve their interests best, but they are more likely to get certified for bone spurs than to see active duty. There are privileged people, fortunate sons in nations who struggle toward democracy, who fight and die for their country. More often, the decision for war is made by the more powerful, the war fought by the less powerful. That is unjust. War should weigh upon us all.

Ensuring that all bear the burdens of war is prudent because their virtues may lead democratic people into unjust or unwise wars. People who love their freedom want others to have it too. People who recognize that rights belong to all people, that they are held in all the bodies of the living, will defend those rights in others. They are angry when they see rights denied and people not permitted to rule themselves. They see the cause is just. They are brave. They are daring and they take risks. Those who call for military intervention may get an easy hearing. We believe, we who long to be free, that we are not for ourselves or our people alone, but for all people.

This has an honorable origin, but it can lead to dishonorable acts. We believe that all people have the capacity to reason and to rule themselves. We believe they have the right to rule themselves as they choose. If their rights are denied, we see that is wrong and believe that the wrong should be fought. Why not by us? There are dangers here. Too often we fail to fully consult the people we intervene to help. Because we all have rights, because we all have reason, we may think we do not need to ask if our intervention is wanted. Of course they want to be free; of course they want their rights. We are all reasonable human beings; we can recognize their needs. When we meet objections from those we hope to help, we may make the mistake of thinking we know better. We fail to recognize the limits of our knowledge; we fail to impose proper limits on our will. We forget that they have the right to decide when and how and with whom they will rebel. We forget that they have the right to choose whom they will be and how to govern themselves together.

The danger of setting consent aside is where the perils of a generous arrogance begin, not where they end. When people think they fight to secure the rights and the freedom of others and find the others less than receptive to their generosity, they may not immediately recognize their mistake. After all, those people are oppressed. They may be resisting aid because they are not free to join and support those who want to fight for them. They may be resisting because they are deluded, still bound by religious or political ideas that prevent them from seeing or choosing freely. The more they resist, the more their resistance may be read as evidence of their oppression. The vehemence of their rejection becomes evidence of their need. This form of justification for wars and military interventions became commonplace—and widely accepted— in the latter part of the twentieth century. It has caused untold harm.

There are other dangers. If the costs of war fall on others, it is easier to call for war. If the costs of war fall unevenly or on the few, it is easier to call for war, easier to use an army of volunteers or those mercenaries some dishonestly call "security contractors." This is neither honorable nor decent. If you are not willing to bear the costs of war on your body and the bodies of those you love, you cannot ask others to bear them for you. There are times when it is honorable to say "I will die with you in this cause," but it is never honorable, never even decent, to ask another to die for you. It is indecent to ask another to die in a cause you choose while you stay safe at home. This applies to women as it does to men, to the old as well as to the young. Where people are free, all bear the burdens of war, all place their bodies at risk.

When the American colonies declared their independence and the British sent an army to deprive them of it, people came from France and Poland, from the German states and Britain itself to fight with them. They believed, as we do, "that all men are created equal, that they are endowed by their creator with certain inalienable rights," and that when those rights are denied, the people have the right to make a new government for themselves. After independence was secured, Americans went out into the world: to France with Paine and Lafayette, to Poland, and to Greece to fight with others in their own struggles to rule themselves. This practice began at the beginning of the republic and continued well into the twentieth century. The Lafayette Escadrille fought with the French in the First World War, before the United States joined in the alliance. The Lincoln Brigade fought with the Republicans against fascism in Spain. They acted honorably.

Those who think that their people, their state, their army, or some mercenaries hired for the purpose should fight in a foreign country should think again. They cannot justly ask others to fight for them. If they think the cause is worth a death, they should offer theirs.

47. Private weapons are offensive to free people.

In undemocratic states, power is secured primarily by force. Secret police who kill in the night, show trials and public executions are the marks of totalitarian regimes. Tyrants rule by violence and the threat of violence. Imperial powers conquer, subdue, and occupy.

Within a democratic country, armed people can claim a similar tyrannical power. They can kill and maim many people with little effort. In doing so, they not only do great physical harm, they have set aside any pretense to equality and any regard for the freedom, rights, and well-being of others. Armed people easily fall prey to this temptation to power. They exercise it not only when they fire the gun or toss the grenade. They exercise it when they carry a gun openly. Carrying the gun is a claim to absolute power over the lives of others.

There is a powerful case for arguing that the people should be given the means to resist their government. Liberal resistance to the right of revolution indicates how much they value order, how dismissive of freedom they can be. Those who claim to defend this right in the United States point to the Second Amendment. Most scholars of constitutional law favor the view that this amendment aims solely at the maintenance of "a well-regulated militia." Many defenders of gun rights argue for the right to defend oneself or, in good liberal terms, one's property. Sanford Levinson has made a more historically and politically powerful argument: that the amendment was, in the strict sense, revolutionary. The Second Amendment, he argued, was an "insurrectionist" amendment. It had little to do with the militia, and less to do with self-defense. The amendment aimed at preserving not only the right but the ability to make a revolution.[1]

When the Constitution was debated, written, and ratified, the Revolution belonged not to historical memory but to experience. "The framers and the founders" knew, none better, that they did not agree with one another about the shape of the state to come. They knew that any government might decay into tyranny. They had the courage to place a defense of rebellion and revolution into a document meant to forestall these. Neither Levinson nor I, however, sees the Second Amendment as providing a defense for the "gun rights" advocates and self-proclaimed militia men of the early twenty-first century. They are not acting as free people: they are acting as dictators. Their aim is not to rebel against tyranny, their aim is to install their own.

Nor is the possession of a gun (or an armory of guns) adequate for revolution. There was a time when the possession of a rifle or two offered security against the possibility of a tyrannical government. Those times are gone. States possess more sophisticated weaponry. States possess more weaponry altogether. More importantly, success at repression, like success at war, depends more on technologies of surveillance and control than it does on weaponry. Effective resistance to state repression requires more and less than weaponry. It requires the right and the ability to evade surveillance and access to the internet outside the control of the state. It requires (as it always has) food and shelter and the provision of other basic needs.

We have reason to doubt not only the tactics but the strategies and motives of those who form militias or assemble arsenals. These are rarely about defending their liberties. They are about diminishing ours.

People who claim the right to automatic, semi-automatic, and assault weapons, who stockpile rifles, hand guns, grenades, and other elements of a private arsenal argue that they need these for their own protection, either against their fellow citizens or against the government. They mark themselves as enemies of their fellow citizens. They show themselves willing to do as tyrants do. They have disdained all forms of discussion or debate with those they target. They refuse to submit to any will but their own, and they insist on imposing their will by force on all others.

Private arms are authoritarian in their intentions and effects. They are intended—and used—to intimidate others, to provoke fear, to give dominant power to those who arm themselves. In acquiring these weapons, people who arm themselves give clear evidence of their willingness to use violence against their own people. They have given themselves not the means to rebel but the means to impose their will on others.

These weapons do little or nothing to preserve the right of revolution or to ensure that people have access to it. The right to revolution is inalienable. The technology of revolution has changed. Make computers and computing universal; enable people to prevent surveillance; remove the internet from the control of private individuals and the state and make it a commons: you will do more to defend the right to revolution than any gun can do.

Those who insist that they need guns "for their own protection" do the same on a smaller scale. They don't want protection; they want special privileges. They want the power to kill if they choose. It is not surprising that we find these weapons used not for revolution but for murders motivated by private aims and pathologies. In every debate, in any quarrel, faced with any shame, armed people want to feel, nestled in a pocket or a purse, the weight of a weapon that will settle any question. They let the people around them know they carry a weapon, relying on the presence of the gun to make others defer to them. The members of Congress who refuse to give up their weapons or walk through metal detectors are not afraid of insurrectionists: they sided with the insurrectionists. They want their colleagues to know they are armed.

Those private citizens who live in suburbs or gated communities and insist on having a weapon betray their fear. They are not afraid of the state. They are afraid of their neighbors. Make no mistake: those guns are aimed at us. These people lack the courage of those who walk through the world unarmed and unafraid. They are not brave enough to be free.

48. Punishment demeans the free.

Simone Weil writes, "There is nothing so marvellous as a punishment."[2] Nothing could be more hostile to the free. Punishment—just punishment—demeans both those who punish and those who are punished. Unjust punishment is a shame too great to mention. Those who are justly punished bear their shame with their punishment; they have demeaned themselves. Those who punish are demeaned by their failure. They acknowledge that they live among those who do wrong and they could not prevent it. They are obliged to do what they can to remedy that wrong. Punishment should be superfluous. The greater people are, the more decent their common life, the lighter their punishments will be.

Weil believes that punishment is "marvellous" because "[w]hen a human being has, by committing a crime, placed himself outside the current of Good, his true punishment consists in his reintegration into the plenitude of that current by means of suffering." In this passage, Weil ignores the difference between crime and wrongdoing. There have been—there are—many good and honorable acts charged as crimes. These do not place human beings outside "the Good." Weil's capitalization suggests that she speaks, as she acknowledges, of the divine. Yet she too easily elides the distinction between law and justice, between the state and the good.

Weil believes in an obedience so profound that one must see "the perfection of inert matter as the perfection of obedience."[3] Perhaps obedience, especially the mindless obedience of the inert, is not the fulfillment of a divine will. Perhaps we are called not to reduce ourselves to inert matter but to raise inert matter. If this is so, labor need not be a form of suffering and divine punishment but a repetition of epiphanies, small manifestations of the divine.

Weil seeks "the radiance of this perfect Obedience." I think it unlikely that free people will find themselves—or the divine—in that. Whether they do or not, they will be diminished when they punish, for in punishing they require an obedience that is compelled by force, and force is a tool that rarely serves the free.

49. Free people are not policed.

IX
Unfinished revolutions

50. We are not democrats yet. We do not yet rule ourselves.

There are places, many places, where people struggle to rule themselves. They elect representatives, propose and vote on referenda. They hold town meetings. They make the case, among the people, for the right of people to rule themselves. They march. They protest injustice. They go to the streets. They resist coups. They fire revolutions. They write constitutions. They make laws. They design institutions. They experiment with governing. They attempt to forestall the efforts of autocrats to take power, aristocrats and the wealthy to retain it. They endure defeats, time after time. They win victories, small and large, and as they do, they build the foundations for democracy. They clear away a few more obstacles; they widen the space for the democratic. They approach democracy, but they are not democrats yet.

There are times and places where people rule themselves. There are countries where the people can claim that their government is one they chose, one they choose in the present, that they make their own laws. There are countries where people have become accustomed to judging: where they turn their demanding gaze on the conduct of officials, of the press, and of the laws themselves. These places can be found on every continent. They are clustered in Scandinavia and the Antipodes, but they can also be found in Africa, Asia, and the Americas. Yet all of these places are, at best, imperfect democracies. In no place are the people free to rule as they choose, unhindered by the power of wealth and the fears of elites.

As Jacques Rancière writes, "We do not live in democracies."

> We live in states of oligarchic law, in other words, in states where the power of the oligarchy is limited by a dual recognition of popular

Wild Democracy. Anne Norton, Oxford University Press. © Oxford University Press 2023.
DOI: 10.1093/oso/9780197644348.003.0009

sovereignty and individual liberties. We know the advantages of these states as well as their limitations.[1]

In a few places—no longer in America—people know there will not be tanks in the street the morning after an election. We know if we are taken to jail, we can call a lawyer. We know our rights and know that they are held within bounds. This cannot be enough for us.

51. Self-rule is a discipline.

The rule of the people is not limited to revolutions, to the moment of contract (mythic or actual), or to those fugitive moments when a people act as one to alter their common course. The rule of the people belongs to the ordinary, to the everyday governance of common matters. Nations and peoples are shaped by the slow working of the people. The evolution of customs, the accretion of conventions comes like a coral reef, from the many who build. These are made from the re-peated actions of many people, acting together even as they act alone. That will happen in a kingdom or a democracy, where people rule and where they are oppressed, where they know their power and where it is hidden from them.

Change comes differently when people know their power. Those who rule themselves come to recognize that they rule in all times and places. They are called upon not only to make the law but to obey it. For many liberals (as well as authoritarians), obedience to the rule of law has primacy. Those who believe that the people rule recognize that the people are also required to judge the law. They are called on, every day, in the ordinary course of their lives, to decide if an offense against the law is serious or trivial, if enforcing the law would be just, officious, or brutal. They decide whether to obey or disobey. They enforce order, and they dispense mercy, often without recognizing that they hold this power.

The rule of the people is not only, not primarily, a matter of citi-zenship, of governments, laws, and institutions. The rule of the people is the governance of the streets and the land, of one another and of themselves. People who are capable of ruling and being ruled must have discipline and self-control. People who are willing to take on the hazards of self-rule must have the courage and the strength to take risks and see them through. Those who have the discipline to rule themselves have the strength to refuse to be ruled. Those who live among the free and the self-ruled are free to refuse to rule.

Mohandas Karamchand Gandhi, who devoted himself to the project of self-rule in every sense, taught that the overcoming of foreign rule depended on the capacity to rule oneself. If Indians were to end British imperial rule, they had to first win through to self-control.

Gandhi knew the power of small things. He thought people who were to rule themselves needed to prize their independence if they were to win it. They would need to be self-sufficient. He taught his people to make their own salt, to spin and weave their own cloth, to grow their own food, to clean their own latrines, and to live simply. They needed to be able to face the enemy with courage—whether that enemy was the British Empire, someone of another faith or caste, or the wolf in themselves. He taught them to face violence without flinching.

The core of *satyagraha* is not only the refusal to use violence but the willingness to endure it. Those who practice *satyagraha* hold stubbornly to the truth. They do not give in when faced with violence. Gandhi's *satyagraha* could be achieved only by the courageous and the steadfast. It depended on people willing to face their enemies—and the violence of their enemies—without fear.

The idea that the people are creatures of passionate appetite, like animals in their desires and appetites, driven by all the passions from greed to revenge, should have fallen away long ago. It is not the people who are driven by their passions and their appetites; it is the privileged.

The wealthy rule because they can. They have means denied to others. They need to learn little about rule because their power depends on force and bribery rather than politics. They can give positions to their friends and punish their enemies. They can practice nepotism. They can establish dynasties. They do. They can use their positions to capture funds from the public purse. They can reward those whose wealth and privilege support their own. They do. They can indulge their appetites, protect their reputations by bribery, by suppression of investigations, by financial control of the media. They do.

Gandhi schooled himself and his people in poverty because poverty teaches self-rule. The rich can eat what they please, when they please. The poor deny themselves so they can feed their children. The rich can buy what they please, when they please. They can replace the lost and the broken. They can waste things. If they do, they will not be harmed. The poor must ration and share. They learn to discipline their appetites. They must consider every purchase, weigh the price, and measure every need. If they waste, they suffer for it.

Poverty is not the only teacher of self-rule. Religions have relied on fasting and prayer, on the demands of ritual, on the demand for adherence to text and law. Too often they rely on fear and the desire for dominion, but at their best, they aim toward ethics and blessing. Learning, sports, and all the arts require discipline. Here, discipline is rewarded with pleasure. At their best, these practices of discipline, great and small, hand their lives to the living. This is what Foucault and the Greeks called *askesis,* or, in Nietzsche's words, how one becomes what one is.

52. We are not yet finished with revolution.

There is a passage in the Qu'ran where Muhammad is reminded that over and over again prophets have called the people to pray and give to the poor. So it has been with justice. Over and over again, people demand freedom and equality, the right to rule themselves, and live as they choose, yet they remain chained. Many of the wrongs we believe we have defeated haunt us in other forms.

The West, in the Old World and the New, is haunted by the feudal.

Feudalism seems, for most of us, to belong to another time, to other places. Historians insist that feudalism describes a specific period and set of governing social and political arrangements. They debate the chronology and contours of the feudal. In popular culture, Hallmark movies, and the quotidian, feudalism persists as a romantic imaginary, the politics of fairy tales and Disney princesses. For some it is a lost past of faith and chivalry, its cruelties softened by time. The present has inherited cathedrals and castles, illuminated manuscripts, icons, carved statues and altarpieces, Gregorian chants and a host of other artifacts of great beauty.

These imaginaries fix the feudal as "once upon time" in a past that has already been overcome. What does it matter if states keep their monarchs and their aristocracies, if a few people remain who are called by archaic titles? They have become mere ornaments and artifacts.

Feudalism is still more alien to Africa and Asia, where the claims of inherited power go by other names. Many scholars, Alexis de Tocqueville and Louis Hartz among them, have argued that America has never known feudalism. They are wrong.

The historian Kathleen Davis points out that the term "feudalism," or (in this early use) *féodalité*, emerged at the moment when French revolutionaries believed they had put an end to it.[2]

Perhaps feudalism has been broken, but if so, we still walk among its shards. Perhaps it began and ended in Europe. Yet the breaking of that system was not an ending but an explosion that spread its structures like shrapnel. Feudalism survives. Those whose titles seem nothing more than empty and archaic survivals still command the power of wealth. More important, feudalism survives not in some lord or *comte*, *graf*, or *contessa* but in structures of law and right and in an altered form of power in the blood.

In the United Kingdom, feudalism has survived the transition from kingdom to constitutional monarchy, country to empire, feudal agriculture to industrial capitalism. The feudal presence can be read on the surface in the survival of titles, the monarchy, and the House of Lords. The survivals are less obvious in those former colonies with avowed commitments to equality, especially Australia, Canada, and the United States. They are, however, present and powerful. They were written into law.

Karen Orren, in her brilliant work, *Belated Feudalism*, observes that the United States contains, "at the core, a belated feudalism, a remnant of the medieval hierarchy of personal relations, a particularized network of law and morality—a system of governance—that the word 'feudalism' conveys."[3] The new United States and, later, Commonwealth nations ruling themselves incorporated great swathes of the feudal order into avowedly republican legal systems.[4] Labor law in those colonies that imported British common law, remained based on the law of master and servant, and kept the hierarchies character-istic of the feudal system. The laws that governed—that still govern—factories, shops, corporations, understood employees to be servants. They are not, as we so often assume, people who have signed a contract to work in a certain place for certain wages. They are servants in the ancient eyes of the law.

There is nothing antique about this. This is law in the present. Law and the practices of the workplace enable employers to silence workers. They are not permitted to speak as they please at work, even about politics. To our shame, we take that for granted. The silencing of workers does not stop there. They can be asked, coerced, or forced to sign nondisclosure agreements. This is a violation of the right of people to speak freely. There is nothing about work that can set the rights of the people aside. They cannot be silenced. As we bring our bodies to work, so do we bring our rights. They are inalienable. They cannot be separated from us.

The denial of natural rights in the workplace is indefensible. Where the body is, there rights are. While these rights are denied, people do not rule themselves. While these rights are denied, no one who works is free, and democracy is fenced out of the times and spaces of work. While there are bosses, there are masters. We do not yet rule ourselves.

There are other, more intimate, and perhaps more devastating inscriptions of feudalism that remain with us. They have taken root at the sites we are accustomed to seeing as most our own: our bodies, our racial and sexual identities.

Feudal titles were inscribed in blood and law. The text of entitlement was written in blood.[5] The nobility held title by descent, in the blood of their ancestors, that most intimate inscription. The expectation of deference shaped their bodies to the form and habitus of entitlement. Sumptuary laws made those claims more visible, more legible, even at a distance.

Power in the body did not pass away; it merely changed its form. The authority written in the blood and worn on the body was more economically inscribed on the body itself. The stigmata of race and sex marked a new form of power in the blood, a new title to dominion in the body. The title to command was no longer "I am your lord" but "I am white," "I am a man."

Racial and sexual hierarchies function as those of the feudal estates once did: as categories outside of and prior to law and politics. Status was given. Status was inscribed on the bodies of those who ruled and those who were ruled. One was born a lord or a serf. Race and the status that went with it were written in the blood.[6]

These enduring structures of dominion inscribe themselves on our bodies and in our conceptions of who and what we are. The persistence of elements of feudal law in the maintenance of sexual hierarchies is familiar indeed: confinement in the household, limits on the holding of property, the licensing of male violence against women, and unhindered male access to the bodies of women in the legal possession of men. It is noteworthy that all of these apply to servants and slaves as well; that is to say, all these can be regarded collectively as encompassed within domestic—familiar—forms of enslavement.

Racial and sexual hierarchies function as those of the feudal estates once did: as categories outside of and prior to law and politics. Status was given. Status was inscribed on the bodies of those who ruled and those who were ruled. Race, and the status that went with it, were written in the blood.

The invention of race was accompanied by the insistence that differences in race were given and biological: the work of nature, or of Nature's God. Race was the work of nature, not of human beings. No one could be held responsible for these hierarchies. No one could question them. Because racial categories—and hierarchies—were biological, no one was at fault. Because they were given, responsibility was occluded. No one could be charged with the creation of hierarchies that were seen to be the work of God or nature. Perhaps they were divinely ordained. Perhaps they were the work of an impersonal nature. Claims of racial superiority and a right to rule were not political claims but affirmations of the sacred or the work of an objective science. Race was placed outside politics and beyond political debate. Responsibility for claims of racial superiority was evaded and the role of the state elided.[7]

The feudal order haunts the West in the all-too-present, all-too-material forms of race and sex, in the bodies we inhabit and the work we do. The West is not alone in this. Every continent has its followers of Iblis, who claim that they are worth more than other people. From a distance, the sheikhs and mansas, maharajahs and obas look as decorative and harmless as European aristocrats. Yet here too, in caste and class and other hierarchies written on the body, people make the claim to power in the blood. Here too some command the work of others. Here too the few silence the many.

Before we can become free people, we must finish the work other revolutions began. We must put an end to all that licenses claims to power in the blood, to the rights of the few against the many, to the claims that some lives are worth more than others.

53. Democracy is not an idyllic state; democracy is a struggle.

Max Weber called politics "strong and slow boring of hard boards."[8] Politics is hard labor, but democracy is harder yet. I do not expect to see the rule of the people accomplished in my time, but I hope to see the work advance. In that work, I may catch sight of the greater work to come.

There is no country in my time that can truly claim that the people rule. In my country we have prisoners to free, prisons to close. We have people to teach. We have wars to end. There are houses to save, people to heal. There are reparations to be made. We must work until "justice rolls down like waters, and righteousness like a mighty stream." Our house is not yet finished. Our work lies long before us, but it is work we can do.

Americans usually understand our history in one of two ways. First there is the history some read in John Locke and Alexis de Tocqueville: Americans are born to freedom, born equal. In this history, God or a benign history gives freedom to us as a gift. This is not true.

In the second history, America is on a road toward freedom. In this history, democracy gradually overcomes obstacles. Freedom is continually expanding. Working men get the vote, the slaves are freed, women get the vote, antisemitism and the old prejudices against Catholics are overcome, and African Americans move steadily toward equality and inclusion. This is Langston Hughes's history, a history of "promises that will come true":

> The plan and pattern is here,
> Woven from the beginning,
> Into the warp and woof of America.[9]

This is the history that won my heart as well, but I no longer believe it to be true.

There is a third history, harder and less triumphal. In this history, the American struggle for freedom is not a history of constant progress. In this understanding, freedom wars against the desire for dominion generation after generation. There is no certainty of victory. In this history, people are not born to a predestined triumph. We are born to struggle, to the long "slow boring of hard boards." The rule of the people, the achievement of justice, the protection of equality, the preservation of the ungoverned and the ungovernable require constant and unceasing work.

This history asks more of us and promises less. This history calls people to take up the burden of past wrongs.

Tzvetan Todorov, writing of the early colonization of what would become the United States of America, dedicated it to the memory of "a Mayan woman devoured by dogs."[10] This moment of colonial cruelty stands for many more. People who have thrown off empire and made themselves anew often believe that in that revolution they have freed themselves from the sins of their past. Perhaps they will find, like us, that they are still haunted and burdened, still facing the work of overcoming that past. Cruelty may live in them, even against their will. This is the history, not of America perhaps, but of American empire. This is the history of the crowded holds of the Middle Passage, of slave trading and the Klan, of the plantation and the overseer. This is the history of conquest: of the decimation and confinement of the First Nations, the Trail of Tears and the emergence of the reservation system, of immigration restriction and border vigilantes, of raids on undocumented workers and the imprisonment of children. This is the history of the prison system. This history records Japanese internment, the Cold War, Hiroshima and My Lai, McCarthyism, Abu Ghraib, Guantanamo, torture, and a culture of surveillance. In this history, imprisonment follows in the footsteps of empire. In this history, greed makes use of violence. This is the history of Haymarket and the Tulsa

Race Massacre. This history testifies against an easy, natural alliance between capitalism and democracy.

Forgetting these histories is neither just nor easily done. Yet there are dangers in recalling them. In remembering this darker history, we fall too easily into seeing a conflict of convictions in which good wars against evil and that the enemies of the democratic remain constant. That is not true. On the contrary, the enemies of democracy in one historical moment may be its friends in another.

Consider the idea of "states' rights" in the United States. It was associated, for about a hundred years, with the preservation of slavery and with white supremacy. Yet in the early years after the Revolution, states' rights were more often associated with preserving freedom rather than taking it away. In those early years, many of the states recognized more rights than the federal government did, and an insistence on states' rights helped, ultimately, to expand these rights to all citizens. In the late twentieth century, it was the states that first recognized the rights of gay people to live freely and to marry. At the opening of the twenty-first century, it was the states that sought to combat climate change, to stand fast against federal agencies and a president captured by the wealthy, the irresponsible, and the ignorant.

Another danger of this dark history is that we forget the moments of triumph. Imperial power has been accompanied in our time by the steady (if uneven) overcoming of racial discrimination. When I was young, there were many signs of the inequality of Black and white. People used racial slurs openly in the North and West where I lived. I remember Civil Rights marchers at Selma and Birmingham, Chicago and Los Angeles. I remember the fire hoses. I remember the dogs.

Those who watched the Civil Rights movement cannot forget those dogs. We saw them made weapons against African American marchers. We saw photographs in the newspapers that froze the snarl of the dogs and enabled us to count every tooth. We saw the forward lunge of the leashed dog on television. We saw the marchers thrust back as sharply as they had been by the fire hoses. We saw the uniformed man that held the dog and urged it forward. The television captured the sound and movement of the march and the attack. The images circulated. This memory persuades some that a history of such evil cannot be overcome, that this is what their nation and their people are. This is what we have been. This is part of what we are. We are called to bear that.

But this is not what we belong to. This is not what we will be. We who watched were changed by that time. We saw the strength and courage of the marchers. As we watched, we learned something about justice and the rights of man. No one who saw this, who saw Emmett Till's mother beside his ruined body, who watched the marchers cross the Edmund Pettus Bridge, can fail to remember that greatness of soul.

There is a passage in the *Republic* where Plato takes up the question of the just man. How would one know the just man? Plato proceeds to treat the just man like Job: "he shall be stripped of everything save justice," and in that naked deprivation the reader is to see what justice is. Antonio Negri saw the labor of Job in his prison cell. We saw it in the photographs from Mississippi and Alabama. The marchers, stripped of the protections of the state, held their rights still. They became rights and right incarnate, and the rights they stood for stood or fell with them.

Americans once found their soul in those who affirmed, "We shall overcome, someday." The Civil Rights marchers kept open the possibility of an America that is not yet. They reminded us of the meaning of the words "We hold these truths to be self evident." They held out to us the possibility that we could be greater than we had been, greater than the founders imagined, far greater than we are.

The slaves, longing for freedom, gave us a greater dream of freedom than did the founders. The Civil Rights marchers—disenfranchised, impoverished, brave—recalled us to that dream. I lived to see my city dance in the streets at the election of a Black president. I lived to see white supremacy rise up again. I lived to march with my people in the city of brotherly love, affirming once again that Black lives matter and that all men are created equal.

Knowing that tragic and disheartening events occur in every age, in every time, among every people, we must reject the idea that democracy progresses inevitably toward freedom. The work is not done. The memory of hardship and shame dedicates us to the cause. Memory of the triumphs enables us to keep our hands on the plow.

54. Democracy is fugitive.

Many of those who have taught me, and those with whom I have worked, have followed Sheldon Wolin in seeing a fugitive democracy. They see democracy in those moments, great and rare, when the people rise up and see themselves as a people: living and acting together in the present. I see democracy growing in the crevices of the everyday, yet I still turn to those moments. Those who have experienced revolutions often write of feeling that they had been born again, or that they were creating a *novus ordo saeculorum,* a new world order. Perhaps these fleeting moments were moments of madness, perhaps they were moments of wisdom, but whatever they were, they were filled with a fragile joy that could not last.

These moments of democracy are fugitive, evanescent. They are also generative and transcendent. In these moments, people recognize themselves as a people. They see their fellow people as their own. They see something beyond themselves, and they reach for it together. For a moment, an idea is made flesh in them. That ecstatic recognition does not remain in its immediacy or in its fullness, but the experience of transcendence alters them. What they see, what they learn in those moments sets them on a course to the future. This is how one becomes what one is.

In the time since Wolin wrote, the idea of a fugitive democracy has been deepened by the work of Black scholars and theorists. They heard the echoes of the Fugitive Slave Act in the idea of fugitive democracy. Surely democracy is fugitive when a government forces free people back into slavery, when the law aligns itself with wealth against rights. Surely democracy lives among those in flight.

Fugitive democracy is not, however, quite as fugitive as it appears. These moments of fugitive joy shape a people, shape people, fill their minds and fire their hopes. The practices they develop in those times can shape their laws and institutions. The strength they hone then will make them democrats.

Perhaps free people are always fugitive, running to ungoverned, ungovernable spaces. Perhaps democracy does fly to anarchy. Perhaps it should.

X
Canon fodder

55. Forget Athens. Forget democratic genealogies.

Democracy is said to have a clear and confirmed genealogy. This is puzzling for a form of life that has had so little presence in the world. Nevertheless, students are confidently told, year after year, that democracy began in Greece, among the Athenians. It is from the Greeks that democracy takes its name, and in Greek history that it is said to find its limits.

If Athens gave us democracy with one hand, it has taken it away with the other.

Athenian democracy was a political practice bounded on every side. Only Athenians could vote, hold office, and decide the fate of those brought before the people for judgment. One could live a lifetime in Athens as a foreigner. Those people, however fully they were bound in the life of the city, however well they served, remained outside its politics. Athens was a slave society, supported by the labor of the enslaved. Politics, as Aristotle observed, required leisure, and slaves had no leisure. Their time, like their bodies, belonged to their masters. The women of Athens, though they grew up in the same land, shared the same ancestry, spoke the same language as their brothers, husbands, and fathers, were also fenced out of politics. Politics, Aristotle argued, was necessary to make one fully human. Women, slaves, foreigners, and immigrants were not free, not wholly Athenian, not judges or lawmakers, and therefore not fully human. They had no place in democratic practice. They had no share in democratic power.

The *demos* was thus small, smaller by far than Athens. It was also tribal. There are tribes who embrace foreigners, taking them in, making them their own. Many of the indigenous tribes of North America made themselves greater in this way. The tribes of Ghana, a proud Ghanaian told me, take immigrants of every race as their own.[1]

Wild Democracy. Anne Norton, Oxford University Press. © Oxford University Press 2023.
DOI: 10.1093/oso/9780197644348.003.0010

The Athenians did not. Their *demos*, divided into tribes, remained closed to immigrants. They deferred to divisions of descent and family, acknowledging their constitutive importance and retaining them as an ordering principle.[2]

The memory of democratic Athens was, for much if not all of the West, filtered through the vivid and varied imagination of the imperial British. Athens proved democracy too wild, too demanding. There were those like Bryon and Shelley who saw something of the democratic promise beyond the limits of Athens, but they died young. British democrats fought for Greek independence, but British diplomats would saddle Greece with an imported king and, worse, with the king's debts. The British, and those they educated, would not remember burdening Greece with the expense of their newly installed Bavarian king or debts to their imperial rulers. Athenian decline had proved the necessity of Roman order and Roman militarism. The British Empire saw the need for a monarch. Athens was a rich inheritance, but a metal too soft for tools or swords. As they hived off the friezes of the Parthenon and carried them away as plunder, so the British would lay claim to Athenian democracy only to enlist it in the service of aristocracy and empire.

Athens was used thereafter to prove that democracy was a Western inheritance. If democracy began in Athens, then it was Western and all other peoples had it only as the gift of the West. Athens was not the wellspring of democracy; it marked democracy's limits. The Athenian origin of democracy was also used to prove its fragility. If Athens, the home of democracy, could not hold it, how could others?

Democracy has been haunted by this Athenian legacy. Democracies must be small, because Athens was; ethnically homogeneous, because Athens was. Democracies could have slaves, because Athens did. Democracies could not include foreigners or immigrants or those whose ancestry was mixed or uncertain, because Athens didn't. The myth of Athenian democracy made the inclusion of women appear unnecessary, perhaps absurd. That legacy has lasted into the present and in areas where reason alone ought to have excluded it. Political scientists enamored of taxonomies and other so-called scholars of democracy act as if the exclusion of women from voting was, if not natural, inevitable, and dismiss the late inclusion of women as a small imperfection in otherwise admirable democracies. Athens excluded women, after all, and Athens was a democracy.

Remember Athens and forget democracy, because Athens proved that democracies cannot last.

Forget Athens; there are other pasts. The American revolutionaries looked to the English country party republicans and to the troops who sat down on the field at Putney to decide how they were to rule themselves. They looked to the Dutch republicans and the brief experiment of the Poles. They looked to the practices of the Haudenosaunee, the Iroquois Confederacy, and other tribes on the American continent. So too do David Graeber and David Wengrow, who show the impact of the thought and practice of the indigenous on their colonizers.[3] We can look elsewhere as well. Massimiliano Tomba has written on the practices of people ruling themselves. He looks to the French commune and the Zapatistas, to the Russian *mir* and the Mexican *ejido*.[4] There is no shortage of places where people work to rule themselves.

Set the practices of the Vikings against those of the Athenians. This, like the old uses of Athens, has an element of hope and fable in it. The *things* and *althings* of the Viking-era Norse were open to all free people, men and women. The *things* and *althings* were simply assemblies of the people. Each person, man and woman alike, had a vote, and all votes were equal. There were no distinctions of wealth or status in the political power of the citizens. There were no distinctions of race (which did not yet exist) or ethnicity. There were law readers at the Icelandic *althing*. These people recited the entirety of the law over a period of three years. The law was made and judgment given by the people assembled. This is not, as the British and even contemporary Icelanders like to claim, "the world's first parliament." The *althing* was not a parliament at all, except, perhaps, in the old sense of the French word *parlement*, a place of speaking. The *althing* was an assembly of the people, without hierarchy, without representation. The Icelanders have a greater history than they know.

This Viking past is an origin story without the haunting memory of tribes. This is democracy untroubled by the inclusion of women, those said to be foreign, or those of mixed blood. This is a better past, a better memory for democrats. It belongs, too, to people whose lives taught them courage and drove them outward. The Vikings sailed off not sure of where they would arrive. They developed techniques of navigation, and they dared to go beyond their reach. They ventured constantly into the unknown, as all people who rule themselves must venture. Though we are usually on land, we democrats, we are always at sea, rarely in the same place, always traveling, often sailing into uncharted waters.

I once asked a Norwegian scholar what they called democracies before they knew the Greek word "democracy." Without hesitation she replied, "Folkestœring." This is conventionally understood as "popular organization." My ear heard "the people, steering," and etymology confirmed it. Written into the word is the recognition that when we rule ourselves, we go constantly into the unknown. Steering belongs not to one man but to the people.

There is, however, no more need for the *althing* than there is for Athens. It is heartening to learn that practices we are told are impossible had a home in the past, to see customs and concepts we can use in Africa and the Andes, but it is not necessary. People need nothing for democracy but themselves. They need to think and speak and act together, in conflict and in common. People can take what they like from Athens. They need no ancestral title to do it. The people can, the people should, plunder the past like pirates. Things that the wealthy and the privileged kept to themselves can be shared out. Things that were once locked up can be carried to new places. Steal the best of politics, and share it out.

There are those who will regret the lost memories of democratic Athens. The democratic Athenians, in love with the new, never yielding for long to tyrants, victorious over empires, shine in a dark past. If I have taken that away from you, I offer another Athens, an Athens of the more recent past, perhaps of the present and the future. This is an Athens of men and women of mixed ancestry or no known ancestry at all, an Athens big enough to include working people and the poor, an Athens where people take to the streets to challenge wealth, privilege, and the dictates of powers that have no democratic warrant. Better to riot with Loukanikos than feast with Alcibiades.

Forget Athens, forget the Vikings, the Germanic tribes, the *panchayat*, the Isle of Man, the Sumerians. We do not need any past at all. Think instead of the Greeks resisting austerity, the people of the Levant struggling for the democratic in the ruins of empire, the indigenous

defending the sacred rights of the people and the earth, of *ubuntu.*
Whatever the place, whenever the time, whoever the people: democracy can begin there. We have all that we need in ourselves.

56. The canon of Western political philosophy was forged against the people.

There are few—if there are any—universities or colleges throughout
the West (and well beyond it) who do not teach some version of the
Western canon of political philosophy. That canon begins with the
Greeks (in some cases with the Old Testament) and (generally leaping
over the medieval period) moves through the writings of Machiavelli,
Hobbes, Locke, Rousseau, possibly Kant, probably Hegel, Marx, and
some selection of Mill, Nietzsche, or Weber. There are no women (with
the still rare exception of Wollstonecraft or Arendt), no one outside
the European heartland. There are no Scandinavians, no Spaniards,
no Greeks past the fifth century BCE, no Huns or Magyars, no Eastern
Europeans, no Turks. This canon is too small for Europe. It is far, far
too small for humanity.

The canon, presented as a civilizational treasure, crowned with the
laurels of democracy, has little that is democratic in it. Scandinavia,
with its long history of popular rule, and the city states of France and
Switzerland with their republican institutions, leave no mark. Medieval
philosophy, with its many defenses of the commons, disappears under
the rubric of religion. The canon moves, as Hegel wrote of History, to
central Europe, reaching its apex in Germany. We should pause here,
in memory of the dead, to consider the full irony of a Western canon
with its heart in Germany. The rule of the people remains an ideal to
struggle for throughout the West, but Germany came late to liberal democracy, and though it is prospering now, it has had a short, hard life
there. There are a few satellite sites. France gives the canon Rousseau,
Montesquieu in some periods, Montaigne and Bodin for connoisseurs.
Italy gives us a few Romans and Machiavelli. For academics and the
cognoscenti, there is Vico, and perhaps Beccaria. The English claim
some space with Hobbes and Locke. The West of the West—the once

colonized Americas, Australia, and New Zealand—have no presence at all. The "Western canon" is not Western. It is not even European.

The canon leaves its defenders with two claims that are hard to reconcile. The West is said to be the creator or inventor of democracy. Whether it begins in Athens (as is generally taught) or among the Germanic tribes, democracy belongs to the West. The Western canon of political philosophy is said to be the wellspring of critical thinking and (for the most arrogant) the source of the West's intellectual preeminence. Yet there is no full-throated defense of democracy in the canon. For virtually all the canonical thinkers, democracy is a danger and an absurdity. For the most liberal, the people are nothing but a problem to be managed.

Too many of those we count among the canonical were simply in the service of tyrants. Plato served the Tyrant of Syracuse. Aristotle served Alexander. Machiavelli served the Medici. Locke and Hobbes tutored the children and enjoyed (or bore with) the patronage of the rich. Over time, the patronage of kings and aristocrats gave way to professional employment. Hegel and Nietzsche worked as professors, Freud as a doctor, Marx as a journalist. Here, too, the need for food and shelter and the limits imposed by newspaper editors, deans, and other administrators (not to mention university donors, the patrons of our age) have limited what one can and cannot say in defense of the right of people to rule themselves.

Those philosophers seen as the sources of liberalism—Hobbes and Locke, for example—regard the rule of the people not an ideal but as a danger to be avoided. Hobbes opens the gate to the rule of the people but closes it as quickly as he can. There is no surer grounding for a government than the consent of the people. Yet for Hobbes the right to consent to one's government lapses with the imposition of order. The sovereignty of the people belongs to one people alone, in one moment, for one act only. Only the dissolution of order can call their sovereignty forth again.

Locke establishes the right of the people to rebel against rulers who infringe on their natural rights or who violate the law of nature. He raised the question "Who shall judge?" when rebellion is justified, and answered, "The People shall Judge," yet he too feared the people.[5] The desire of the people to rebel against tyranny, to consent to rule imposed upon them is admirable and it is just, but it is also a problem to be solved, a danger to be managed.

Marx, whose work transformed both scholarship and rebellion, praised the transformative effects of imperialism.

This is no democratic canon. These are not the writings of our emancipatory ancestors. These are the writings of our enemies.

There are resources for democrats in the interstices of the canon. Those who long to see the people rule can hunt them down and bring them forward There is always something lawless and transgressive about this. We seize on Machiavelli's messages to the people like slaves passing notes of a possible escape route from one to another. We plunder Hobbes and Locke like Diné raiders. Hobbes gives us the Leviathan. We stop at the moment he says the people choose to place themselves under a government and that they make a contract or covenant to secure their own welfare. Locke gives us money. We refuse it. We stop at his description of the commons, where all can take what they need if they leave "enough and as good for others."⁶ Marx is redeemed in the service of anticolonial revolution. There are defenses of the democratic to be found in the canon, but they are accessible only to pirates, raiders, the disobedient, and the irreverent.

I was educated in the canon and have worked in and upon it the entirety of my working life. The more I have read, the more I have come to see its virtues and its inadequacies. There is great thought here, and I will feed off it until I die, yet its claims are too large and its reach too small. The claims of the canon to offer the thought of political philosophy as a whole, or—more modestly—Western political philosophy, are too large for the small number of books and figures that even a generous counting of the canonical would offer. There is far too much in the canon that serves tyranny and imperialism. The canon is confined like a prisoner in so small a space that those within it are unable to speak to others. Their ties to other places, to other currents of thought are broken. They become civilizational thinkers, not human ones, and they are diminished. Above all, over and over again the canon speaks for the rich against the poor, for the powerful against the people.

Contemporary political theory is little better. Though most people in the West would describe themselves as democrats (social or Christian), republicans, or liberals, there are still few to be found who do not fear the idea that people should rule themselves. Rawls, who spoke and wrote the common sense of many liberals, concerned himself with just outcomes and neutral procedures. His proceduralism, like that of Habermas, still sees the people as Aristotle saw them: vulnerable to demagogues and tyrants, lacking the intellect or education to rule wisely. As critics noted in the wake of *A Theory of Justice*, Rawls's account assumed human beings who too closely resembled white Anglo-European men.[7] Derrida sought to still the seeking for democracy by a double strategy. Democracy was suicidal, "auto-immune," destroying itself (as generation after generation of theorists and philosophers had argued) from within. The people were dangerous. Democracy belonged to the eveningland, the land of death, and it should be left there in the realm of the infinitely deferred. Habermas, whose early work showed a love for as well as an anxiety concerning democracy, grew ever more concerned with the technical requirements of communication. Where, then, does our veneration for democracy come from? Where are those who speak for the rule of the people?

There are at least three answers to this, and all are true. The Western canon of democracy has resources for democrats. There is truth in that, but it is insufficient and misleading. There is no canon of democracy. There are pamphlets and manifestos, court records, poetry, and songs that record the struggles of the people for justice. The right of the people to rule themselves has been forged not in the texts of the wise but in the practices of the many. That is the canon we have neglected.

We might pause to wonder what the canon would look like if we turned to the places where democracy has prospered.

Tomba's *Insurgent Universality* brings some of those forgotten democratic practices before us. Tomba looks not at the practices of statesmen, official documents, or the memoirs of "great men" but at how people have ruled themselves. Russian villagers adapted the *mir*, a long-established, traditional form of peasant life, in which the peasants governed their land in common. This was quite distinct from—and ultimately in opposition to—collectivization. The *mir* differed both from private possession and from collective ownership, and each successive system had sought to eradicate it. The land was held not by a collective but in common, which is to say it was not owned at all. Most importantly, it was governed democratically. The *mir*, not the state, allocated land. Land was given to households, which were then free to decide how much to plant, what to plant, and where to plant it.

The revolutionaries of the Commune tried one experiment after another in the short weeks of their rule.[8] They knew the past had failed them. That knowledge freed them to look beyond the inherited past to practices that had been lost or scorned. It freed them to take the paths that had not been chosen and see where those would lead them. It freed them to leave the past behind and find their own way. We watch as one revolutionary uprising after another struggles to find new ways to make decisions together, to act together, to build a more just order where they stand.

There is a democratic canon. There are books and speeches, manifestos and petitions. They are records of debates. There are the trials and confessions of those who advocated the right of the people to rule themselves, even under torture. There are the records of those who were thought unimportant: slaves, the subaltern, the poor. The slave narratives collected under the U.S. Works Progress Administration in the Depression, the work of the subaltern studies historians belong to this democratic canon. E. P. Thompson, Christopher Hill, Thomas Holt, Eric Hobsbawm, Peter Linebaugh, and Marcus Rediker have recorded the histories of working people and dissenters, rebels and bandits, opening the way to a canon of the many rather than the few.

This canon is not settled; it is unsettled and unsettling. We make and unmake it, and as we do, we learn of more people we can study. This canon has no home. This canon draws from every corner of the world. This canon is intimate and familiar, alien and cosmopolitan.

Our hope lies not in the silence of the powerful and the learned but in the convictions of the people. Though both our educations and our institutions speak against it, there are still people who believe that they have the right to rule themselves.

Our time lies in the past, present, and future.

XI
Democratic times

57. Democracy is episodic.

The people's rule is omnipresent as a source of legitimacy, a point of orientation, and a presence that governs the conduct of all. It is experienced as a constant presence in mind and as an episodic presence in the lives of the people. The revolutionary moments that bring the people into being, and the moments when the people make themselves anew, are fugitive and fleeting. They live in history and memory, in the knowledge of the ideals they change, the standards they set, and the worlds they build, but their presence thereafter is partial and allusive. Revolutions follow no set calendar, no predictable cycle. The rule of the people can, however, also be episodic. The people can agree to call themselves into being on a regular basis.

Whatever institutional forms the rule of the people takes, that rule will always be interrupted.

58. The time of democracy is a time of celebration.

One of my teachers, Aristide Zolberg, Holocaust survivor and refugee, an immigrant and an authority on immigration, wrote that revolutions are marked by "moments of madness." He was thinking not of the rabid insanity of the crowd that so many have feared, but the transcendent joy that people feel in moments of revolutionary change. He quotes Simone de Beauvoir writing of the liberation of Paris from the Nazis. They were, she wrote, "swept away by joy."

> Day and night with our friends, talking, drinking, strolling, laughing, we celebrated our liberation. And all those who celebrated it as we did, nearby or far away, became our friends.
> What an orgy of brotherhood![1]

Wild Democracy. Anne Norton, Oxford University Press. © Oxford University Press 2023.
DOI: 10.1093/oso/9780197644348.003.0011

In these moments, Zolberg argued, politics becomes prophetic. People believe that "all is possible." They are ecstatic. They say of themselves that they "live a dream more beautiful than dreams, a dream which they have not imagined," that they inhabit a moment of "volcanic happiness," of "absolute magic."[2] Henri Lefèbvre wrote:

> The Paris Commune! It was first of all an immense, a grandiose festival, a festival which the people of Paris offered to themselves and offered to the world. Festival of spring in the City, festival of the disinherited and of the proletariat, revolutionary festival and festival of the Revolution, total festival. . . . [I]t unfolds first in magnificence and joy.[3]

People who experience revolutions write of being born again, of their joy at being one with the people around them. Lefèbvre, writing of the Commune, concluded, "For a few days, this utopia, this so-called myth, was actualized and entered into life."[4]

Many people look at these moments of popular celebration and democratic joy as simply fugitive: moments of transcendence that, like joy itself, cannot endure. Lefèbvre saw it otherwise. When he looked at the Commune, he saw more than a celebration: he saw a proof. The communards were not simply celebrating an evanescent moment of triumph and freedom. They had proven their hopes: "For a few days, this utopia, this so-called myth, was actualized and entered into life." The brevity of that life was beside the point. Like a scientist who, for a brief moment, produces electric light or a surgeon who performs a heart transplant on a patient who lives only for a few days, Lefèbvre saw not a fugitive moment but an opening of possibilities. Things thought impossible had become possible. That brief interruption had set aside "layers of sediment: the State, bureaucracy, institutions, dead culture."[5] People saw that it could be otherwise. Their sense of the possible was changed. It was no longer possible to say that the people could not govern themselves or live without bosses. They already had.

They did so, moreover, in a manner that confounded fears of popular violence. Tocqueville had feared the downfall of the July Monarchy, feared (as so many have, as so many do) the violence of an unleashed— a free—people. Yet as he walked through the streets he was struck instead by a peace as profound as a Sunday morning and the atmosphere of fraternity that joined defeated soldiers with the young citizens who had disarmed them. Tocqueville, as any reader knows, was a man preoccupied with loss, but also a man who could see and judge fairly, overcoming his fears:

> When I came to peer attentively into the deepest reaches of my own heart, I discovered there, with some surprise, and a certain relief, a sort of joy mixed with all the sadness and all the fears which the revolution was bringing to life. This terrifying event made me suffer on behalf of my country, but it was clear I did not suffer on my own behalf. . . . I was breathing more freely than before the catastrophe.

Nor was he alone. He notes that the "priests, the old aristocracy, and the people were meeting in a common sentiment." They were not afraid. Even for the defeated soldiers, "all other feelings seemed to be absorbed by the pleasure of finding themselves free. They walked without care, stepping lightly."[6]

Everyone sees the joy, the festivity of the revolutionaries. This is not, however, simply a moment of release, a kind of political Saturnalia in which, just for a day or two, the world turns upside down and people feel that all is possible. There is a strong note of practicality in these popular celebrations. For one thing, people clean up after themselves. Anyone who watched the Egyptian Revolution unfold in Tahrir Square, or the Lebanese uprising, could see the people organizing themselves to pick up rubbish and the debris of demonstrations. They went further; they scrubbed the place clean. When the Egyptian revolutionaries were asked about their pails and scrub brushes, they answered that it was their country now, and they would keep it clean. The people of Tahrir Square, men and women, rich and poor, secular and religious, organized food and medical care for themselves. The secular protected the religious while they prayed. Revolutionaries may be filled with an evanescent joy as they see their people around them and know themselves as rulers together, but they also know the enduring joy that transforms mundane acts. They are transfigured as they come to power, and the world is transfigured for them. Their ordinary work has become divine.

59. The time of democracy is a time of danger.

The rule of the people is always dangerous. The canon of every philosophy warns, over and over unceasingly, of the hazards of democracy. The people, statesmen and philosophers warn, will rob the rich to feed the poor. (Though I will bless them if they do, I see no evidence of this.) The people are licentious. Once they are free to rule, they will give in to all their appetites. (Decadence seems to me to be a problem more of the privileged than the people.) The people are passionate. Once they are free to rule, they will do whatever they please, and do it with a passion that no one can stand against. (Considered against the whims of dictators, the passions of the people may seem less threatening.) Except possibly for the last, none of these dangers are more to be feared in democracy than in another form of rule. The last is different.

When the people are free to rule, they will indeed do what they please. Perhaps (it is my hope) they will do it with a passion that no one can stand against. For some this is a threat. For others (I am among them) it opens up a horizon of promise and possibility that I cannot dream of seeing in my time (though still I hope).

What will the people do? Ask instead: What do people do? Do they forget the past and rush headlong into utopian projects? Sometimes. More often they look to the past for guidance. They seek to recover goods they have lost. They try to emulate those they admire. They seek to preserve what they love and honor in their own history and experience. They are more likely to regard the past in the rosy glow of myth and memory than they are to abandon it. Will they then lose the drive to exploration and invention? Some never have that. Others always do. In the darkest times, in places of the most abject poverty, there are thinkers, inventors, and explorers. There may be those who choose to be comfortable, to live like Patrick Henry's citizen and enjoy "the fruits of his labor under his own fig tree, with his wife and children about him, in peace and security."[7] They can live, sheltered and fed among the people, and the people can be proud that such are safe and content among them. People have learned that those who live peaceful lives, cultivate their gardens and their families, can make good neighbors and good friends. Some, like Wendell Berry, have written of them as if they were the guardians of something precious to us all. Perhaps they are. Perhaps they are the gardeners of our common country.

Will people turn on one another and try to re-create a world free from their enemies? Will they kill one another? Sometimes. They do that now, seized by a demonic myth of religious or racial superiority, by a conviction of righteousness, by mere greed, or in great fear. These killings take place in all places and times I know, though they take place least where the people have more power. Mindful, as Hobbes and experience have taught us, that anyone may kill anyone else, we cannot wholly escape the danger we pose to one another. We cannot escape the need for courage.

60. The time of democracy is a time of creation.

One of the great contributions of the social contract theorists was their recognition that people make the sovereign, make the state, make themselves.

When the people rule, they build. They build in common. They build as individuals. Free from the fear of coercion and dependence on the powerful, they can live as they choose, think as they choose. Their thoughts—and their ambitions—will have more range and more focus. People who are free to speak and write as they choose can write honestly. They can explore the past, examine the present, and plan the future with clear eyes.

They build in common. They will debate, as they should, the virtues of different plans and projects. Some will see the virtues of highways, others of mass transit or the hyperloop. They will argue over sources of energy. They will have more to argue over because the inventiveness that independence unleashes will open unexpected possibilities. Those with a passion for planning will be limited in their ambition to order, and in their power, by the anarchic.

People who rule themselves, who secure freedom and equality among themselves, open reservoirs of creativity dammed up by autocrats, by aristocracy, by inequalities of wealth and power. They are more just and more honorable, to be sure, but they are also more inventive and more daring.

61.   Democratic time is sacred time.

St. Augustine saw that sacred and secular time could exist, did exist, in the same place, at the same moment.[8] We are at once body and soul. The time of the soul and the time of the mind are not the same as the time of the body. The time of the body seems inexorable to the mind: too slow for the young who long for adventures and power, too rapid for the old who have fallen in love with the world. The mind is not bound wholly to the time the body inhabits but wanders through the past and into the future. Has the soul the timelessness we claim for it? Perhaps. One who belongs to a people belongs at once to the time the body inhabits, the time of the surrounding world, and to the time of that people: to the past of the people and to the people's future.

Those moments when people, knowing they are the eyes and hands of the sovereign, bring a people into being, are sacred times. They are moments removed from the mundane, moments out of time. The dead call to the living and the living to the dead. Living and dead call to those yet to come. Law and custom vanish, and the sacred enters.

62.   Democratic time is before, after, and now.

The placement of democracy in Athens, or among the Haudenosaunee, in medieval city states, among the Vikings, or in some other place is both true and false. There were people at these sites, and many others, who struggled to ensure that they ruled themselves. There is a democratic past—indeed, there may be more democratic pasts than we have yet discovered. The conviction that a people can rule themselves is strengthened by the example of those who did so in the past, however brief their success. When we struggle to rule ourselves, we can look to those who struggled before us, learn from their errors, and honor their memory. Episodic, fractured moments of political courage give us a time before. That time serves not as an anchor but as a proof, securing confidence that what has been done before can be done again.

Perhaps the people will not rule themselves, fully and honorably, in my time. For me, then, the time of democracy is the time to come. The rule of the people in its fullness belongs to a future I may never see.

And yet it is mine. This is the call that animated King's speech the night before he died: "I've seen the promised land. I may not get there with you. But I want you to know tonight, that we, as a people, will get to the promised land."9 That is my country, the longed for country that is not yet, the only country that commands my allegiance.

The promised land opened to King not because he dreamed of the future, but because his dreaming was fired by "the fierce urgency of now." Democracy belongs to those who struggle to rule themselves in the present. Democracy is made by—and in—those ordinary moments of judgment in which people make, follow, question, critique, reject, and disobey the laws. Democracy is made in those frustrating, seemingly futile moments when people struggle to use the worn, blunt tools they have. The vote cast for a disappointing candidate, the unsuccessful campaign, the books and articles, the email sent to an unresponsive senator, the unpublished letters to the editor, the marches in the sun and the rain, the seemingly fruitless organizing, are all working toward the people's rule. Each testifies to the person's commitment. Each offers a hard training in the discipline of being ruled. Each demonstrates the will to speak, to be heard, to rule. Each binds an uncertain future to the fierce urgency of now.

XII
The direction of the democratic

63. Democrats are conservative, progressive, and radical.

The idea that the people rule remains a radical idea. It goes to the root. In advancing it we "lay the axe to the root and teach governments humanity."[1] Yet anyone who looks at what people do, what they ask, what they long for, will find that they are not ready to abandon the past. Paine's great antagonist, Edmund Burke, is remembered as a conservative, but his conservatism had a profound respect for the wisdom of the people. Burke's belief that we should defer to custom and convention has a democratic cast; it speaks to democratic history and democratic sensibilities. At the very moment when the American Revolution caught fire, the Declaration noted that people endure hardships and evils for the sake of stability, that they change unwillingly. When people decide important matters, they turn to the past. They look to history and custom, they consult the advice, the wisdom and the dreams of the past. They are not bound by the past, but they bear it in mind. The past does not rule them, but they go forward mindful of those who came before.

Many people see the rule of the people as rooted: rooted in custom, rooted in history, rooted in their communities, rooted in the life of people who have a shared life in a place they hold in common. Wendell Berry wrote that the commonwealth, "household, neighborhood, and community," is "the foundation and practical means" of democracy.[2] Those from Tocqueville to the present who admire the New England township, those who write wistfully of the villages of England, Kenya, and Rajasthan hold to this as well. There are left Burkeans to be sure, and there are also conservative Gandhians: people who hold to the virtue of the old ways of small communities and ancient crafts.

Wild Democracy. Anne Norton, Oxford University Press. © Oxford University Press 2023.
DOI: 10.1093/oso/9780197644348.003.0012

People see the boundaries of their common life as enfolding both the living and the dead. They believe they owe something to the past. They protect things they treasure in museums. They remind themselves of people and events in the past. These are often, but not always, people to be honored. There are memorials of many kinds: the Maison des Esclaves on Gorée Island; the graves in Westminster Cathedral; Yad Vashem; the tombs of unknown soldiers in Paris, Washington, and Delhi; the Lincoln Memorial in the United States; the Panthéon in Paris. Statues are put up and taken down as what is honored and what is rejected changes in the eyes of the people. The *Stolpersteine* in Germany are small bronze caps, each covering a cobblestone, recording the names of people who were taken from their homes during the Holocaust. They are called *Stolpersteine*, "stumbling stones," because they are meant to stop you for a moment, to interrupt a steady pace with a moment of recollection.[3] Museums of lynching and slavery in the United States, the bullet-riddled walls in the heart of a restored Beirut recall past wrongs that are not to be repeated. There are monuments, museums, and exhibits that record a more troubled and uncertain history. The pyramids in Egypt and Mexico recall a history of glory and exploitation, achievements and suffering. India's Taj Mahal is a building of surpassing beauty, but it also recalls a history of conquest, religious strife, and discrimination. People seek to record and remember not only their victories and achievements but their self-betrayals and injustices. This speaks powerfully for their integrity, their honesty, and their commitment to rule themselves.

The decision to take down or put up monuments is not a sign of frivolity or lightmindedness. It is the result of thought, debate, and deliberation. This is what happens when people look around and ask "Who is honored here? What is remembered here?" and then "Is this just? Is this who we are? Is this what we honor?" This is the work of people who examine their life together.

Conservatism, like all political positions, has the vices of its virtues and the virtues of its vices. At its worst, conservatism is no more than a small-minded love of one's own, a belief in one's superiority, an indolent indifference to the intellectual riches of the world, a fear of change, an acceptance of inequality if not a love for it, and the willingness to hold others back against their will. At its best, conservatism respects the judgment of ordinary people over generations; reminds us of our failings, our frailties, and our errors; cautions us against arrogance; and honors the ancestors. At their best, conservatives protect the learning and the arts of all people, not only their own. At their best, they may be, as Patrick Henry called himself, conservatives for liberty, committed to a set of principles and a discipline that keep the people ruling themselves.

People who rule themselves look to the future as well. The desire to go forward willingly into the unknown, the daring that greets the future as its home, belong to all those who struggle to rule themselves. Those who rule themselves have already committed themselves to a dangerous and uncertain journey. Progressives believe that journey is inevitably a journey forward, a project that struggles toward a future and a future people, that surpass the plans and dreams of the present.

There are hazards in the vision, in even the idea of progress. Those who know those dangers may hold to a vision of progress nonetheless, for there are virtues in it as well. The idea of progress reminds a fallible, imperfect people that they have work to do. The idea of progress reminds them that they can be better than they were, better indeed than anyone has ever been. The will to make progress drives people beyond the limits of the present and the past. They recognize the simple truth that the past is not the limit of the future, that history is not a boundary wall. For them, the only limit is an ever-receding horizon that draws them forward.

Progressivism, like conservatism, can bind people to both the dead and the unborn. The commitment to a better future is easy to see: it is declared in every progressive plan, poem, and manifesto. The commitment to the past is more subtle but very much present. Progressives see the course of the people like an arrow shot toward a distant target. They see their people on a hard journey to a promised land. They see their commitment to progress as keeping faith with that past. They see themselves as following in the footsteps of their ancestors, continuing the work of those who came before them.

Progressives recognize the inadequacy of the present. At their best, they recognize their own fallibility. They drive forward knowing their failures, their inadequacy, their limits and striving to overcome them. They have an iron discipline and transcendent hope. At their worst, they fail to see that the limits of the present are their limits as well. Blind to their own fallibility, indifferent to the virtues of others, they insist that they know what is best, and their drive to a better future becomes a forced march to an iron cage.

The belief that progress is predestined, that we shall overcome someday, gives comfort in hard times. Those who suffer injustice rest in the hope that better days will come. Those whose courage and virtue are not matched by those around them move like horses running for home, fueled by the hope that the country they call their own can still be reached in their time. Their strength can become the strength of their people.

Those who do not believe that progress is inevitable, who distrust promises of either a heavenly or an earthly paradise, who have no faith that we shall overcome one day may still take heart from those who do. For us there is no promise but our promise, no redemption but in our own work.

Those who believe that the people should rule themselves, who agree to rule and to be ruled in turn, hoping for none to be ruled at all, who are convinced that all men are created equal, that everyone has a life to live, are radicals all. They go to the root. Everybody, everybody walking on the earth, living and breathing, hungry and thirsty, thinking and planning, has a life to live. I ground rights in the needs and demands of those bodies and the souls they shelter within them. This is the ground of equality. The right to live freely, to live life apart and in common, is rooted here.

The right of people to rule themselves is radical in another, more common sense. Much must be changed to make that possible. There are institutions to take down, rules to break, laws to disobey.

Praise of the conservative preservers and the progressives on their predestined progress neglects the revolutionary power of the uprooted and the rootless. These, exiles and refugees, dissidents and heretics, are how newness enters the world. The world has failed them or launched them into the unknown. Nothing holds them. They are unbounded.

Conservative or liberal, progressive or radical, democrats are always fugitives. They are pursued on every side. Those who distrust the people fear that they will unleash the mob. Those who want to rule are always trying to corral them. Liberals and conservatives want to tame them, make them calm domestic animals who submit to their betters.

Yet even when the people rule, they find themselves on the run. They are always seeking something more. They struggle to escape the dead hand of the past. They will not accept that history fences them in. They fly from the errors, the defects, and the limits of the present. They fly to utopian visions, to experiments, to the ever-receding horizon of their hopes, their curiosity, and their will to discover more.

They fly.[4]

64. Democracy moves upward.

The rule of the people, Whitman saw, comes out of the ground like grass,

> a uniform hieroglyphic, and it means
> Sprouting alike in broad zones and narrow zones.[5]

It remains close to the ground. The right of the people to rule, the power of the people to rule, is present in each of them, no matter how poor, no matter how abject. The conviction that the people should rule draws them upward. They stand tall, metaphorically but also in practice. When the people rule, they walk without fear. They stand firm in the knowledge of their right to rule.

Democracy begins among the people and spreads, far too slowly, upward, until the arrogance of the rich and privileged is shamed.

The rule of the people moves upward in another sense. The people build. The spread of equality gives power to the creativity of the many. Where a few once invented, discovered, explored, many do. The concentration of wealth in a few hands is often defended by arguing that a fairer redistribution would stifle creativity and limit invention. The opposite is true. The capacity for invention, research, discovery—yes, "wealth creation"—is not concentrated in the hands of a few. When people are given tools and education, the freedom to invent and experiment, many create wealth where few did before. That wealth is spread more broadly, and as it spreads, more people are freed and inspired to build.

The demands of self-rule raise standards of conduct. In asserting this, I am, of course, directly contradicting the greater part of the canon of Western political philosophy. I do so proudly. That canon was written in the service of tyrants and for the advancement of the few. These men claimed that free people would give themselves up to appetite and license. We have seen that the closer people come to ruling themselves, the more responsibility they assume.

When people follow tyrants, demagogues, and autocrats, they abandon their pride, their responsibility, and their self-discipline. The autocrat's misconduct licenses every offense, every vulgarity, every abandonment of responsibility. The followers abandon ethics for the guidance of the corrupt, abandon responsibility for indolence, pride for the pleasures of abjection.

It is otherwise with free people. The more responsibility they assume, the more carefully they govern their own conduct. They learn to judge, and they turn that judgment on themselves. Little is required of them but much is asked. They learn to fend for themselves and to provide for others. They learn discipline, and they learn power. They learn to stand up for themselves and for others.

They rise.

People who rule themselves reach upward to the divine.

65. Democracy moves downward.

Democrats rise, but in the common phrase they remember where they came from. This is our common sense: the sense, held in common, that we are all mortal, we are all fragile, we are all at risk. The rule of the people looks to people in their simplicity: as mortals with all the needs and frailties of embodied beings. Mindful that everyone has a life to live, democracies direct their resources downward. Democracy has the poor in its heart. People who rule themselves ensure that all are fed, all are sheltered, all are cared for in times of need. Mindful that they will not only rule but be ruled, they ensure that all are educated, that all have the tools they need to cultivate their talents, that all have the means to resist when resistance is necessary, that all have a place to shelter in hard times, and, at all times, places where they cannot be ruled.

The rule of the people moves downward in another sense. Power, even the power of the ruling people, is not to be concentrated at a single site, certainly not at the top. The decentralization that extends democracy and shields the power of the people in hard times moves downward. Power moves through the whole of the people, living, dead, and yet to come, but it flows most powerfully among the living people. Democratic rule depends on the presence and the lived experience of power in all people. Every one of the people should know their power and seize their right to rule. Every one of the people should be willing to submit to rule by their own people.

Everyone must resist unjust rule, even—especially—among their own. "The people shall judge" applies not only to the right of revolution and the need for it but to the ordinary conduct of a common life. The people judge. They execute the laws they judge to be just in the ways that they think best. Everyone must be ready to correct injustices, great and small, and to call for revolution when revolution is necessary. Each person builds their world, making it anew at every moment of their common life.

People work to ensure that "justice rolls down like waters, and righteousness like a mighty stream."[6]

When the people rule, they will make mistakes. They will try strategies that fail. They will have plans with catastrophic consequences. Even when they move wisely, they will encounter obstacles. They will advance, and they will fall back. They keep the faith. They keep their hands on the plow.

XIII

Democratic spaces

66. People preserve the anarchic and nurture the democratic when they assemble.

The people are never visible as a whole, for the people include in their understanding of themselves the living, the dead, and those yet to come. When the American people speak in the Constitution, we establish a government "for ourselves and for our posterity." All people move forward. When they come to know themselves as a people, they look both to those they take as their compatriots in the past and to their own presence, the presence of their children and their children's children, in the future. A people in its wholeness is thus hidden from us. The closest we come to that vision of the whole is of the people assembled. The sight of people stretched beyond the line of vision calls up the vision of the people we cannot see. In that assembly we see the people whose power and whose right to rule stands before and beyond law and government. It is for this reason that demonstrations still serve to call governments to account. Demonstrations remind governments, institutions, officials that they serve at the pleasure of the people and that they must answer to the people.

When people assemble they call up the people, but that call will be judged by their compatriots, living and yet to come, perhaps even by the dead. Their assembly calls people to ask: Do they stand for the people? Do they stand for me? The answer to that question shapes the constitution of the people.

National assemblies, congresses, and parliaments gesture visually toward the presence of the people. They are, in themselves, the work of the people's will in choosing their forms of governance and the representatives themselves. The spectacle of deliberation and debate—especially debate—makes two aspects of popular rule visible. Representatives, and those who watch them, confront the differences

Wild Democracy. Anne Norton, Oxford University Press. © Oxford University Press 2023.
DOI: 10.1093/oso/9780197644348.003.0013

and enmities among the people. They are reminded that though the people are one people, they are also many people. We differ profoundly, in practice and in principle, in our interests and in our ideals. Only in the simultaneous presence of likeness and difference can the people be seen.

67. Democracy lives in the city.

Cities intensify. There is more art, more commerce, more crime, more law enforcement, more politics, more scholarship, and more religion in the cities than there is among the farms and ranches of the country or the malls and developments of the suburbs. The weight of governance is felt more heavily. Every level of a decentralized government is visible and active in the city. If government is centralized, it will be in the city that its power is greatest. If it is decentralized, it will take on myriad forms in cities. If it is liberal, the city will be hedged about with regulations, which will be endlessly debated and modified. If it is autocratic, it is in the city that the full weight of dictatorial rule will be felt. The work of government will be visible to all: in buildings, in meetings, in posted regulations. No one will be able to walk the streets without seeing it. The work of the governing people is visible there and in the contests surrounding issues and events. Sovereignty shows itself in the city. Power shows itself in the city.

The simplest aspect of cities may be the most important. There are more people. Cities are magnetic. They attract people who are looking for jobs for there are many jobs, far more than are to be found in the countryside. They attract people who want to study. There are universities in the country, to be sure, but the city has not only colleges and universities but art schools and conservatories. People bring their pasts, their hopes, their interests, and their ideals with them to the city. People flee to the city from places where they felt lost, alone, abandoned, or alien. They mix with others like and unlike themselves. They are confronted by new ideas, new questions, new possibilities. The pleasures and dangers of living with other people, unknown, dangerous people, are familiar to them. They can acquire the common courage that comes from living with difference, in and among the unknown.

68. Democracy lives in the countryside.

Eighteenth-, nineteenth-, and even twentieth-century democrats have tended to favor the country over the city. Jefferson envisioned the yeoman farmer in a fertile country furnishing people with food and shelter and thereby securing their independence, and the farmer's own. These agrarian philosophers, and those who followed them, also saw life close to the land as offering more freedom, more leisure, and thus more opportunities for politics and learning.

The agrarians, like the striking textile workers of the Northeast, saw that people need not only bread but roses. They need time: time to study and time to organize, time to deliberate and time to argue with one another about the issues of the day. Some forms of farming and ranching give people that time; most demand as much intensive labor as any factory. In the late nineteenth and early twentieth centuries the demands of labor made time shorter still. If one could read when the fields were fallow, one might be hard put to find the books to read. People who read might well read and think and debate in solitude for neighbors were far away, and the nearest neighbors might not be drawn to the same books. The time to reflect and debate that Jefferson valued was made greater by distance, and candidates, like books, might be hard to come by. Time was both an aid and an obstacle to rural politics. Candidates might not travel to far-flung farms, and the courthouse lawns where they made their speeches might be a long ride away. People might meet in church, but churches are notoriously poor places for political debates.

It was this that made the granges so important. The granges were to farmers as the union halls were to dockworkers, miners and factory workers: they provided a place for rural people to meet, talk, and organize. They were places where books and pamphlets could be shared, candidates and ideas debated. They made political organizing possible. They kindled a prairie fire. They made the reforms of the People's

Party and the Progressives possible and fueled them with the urgency of need.

The country is a place of solidarity and solitude. People help one another. There is often nowhere else to turn. They combine, as they did in granges, ranging themselves against the absent powers of banks, other corporations, and the state. They learn to provide for themselves. They can grow, hunt, fish, and forage for their own food. They learn to build. They learn skills people in cities may never need. They strive to be free from dependence on others, yet they give to their neighbors with an open hand.

The country can also be a place where anarchy spreads its branches, where people live as they choose, and new ways of life are born and take root.

There is a simpler way to state the preceding two theses: "In the city the people rule" and "In the country the people rule." One of the shortcomings of the word "democracy" is its concealment of this simple idea. I wrote the theses as I did because each holds a political history within it. "Democracy belongs to the city" calls up the many efforts to cast cities as places of sin and degradation. Many of the state constitutions written after the American Civil War gave cities less representation, and less power, than rural areas. Trump's characterization of Baltimore as "a disgusting rat and rodent infested mess" echoes a long history of hostility to cities and their people. "Democracy belongs to the country" counters a history of portraying rural people as ignorant and parochial. It recalls a neglected history of Midwestern radicalism in the search for justice. Both are charged with a predilection for violence: the gangs of the city, the vigilantes of the countryside. Both are feared as places of anarchy.

Let them be.

69. Free people carry the democratic with them. They carry it into the factory, the shop, the school.

We Americans call ourselves democrats and republicans, but we have steadily eroded the reach and power and responsibility of citizens— of all people—in the United States. We speak of our republic and our democracy, but we have diminished ourselves, fencing our principles, our rights, and the democratic practices we have into smaller and smaller spaces. We say we believe in free speech, but no one in America thinks they can speak freely at work. Politics, we are told, belongs outside of work. It appears we have our rights—to assembly, to free speech, to freedom of religion—only in those hours of the day that we are not working (one job or two or three) or eating or sleeping. We don't have them when we are shopping, for malls are private spaces and we are not permitted to assemble or speak freely there. We don't have them on the streets, for the streets are policed and assemblies require a permit.

This is absurd. We carry our rights within us.

Forget these boundaries. Refuse these restrictions. Rights are born in us. They are inalienable. Whether they are recognized or not, rights remain with us always. They are carried into the schoolroom, onto the shop floor, into the church, into the office, onto the streets.

This is no easy business. This is no simple project. Anyone who has worked in a subordinate position knows that to speak at work is to speak not as an equal but as someone who can be fired and who needs that job.

Schools, masjids, temples, and churches have hierarchies and inequalities as well. These are not, in general, as burdensome or as unjust as the inequalities at work, though there are shameful exceptions. This is not simply because they are, as many have argued, "natural" and "just" inequalities. The teacher who looks out on the class should think, my teachers taught me, that there is someone in that class who is smarter than you, and someone who is more moral. Perhaps they all are. If they are not now, they may come to be so. In teaching, the brilliance and the goodness of these students is revealed. This is a source of both humility and joy. No one can teach and not be reproached, day after day, by students who silently (but not always silently) remind you how much you do not know, how much you have to learn. No one can watch people learn and not be awed by their transcendence, their transfigurations.

In all the religious traditions I know, something similar is present. There may be (there usually is) a hierarchy. There may be norms of deference to authority, and rules enforcing doctrine. There may be customs and rituals arguing silently and insistently for the powerful, but there is something more. There is grace. There is prophecy. There is saintliness. Grace, *mana*, *baraka*, whatever name it bears, comes without warning, to the great but more often to the poor and the scorned. In the midst of the Peasant Wars, Thomas Müntzer, a brave priest who defended the peasants when too many priests ranged themselves with the lords, reproached those who wrote that the times of prophecy were past and it was "fantastic and fool-headed, and that it is most impossible." Müntzer insisted, even under torture, that "now, in our times, God also sends his light into the world."[1]

The democratic is carried into the world, fought and secured, in each human body. The sovereignty of the people is decentralized, disseminated, scattered through the world, in the bodies of those who make up the people. The people, together and singly, are the voice and hands of the sovereign. The ethical, democratic, acts of the people, far more than institutions, secure democracy.

70. Democracy cannot be fenced out of the economic realm or separated from the social.

Political theory and political practice have divided the world again. Statesmen and theorists have taught that there are separate realms, public and private, ruled by different regimes. Where rights are concerned, these divisions must be considered carefully, used carefully, for they are a weapon that can turn in the hand. The distinction between public and private can protect the people. The idea that some space is private, that it cannot be entered by the state or by others can give people shelter: shelter for their beliefs, for their practices, for whatever they choose to keep to themselves. Holding that space, caring for what lies within it, teaches them to rule. We have learned, however, that the distinction between public and private gave some people unjust, tyrannical power over others. For women, for slaves, for servants, even for children, the private realm has been made a prison. The idea of the private, holding homes and corporations, has concealed the power of the wealth and the persistence of feudal power in the aptly named economic realm.

Businesses and corporations have claimed the right to govern spaces that would otherwise be public: places where people meet, discuss, debate. The shopping mall might seem open, but it is a private space. Politics is fenced out. The owner decides who will enter and who can be forced (by guards with guns) to leave. You can speak freely to your friends about political issues, but if you speak too loudly, if you speak to the people around you, if you speak without the permission of the owner, if you speak for something the owner opposes, you can (and you probably will) be silenced. Freedom of assembly is denied. Within that space, people are not free, not equal. Some people are denied entrance altogether. The visibly poor are treated like unwanted wildlife, captured and persuaded to leave. Members of a minority race or religion, even the wealthy, find that they are excluded. The bell they ring does not admit them, or they enter only to find themselves unwelcome. In these places of commerce, the few can buy what they choose. The many are denied. The few are taught that their wealth makes them free. The many learn that they are not. All see, whether they acknowledge it or not, that the people do not rule in these spaces. Rights are not recognized. There is no democracy there. These are spaces of autocratic power.

The idea of the private has made the spaces of banks and businesses curiously immune to protest. Occupy Wall Street protested against the power of the 1%, the power of corporations whose careless rapacity made millions homeless. The protesters occupied Zuccotti Park and held it against several police efforts to evict them. The park was a "privately owned public space," a privately owned space the owners are required to keep open to the public (more or less). The Occupy movement spread from this curious liminal space to streets and plazas around the world. The protesters did not occupy the businesses they protested. They could not, for these are fortresses. They are more difficult to enter than, more closely guarded than, and as dangerous to breach as the state buildings of any other dictatorship.

Make no mistake, these are dictatorships. They may have boards, as dictators have advisers. They may have shareholders who vote, in which case the dictatorship is oligarchic. They may be large, bureaucratic, totalitarian regimes of rules and surveillance. Except in the rare cases where those who work in the company own it as well, there is nothing democratic here, nothing republican. This is alien territory for people who intend to rule themselves. Here, the boss rules.[2] This is true for Goldman Sachs and Santander, Nando's and McDonald's, for the man who owns a corner store and the man who owns Amazon. For generations, for hundreds of years, people who believe themselves to be democrats, who have built republics and struggled to establish at least representative institutions have spent most of their lives under the rule of one boss or another.

Is there anyone reading this who has not worked under a boss? There are few, I expect, who have not worked under a bad one.

There are places, of course, liberal or striving toward the democratic (even some totalitarian orders) where the boss is constrained. Slavery is forbidden. Children under fourteen or fifteen or still in school are forbidden to work, or are allowed to work only when the work is not hazardous. The hours a person can work are limited. Working conditions are regulated for safety. Some workers are allowed to unionize. In liberal places, places where people have worked to introduce elements of democracy in their institutions, these constraints were won only after hundreds of years of struggle and suffering. They are still evaded or ignored.[3] And though in music and art, in every medium, people recognize that the boss is a tyrant, the company's rules foolish, and the law powerless; though people talk, quietly and discreetly, in the corners of the workplace, the rule of the boss is accepted, even praised, as essential to capitalism and wholly consonant with—perhaps even necessary to—democracy. This is wrong.

Rights are held in the body, in your body, in our bodies. There is no invisible process that strips them from you, silently and thoroughly, as you enter the workplace. There is no boundary that that rights cannot cross. The powers bosses claim and states license are illegitimate and indefensible.

The idea that the workplace can be democratic may seem absurd and unimaginable. Yet there have been many times when people not only struggled for their natural rights in the workplace; they expected them. The young women hired in newly established New England textile mills assumed that they carried their rights to speech and assembly into the mills. They assumed that decisions about the mill would be made democratically. After all, were they not still in a democracy? That claim was answered with brute force, yet their question remains.

If people are to rule themselves, then they must do so everywhere, not just outside the workplace and not for (allowing for eating and sleeping) something less than six hours a day.

The same should be said of that amorphous zone called "the social order." Hannah Arendt argued, in "Reflections on Little Rock," that segregation was permissible in the United States because it belonged not to the political but to the social order. Arendt believed that there were no rights outside politics, indeed no rights for any people without a state. The condition of the stateless thus was, for her, one of complete abjection. They could make no demands, for they had no rights. Rights came from laws. Rights came from states.[4] She could not bring herself to ask for more for the stateless than "the right to have rights." In making the argument that the social order stood apart from politics, Arendt made her politics smaller. She denied that politics takes place outside law and governance. Politics observes no such boundaries. The denial of equality and power to a slave or a wife in the home is political. Caste and racial hierarchies are no less political because they are "social distinctions." Hierarchies of wealth and poverty are no less political because they are social (or economic). Arendt, Wendy Brown notes, laid every sin of modernity at the feet of the "overtaking of everything by the social." Arendt praised the American Revolution for avoiding "the social question in the form of the terrifying predicament of mass poverty."[5] Arendt's imaginary of an American Revolution raised above concern for poverty conceals the revolutionary importance of the Dorr Rebellion and the Whiskey Rebellion, the continuing pressure for veterans' pensions, and the text of the Declaration. Equality grounded the revolution. Equality grounds democracy.

71. The rule of the people lives and is endangered in each person's body.

Where the people rule, each person carries the right to rule. More than this, each person does the work of judging politics every day. They make law together. They judge the law, they judge offenders, every day.

They execute the law, obeying when they think it best and ensuring that others obey. The work of politics is thoroughly decentralized. Responsibility belongs to every person.

The people are always present, not only in the form of an idea but in the flesh. They do not simply "hover above the world," as Tocqueville wrote. They are in the world, doing the work that belongs to us all. That presence, however, is only a partial one. Each of us is a part of the people. Each of us stands apart from the people. We are partial to those we love, to a place perhaps, or a party, to a particular set of sentiments and ideas. We carry with us a particular set of experiences, of love and loss, victories and frustrations. We carry knowledge and memory, tastes and dispositions. We have some skills and not others. We learn some things and make some errors. Yet it is in us, through us, and as us that the sovereign people is present in the world.

It is in the thoughts and practices of particular people that the idea of the people is called forth in the world. It is in and through the actions of particular people that the people act.

Donne's observation "Any man's death diminishes me because I am in involved in mankind" becomes more intimate and more political here. There is only one way in which the people appear in the world. The people appear in the people. My people appear in me. I am called to act for, to act as my people in the world. There is no other way to call a people into being. There is no other way for a people to be born, to live, to thrive, to decay, to be lost except in its people.

There is, I have been told, a Hasidic belief that there is a person in every generation who has the potential to become the Messiah. The democratic call is broader than that. This is not a question of the possibility of greatness in one. All are called, and all are chosen. All bear the universal within them. Each person is a gate, and through that gate the future comes into the world. When we belong to a people it is through us, in us, as us that the people live or die, suffer or thrive.

XIV
Friends and enemies

72. Equality is proper to democracy.

Say this, as Wendy Brown has, in the clearest way: "Political equality is democracy's foundation."[1] When Americans declared their independence, they began here. They addressed not their overlords but all mankind. They began not with their grievances but with truths anyone could hear and understand. First among these was equality: "We hold these truths to be self-evident, that all men are created equal." Those words have returned to us from the Diné, the Muscogee, the Lenape; from African Americans and Asian Americans; from Filipinos and Puerto Ricans; from the interned, the deported, and the tortured. The words are greater than we are. They set an enduring truth before us, before all. They command us.

When the great army that brought down the English monarchy saw Charles Stuart captured, they sat down in the fields outside London and began to debate what form of government they would have. These debates, the Putney Debates, are one of the most heartening moments in history, for they show us a people willing to make themselves anew. There is much that is admirable in these debates, but one moment has come to stand for the whole: Rainsborough's declaration "I think the poorest he that is in England has a life to live, as the greatest he."[2] Everyone has a life to live. Everyone is bound within the small compass of a single body. Everyone has a need for food, for shelter. Everyone has been born. Everyone will die. If we are born and live and die in the solitude of the body, yet we know that all people do the same. Our rights to life and liberty are grounded in the strength and fragility of the mortal body, and the mind and soul sheltered within it.

Every person has uncertain potential; each has immeasurable promise. Rainsborough might have said with the Talmud, "Every

Wild Democracy. Anne Norton, Oxford University Press. © Oxford University Press 2023.
DOI: 10.1093/oso/9780197644348.003.0014

death is the loss of a world." This is the equality that is proper to democracy: that each person is of incalculable worth.

The British set equality aside, preserving monarchs and aristocrats, building an empire. Nevertheless, the words remained, driving the British beyond empire and toward justice.

Americans set equality aside when they held slaves, against the principles of the Declaration. We have not succeeded in overcoming the effects of slavery or the other inequalities that diminish us as a people and as a people. Nevertheless the words remain, driving us toward justice.

The struggle for freedom in Europe's colonies, in Ghana and Algeria, India and South Africa, fired the hearts of people far away. The demand that the equality of each person be recognized could not be separated from the demand that people be free to rule themselves as they chose. The demand for freedom and independence was grounded in the recognition of equality.

73. Inequality corrupts democracy.

Inequality of wealth is inequality of power. It is therefore a constant obstacle to people who will rule themselves. They may overcome that obstacle, they may endure the burdens it places upon them, yet it remains an obstacle to their freedom and an offense against justice.

In many ways inequality of wealth may seem to be a trivial concern. It does not trouble me if my neighbor drives a Lamborghini or wears a large diamond. I have enough to live the life I choose, and I have never been fond of cars or diamonds. There are other uses for wealth that should trouble us. Wealth robs us of our rights. We all have the right to speak freely. The wealthy have the ability to make themselves heard. We can write a letter to the editor. The wealthy own the newspapers. They can decide who or what appears there. We can voice our concerns on the streets and in public meetings. The wealthy own radio and television stations. They can decide who is seen and heard. Money buys voice. We are silenced, but this inequality of speech does more: it prevents us from hearing what others have to say. Money buys power. Where bribes are taken, influence and power are bought directly. Where bribery is forbidden, there are other avenues of influence. A campaign contribution of sufficient size buys access. Indeed, wealth alone buys access. Even the uncorrupted bow before wealth.

They know that wealth is power and believe that in order to serve the common good they need to court the wealthy.

Wealth divides. We do not see the very wealthy; they have set themselves apart from us, but we know that they are there. We know that there are those who could not spend their wealth in many lifetimes, but we do not see them. We see the poor. We know that there are those who have so little that their lives are shortened, their creative abilities stunted, their potential fenced in at every turn.

If wealth does not trouble us, poverty should. It should trouble us all to see people begging on the streets.

> C is a contrast, revolting but true
> Want with the many, excess with the few.[3]

Our eyes find this excess revolting. What of our minds? That excess should appall us. Spare us the dangers posed by the poor. Consider the greater dangers posed by the rich. The contrast revolts our eyes and our minds; it is at once ugly and unjust. The longer it remains, the more it is seen, the more culpable we are for failing to do our duty, for failing to refuse this.

There is no common, no democratic life when people are divided between rich and poor, when voice, action, and justice under law have become commodities for purchase. A common life, a democratic life, requires equality.

74. Friendship teaches people to live as democrats.

The Greeks, and the old Norse who surpassed them in democratic ethics, both valued friendship. "In antiquity," Nietzsche wrote of the Greeks, "the feeling of friendship was considered the highest feeling, even higher than the most celebrated pride of the self-sufficient sage—somehow as the sole and sacred sibling of this pride."[4] The *Hávamál* holds, "No man is whole," and offers the practical advice:

> If you know you have a friend, and that she is true
> And that you will get good from her,
> share your mind with her, exchange gifts,
> and visit her often.[5]

Friends, as Aristotle wrote, have everything in common. In friendship we learn to practice holding things in common. In friendship we learn that individuality prospers in the commons. It is with those with whom we hold a commons that we are most fully ourselves. Friendship, however, is predicated not only on similarity but on difference. Friends are sought for the lacks they remedy. Aristotle distinguished between the friends of need and convenience and "true friendship," which arises between different people seeking understanding not yet within their reach. These friendships are marked by pleasure in the other's distinct, otherwise unknown and alien thoughts and insights. The pleasures of friendship are the pleasures of diversity in a common life.[6]

Some philosophers have been wise enough to value friendship far more highly than companionate marriage or sexual love. Sexuality, after all, belongs to many beings. A bond rooted in sexuality may be intimate indeed but, like the bonds between those Aristotle so evocatively called "peers of the mess" or "companions of the cupboard," it is not linked to the political.[7] It is language that binds us in the highest forms of friendship, language that enables us to become political and, thereafter, fully human. Friendship trains us in democratic ethics: in respect, in dignity, in risk-taking. Friendship trains us for politics. Friendship teaches us a solidarity that will not be impaired by debate. Friendship makes us at home with diversity. A friend is never wholly one's own, never one flesh, never wholly like us. Each encounter with a friend is at once familiar and astonishing, intimate and alien. The friend is always known and unknown. The friend opens another world. Friendship teaches that diversity may be not only a threat but the greatest gift, not only a danger but a source of power and joy. This is a relation of equals.

75. Who are the enemies of democracy? What is to be done with them?

The enemies of democracy are the fearful: those who seek glory, autocrats, aristocrats, and all those who claim that their lives are worth more than others'.

What is to be done with them? The fearful can be taught not to fear. Children learn to overcome many fears: the darkness, loud noises, the new school, strange foods, and the monster under the bed. That capacity remains in all people. The fearful can learn. They can learn to see foreigners as people who, like them, are hungry and thirsty, who need shelter and protection. They can learn to see them as people with useful strengths and skills. They can learn to look with interest and curiosity at the strange appearances and practices of foreigners. Perhaps they can do more. Perhaps the fearful can learn the courage of the explorers. They can learn that new places, new people, new things, new ways can be useful and pleasurable rather than threatening. They can learn that the one they feared can be a fellow worker, a colleague, a friend.

Perhaps they can learn, as soldiers must, to face the enemy calmly. Faced with those who truly threaten them, they can pretend to set their fears aside and, as they do, find a courage to fill their pretense. Those who fear change can be taught to be at home with it. Like a person who has never sailed, they can learn to shift their weight on the deck, to tack, to jibe, to feel pleasure rather than fear when the boat heels.

Aristocracy, Tom Paine wrote, is infantile and silly, "it talks about its fine *blue ribbon* like a girl, and shows its new *garter* like a child": "The world has seen this folly fall, and it has fallen by being laughed at."[8] In Paine's time there were still those who held in their hands the lives of the untitled poor, who claimed wealth and privilege and power on a claim no stronger than that of a purebred dog. In Europe, that claim would still hold fast, for a time.

Aristocracy fell so far and so hard in America that Paine could say, "If I ask a man in America if he wants a King, he retorts and asks me if I take him for an idiot?"[9] That strength has held fast. No one wants a king. Claims to the privileges or trappings of a lord would be mocked unmercifully. Yet elements of the feudal order remain very much with us, embedded in the law. The old law of master and servant lives disguised in the laws that govern employers and employees.[10] The idea of power in the blood, preserved in hierarchies of race and sex has been hard to dislodge. Racial and sexual claims to power over others are among the shards of feudalism. There are still men who demand deference simply for being men, with men's bodies. There are still women who are beaten for not accepting this. There are those who insist people bear the bodies they were born with. There are, we have learned to our sorrow, still people who long to claim title in their ancestry, who believe that "whiteness" is a title to power. This is the whiteness of the empty page, the whiteness of old bones. It bears a family resemblance to the claims of aristocracy, in the absurdity of its claims and in the cruelty of its exactions. We cannot yet ridicule the claims of race; we are too close to the bodies hanging from the trees, the bodies shot in the street. We cannot yet claim to have ended the subjection of women or the persecution of the queer. We remain under the tyranny of regimes of sex and sexuality. We will not be free of the feudal until we end the claims of power in the blood.

Those who seek glory look for a more honorable way to make the claims aristocrats made. Their efforts are as silly as those of any aristocrat. The prizing of a number of "Facebook friends" or hits on social media, the self-exposures of celebrities and others famous for being famous are as easily dismissed as claims to an illustrious ancestry or an ancient title.

We have more to fear from those who long for money and power. There are still ambitious people ready to lead (they always mean to lead) their countries into empire, who persist in the acquisition of wealth beyond all reason and the exercise of the personal power that goes with it. We have learned, to our great cost, that there is no limit to the appetites of the wealthy. They will amass as much power as they can and use it as they wish. We should be prevent them from using it to rule others.

We have learned that it is not the passions and appetites of the people that are to be feared, but the passions and appetites of would-be autocrats. Our capacity to rule ourselves depends on our ability to stand against these, to learn the art of not being governed, to make space for anarchy and in that space cultivate the courage and resources to rule ourselves.

What do we do with the enemies of democracy? When the people rule, nothing needs to be done with them at all. They will not become dangerous in the passion for glory. They will not spread their fears. They may be a nuisance, but not more. We can carry a few parasites. When the people rule, they have the strength to carry the weak and shelter the fearful. People with the strength anarchy builds can ignore claims to superiority of blood or descent, race or sex or wealth. Such claims hold no commanding power when everyone rules and is ruled, when everyone has rights in common. People who rule themselves learn to set their fears aside, to act with courage in times of crisis, to place the needs of others before their desires—or their fears. People who consent to be ruled learn to walk among their enemies unafraid. We keep our ability to rule ourselves while we keep our courage.

XV
Democratic divinity

76. In ruling themselves, people become divine.

Alexis de Tocqueville is most often remembered not as one who loved democracy but as one who feared it. Tocqueville's writings are filled with an anxious melancholy. He grieves for the lost glory of aristocrats and Indians. He fears that art and philosophy, poetry and statesmanship will prove hard to find among the untutored peasants, smallholders, and frontiersmen of new democracies. His melancholy envelops readers. His anxieties are read as prophetic. Tocqueville feared that equality was the aim of democracy, the end of greatness. The end of inequality seemed to him to entail the loss of glory, beauty, and grace. He writes, "the sight of such uniformity saddens and chills me, and I am tempted to regret the state of society that has ceased to be." Yet in the end, Tocqueville comes to think otherwise. Divine judgment speaks for democracy:

> It is natural to suppose that not the particular prosperity of the few, but the greater well-being of all, is most pleasing in the sight of the Creator and Preserver of men. What seems to me decay is in His eyes progress; what pains me is acceptable to Him. Equality may be less elevated, but it is more just, and in its justice lies its greatness and beauty.

Tocqueville sees that it is his duty to understand "this divine view of the world."[1]

We who have seen democratic glory and beauty need have no fear. We have read the poetry of Whitman and Ginsberg, Dickinson and Merrill, the novels of Morrison and Melville. We have seen the paintings of Eakins, Whistler, and O'Keefe, Johns and Rauschenberg. We have learned to see that courage in battle lies not only in the

Wild Democracy. Anne Norton, Oxford University Press. © Oxford University Press 2023.
DOI: 10.1093/oso/9780197644348.003.0015

commander who stands apart but in those who fill the trenches. We have learned, like e. e. cummings, to see courage in the conscientious objector, "more brave than me, more blond than you."[2]

All of us who long to rule ourselves have seen that greatness and beauty escape and exceed wealth and privilege. Beauty belongs not only to Blenheim and the Forbidden City but to the ruins of Chaco Canyon, the simplicity of a wooden house rising above a *klong* on the outskirts of Bangkok. There is Ming pottery, and there is Acoma pottery. There are the paintings of Velasquez, and those of Diego Rivera. The wisdom of Supreme Court justices falls before the hopes of slaves and workers.

Beauty and grace, courage and wisdom are not found only among the great, whether the great are aristocrats or common people. Tocqueville saw that, in the sight of the divine, beauty belonged to masses of people who are fed, sheltered, educated and free and who have made that world together. There is great beauty in the sight of people studying, working, moving, speaking freely. Beauty belongs to clean cities with clean water, unsoiled by litter; to clear rivers, filled with healthy leaping fish; to open beaches free to all.

Divine beauty, Tocqueville saw, belongs not to the few but to the many, not to evanescent moments but to the constant and enduring good in ordinary lives. People who live justly, who see that rights are honored, that people are fed and clothed, cared for and educated, who think and act freely, build a more just world. "In its justice lies its greatness and beauty."

77. The voice of the people is the voice of God.

Accounts of divinity show us the presence of the people in the *umma* and the work of *ijma*, in the Holy Spirit, in Pentecost, and in the constant unceasing work of people whose homeland is the text. The Muslim idea of the *umma* conceives of a people united by faith and a commitment to a particular text and form of life. They do not, cannot all live together, for they are spread across the world. The Prophet Muhammad, peace be upon him, said, "My people will not agree upon an error."[3] This *hadith* (a verified statement or act of the Prophet) captures one of many moments in which the people are understood as able to speak in accordance with divine will.

The canon gives us the sly, irreverent awe of Rousseau and Machiavelli. When listing great lawgivers, Machiavelli turns not to monarchs or statesmen but to the prophets. Rousseau writes, "Gods are needed to give men laws."[4] When people give laws to themselves, they become divine.

There are many qualities attributed to gods and other divine beings. These are not always to be admired. They are said to be merciful, creative, generous with their blessings, cruel, and destructive. These qualities can be found in animals as well as divinities. Certain attributes, however, speak directly to the political. In divinity, beings transcend the limits of time, space, and mortality. These attributes also belong to people who have become political. Those who are part of a people live in that people. They transcend the limits of their mortality. This is not merely a matter of memory. Those people may be forgotten. Nevertheless, they remain. They are and will always be part of that people. They are divine in their transcendence. The social contract, the agreement among people to become a people, transforms each individual human being and "from a stupid and limited animal makes him an intelligent being and a man."[5] Rousseau thought that the creation of the human was done by man in the form of the divine. Is this another theory of the Incarnation? Perhaps.

Justice and morality follow in the wake of divinity. There are many monarchs—Solon and Augustus, Justinian and Alfred, Kanunî Sultan Süleyman and Napoléon—who have given laws to their people. They are remembered and venerated, but they are not divine. The capacity to give the law to oneself calls forth the divine in one and in all. People who rule themselves have divinity in them. That rule is democratic.

The dominant understandings of sovereignty in our time tend to be radically undemocratic. The first is the notion, popular among lawyers, that sovereignty is a legal question, to be settled by laws and experts. In this view, sovereignty belongs to states (or international organizations) and operates through existing institutions. This view has no place for rebellion, and often no place for reform.

The second concept of sovereignty was developed by Carl Schmitt. It is also, not surprisingly, popular with authoritarian political figures.

Monarchical, authoritarian rule is the form that animates Schmitt's concept of sovereignty, effectively eliding the distinction between the sovereign and the executive. Schmitt erases the distinction between executive and sovereign power. He and his followers are committed to an understanding of sovereignty as decisionistic and personalistic for political and religious reasons. Politically, Schmitt seeks to strengthen executive power, to reinstall the powers of the sovereign in the executive and thus recapture what the revolutions of the Enlightenment had stripped from monarchy. Religiously, Schmitt is committed to the primacy of the Incarnation, to the presence of God's divine sovereignty in the person of Christ.

Schmitt's religious imperative may be attractive to those Christian evangelicals who, committed to the notion of a personal God in a quite different sense, likewise insist upon the primacy of the incarnate form of the divine sovereign. It may be attractive to the partisans of ambiguous secularization who wish to preserve the political theology undergirding the not quite secular state. Schmitt's political imperative has also found contemporary allies for what American neoconservatives call "a more authoritarian presidency" and "a more disciplined democracy." These commitments are hardly compelling to democrats—or to republicans. But this is not the only reading available within a secularized Christian theology, even within Schmitt.

In *Political Theology*, Schmitt gestures, briefly and allusively, to another form of sovereignty:

> In America, this manifested itself in the reasonable and pragmatic belief that the voice of the people is the voice of God—a belief that is at the foundation of Jefferson's victory of 1801. Tocqueville in his account of American democracy observed that in democratic thought the people hover above the entire life of the state, just as God does above the world, as the cause and end of all things, as the point from which everything emanates and to which everything returns.[6]

If the installation of sovereignty within the executive is the secularization of the Incarnation, we can look to the confluence of language and diaspora in Pentecost and see a recognition of the sovereignty of the people.

In Pentecost, the power and sovereignty of the divine comes not to one but to the many. The divine comes not in the flesh but as the word. The divine is sent not to one chosen people but to all peoples. The divine takes form not as a man but as language. I do not mean this as a return to Christianity alone. Belief in the divinity of language belongs not to one faith but many. Jews call themselves the people of the book. Muslims hold the word sacred. For all the children of Abraham, the word is sacred.

The word is greater than this. Recognition of the divine belongs to learning as well as religion. In language, people transform themselves. Alone, in families, in villages, and under the rule of kings—or any authoritarian ruler—people live as animals. They may, if they are fortunate, be well provided for. They might even prosper economically. But they are not fully human. It is only in politics that people become truly human. And politics is politics only when it is in the hands of the people, when they gather, debate, deliberate, and give judgment.

Democratic politics is the politics of the word made flesh. People debate with passion as well as reason, for language is meant to carry both. Democratic people make laws and follow them; they rule and are ruled in turn. It is in politics—democratic politics—that people become fully human, for politics is conducted in language, and language sets us beyond the animal and close to the divine. Politics permits us transcendence and enables us to approach a common divinity.

In politics people live beyond the limits of a single life. In politics, people may live according to ideas greater than their own. In politics, people overcome their individual flaws and collectively find a wisdom beyond the individual. It is for this reason that in many times, in many places, and in many languages, people have recognized *vox populi, vox dei*: the voice of the people is the voice of God.

In this understanding, in the political theology of a democratic Pentecost, sovereignty belongs not to the one "who decides on the exception" but to the people, whose spirit animates democracy like tongues of fire.

When we are in the midst of the hard work of democratic politics—building institutions, questioning them, correcting them—democracy may seem very far indeed from the divine. It may seem very far from the possible. In this long struggle, belief in the people is hard to come by. The fire is kept alive in the ashes by memory and by forgetting.

We must forget, we democrats, that kings and priests were said to be divinely ordained, that the order of wealth and privilege was said to be the work of God or nature or the market. Forget those myths that furnished—that still furnish—the license for oppression. Power lies in anarchist refusal: "No gods, no masters." Forget that we have been scorned and humiliated: walk like gods. Remember those times when the people rose up and, for a moment, gave the divine speech and strength and hands to work in the world.

78. The people sing.

I do not know why, but I know the people sing. This will come as no surprise to those who have heard people singing "We Shall Overcome" in dark times. The jailers who heard them in Selma and Birmingham knew that what they heard was not only the voices of the imprisoned but the voice of the people, the voice of God.[7] The people who heard them heard their own voice raised. So it has been with "Bella Ciao," "Glory to Hong Kong," "Solidarity Forever," and other songs sung in hopeful and in desperate times. The people who sang called forth the divine.

I do not know why the people sing. I know that when they sing, their voices join. They speak, they sing with one voice. When the people sing, their differences are lost in the sea of sound. It does not matter if you sing well or badly, your voice joins with the others in that ocean. Rich and poor, old and young, people of every sex and race sing. They sing as one. Their bodies vibrate to that singing. Their voices come out, join with one another, and as they do the surrounding people feel the sound of those voices near their heart. They speak and they hear in the same moment. They sing and they feel the sound. I know that when the people sing, their bodies carry the common, and yet each one sings. In singing, the solitude of the body is, for a moment, affirmed and overcome.

79. The earth belongs to the living.

In the American democracy, Tocqueville wrote, "the people hover above the entire life of the state, just as God does above the world, as the cause and end of all things, as the point from which everything emanates and to which everything returns."

Tocqueville's passage puts the embodiment of the people in doubt. Are the people present on earth and in the flesh? Thomas Jefferson and Thomas Paine argued that the earth belonged to the living, to the present people in all their mortal power and fragility. Surely the consent of the governed means the consent of the living people, who bear the burden of rule. Yet I have learned that for the people themselves this is not the case. All the people (and all the peoples) I know look to the dead and the unborn, to their ancestors and to their posterity. They see themselves as present in the past and the future. They gather in those people of the past whom they believe belong to them. They look to them for guidance. They feel a duty to their ancestors. They feel a duty to the dead. They feel a still greater duty to those who are yet to come. When a people makes itself in the world, speaks itself into being, sees itself, the people who do the making see beyond the present. They open to the future.[8]

Living people hold the past and the future within them. The transcendent people, living and dead and yet to come, enfold and empower the living people. This transcendent being, this ineffable sovereignty is held in the bodies of living people. People hold the memories of the past, visions of the future, the presence of the past, and the material beginnings of posterity in their bodies. Sovereignty is inscribed in soul and cell and synapse.

The presence of a people extends into their memories and their records of the past, into their plans and hopes for a future they can build together. Yet it is not in the past or in the future that we should look for people ruling themselves; it is in the present.

The recognition that the earth belongs to the living is at once a burden and a liberation. We are free to set the past aside. History cannot bind us completely; the limits of custom and tradition can be overcome. When we become people who rule ourselves, we can do as we think best. The earth is ours, not as a possession but as mother and child. We are held in it, we are fed by it, we care for it in our turn. Because we are in this place and in this time we have a duty. We are called to do justice in the present. That duty falls on each of us. Everyone is called, every person living in the radical solitude of the mortal body.

We live in the knowledge of death. As democrats, we know what it is to face the prospect of our annihilation with courage. Because we are before death, life is imperative for us. We have a calling. God calls, the prophets call, the people in their divinity call to one another.

We may warm our hands before the ashes of old struggles. We may fire our hearts with the desire for justice in the future. Yet it is only in the present that we can rule ourselves. We are called not to endure but to overcome. In the song of that name, it is not the refrain "We shall overcome, someday" that we should sing; it is "We are not afraid today."

Appendix of imperatives

Have courage. Fear is your enemy, courage your weapon and your
defense. Walk proudly among your enemies.

Keep the open spaces of anarchy.

We are all of equal worth. Act accordingly.

Every right entails a command, an obligation, a duty.

People have a right to self-preservation, to life. Therefore they have
a right to food, to shelter, and to healthcare. We are called both to
demand and to provide these.

People have the right to make themselves as they choose. They have
a right to education, to the tools for their work. They have the
right to move. They have the duty to open the world to others.

Undo empires. Decolonize.

Your rights are yours. They do not depend on legal recognition.
Seize them.

Your rights move with your body into the school, the factory, the
job site, the church, the masjid, and the synagogue, on the road,
in private and in public space. Do not ask permission to exercise
them. Obey their commands.

Assemble. In the flesh, on the internet. You need not ask permission.

Don't begrudge taxes. Taxes are how we pay for the work we do
together.

Judge. Judge the laws, judge officials, judge others, judge yourself.

Defend the commons. Extend the commons.

Rule the law.

Support no war you will not fight in yourself. Do not ask anyone to
die for you.

Tell the truth. Democracy depends on truth.

Truth depends on democracy. No media or news source should be concentrated in a few hands or controlled by any concentrated power: not by the state, not by the wealthy.

Sing.

Acknowledgments

I have debts to both the living and the dead. The Declaration of Independence, the writings of the Levellers, the Swabian peasants who gave us their *Twelve Theses*, Langston Hughes, Vachel Lindsay, Philip Levine, Allen Ginsberg, e. e. cummings, Sheldon Wolin, Michael Rogin, Christopher Hill, and Eric Hobsbawm: people I have known in the flesh and people I have known only on paper are not among the living, and yet they live for me. Though she is dead now, the deep democratic sensibility of my mother lives in me, my sister, and my brother. She was the daughter of a coal miner and farmer, granddaughter of immigrant peasants from every corner of Europe, admirer of the Diné way. She came out of the open prairie of Illinois and kept that intimate immensity within her. She taught us democratic manners, a democratic ethic, and democratic principles. My father taught me what honor is among free people. He was a sailor who became an officer, a captain of ships at war who came to mourn the lives he had taken. When I saw him, I saw Hector, who took off his plumed helmet so it would not frighten a child. I watched him live with courage and passion, love and generosity. He taught me poetry, Japanese aesthetics, and the shape of stories, to give with an open hand, and to reach for courage.

When I look back on what I have written I see Adolph Reed, Rogers Smith, Asim Qureshi, Bruce Kapferer, Thorvald Sirnes, Neil Roberts, Jane Gordon, Lewis Gordon, Drucilla Cornell, Uday Mehta, Jeff Green, Michael Hanchard, Eve Troutt Powell, Jim Johnson, Jeffrey Tulis, Sami al-Arian, James Scott, Joan Scott, Murad Idris, Rob Nichols, Wendy Brown, Judith Butler, Joe Lowndes, Kevin Bruyneel, K-Sue Park, Elizabeth Anker, Victoria Hattam, and Deborah Harrold in the pages of this book. I know I have not done them justice or honored their work properly. I fear there are those I have forgotten. Joan Scott, Laurie Balfour, Aisha Ghani, Timothy Pachirat, Jeff Green, Rogers Smith, and

Jim Morone read versions of the book and guided me to its present form. Ruth O'Brien and Angela Chnapko are sorcerors of publishing, swift and daring. Didier Fassin, Bonnie Honig, Susan Buck-Morss, and Seyla Benhabib, unsurprisingly, surprised me with wisdom at critical moments. Massimiliano Tomba and Banu Bargu remade my world. Together in Princeton, we shared food and thought, laughter and struggle, work, transgression, and love for Teo. None of my work will have their learning and scholarship, but it will carry their thinking all the same.

Seminars at the University of California–Santa Cruz, the Graduate Center of the City University of New York, Deakin University, the University of Bergen, Columbia University, the University of Virginia, the University of Calgary, and the Center for Islam and Global Studies at Sabahattin Zaim University contributed to this work in ways that leave me in their debt. The Institute for Advanced Study gave me time, a home, new thinking, and new people. I have never been at a better place. That was the year of Brood X. The rising of the cicadas sounds like the sea. They come out of the ground en masse, they change, they fly. They renew the world. I learned from the cicadas as Whitman learned from the grass.

The people closest to this book have been the graduate students I worked with in these years, especially Andrew Barnard, Yara Damaj, Rosie DuBrin, Mackenzie Fierceton, Ashley Gorham, Archana Kaku, Juman Kim, Gregory Koutnik, Clancy Murray, Gabriel Salgado, Miranda Sklaroff, and Kimberly White. They will light their time in their own ways.

Notes

I

1. Abraham Lincoln, "The Perpetuation of Our Political Institutions: Address before the Young Men's Lyceum of Springfield, Illinois," January 27, 1838. http://abrahamlincolnonline.org/lincoln/speeches/lyceum.htm.
2. Timothy Mitchell, *Rule of Experts* (Berkeley: University of California Press, 2002).
3. Wendy Brown, *In the Ruins of Neoliberalism: The Rise of Antidemocratic Politics in the West* (New York: Columbia University Press, 2019), 25.
4. Alexis de Tocqueville, *Democracy in America*, trans. George Lawrence, ed. J. P. Mayer (New York: Harper Collins, 2006), vol. 2, part 4, chap. 1, 667.
5. Xenophon, "Hiero, or On Tyranny," in Leo Strauss, *On Tyranny* (Ithaca, NY: Cornell University Press, 1963), 7. Xenophon holds, against Derrida, that it is tyranny, not democracy, that is "autoimmune" and inevitably calls forth its own destruction.
6. Hannah Arendt, *Origins of Totalitarianism* (New York: Harcourt Brace Jovanovich, 1979), 430, 431, 432–433.
7. Patrick Henry, speech in the Virginia Ratifying Convention, June 5, 1788, in *The Anti-Federalist: Writings by the Opponents of the Constitution*, ed. Herbert J. Storing (Chicago: University of Chicago Press, 1985), 305.
8. Walt Whitman, "Song of the Broad-Axe," in *Walt Whitman: The Complete Poems*, ed. Francis Murphy (New York: Penguin, 1979), 219.
9. James Scott has written many important and fascinating books on the power of the state and how people evade it. Two of my favorites are *Weapons of the Weak: Everyday Forms of Peasant Resistance* (New Haven, CT: Yale University Press, 1987) and *The Art of Not Being Governed: An Anarchist History of Upland Southeast Asia* (New Haven, CT: Yale University Press, 2010). Christopher Hill, *Liberty against the Law: Some Seventeenth Century Controversies* (New York: Viking, 1996); Eric Hobsbawm, *Bandits* (1969; New York: New Press, 2000); Paul Gilroy, *The Black Atlantic: Modernity and Double Consciousness* (Cambridge, MA: Harvard University Press, 1993).
10. Hobsbawm, *Bandits*; Scott, *The Art of Not Being Governed*.

11. Woody Guthrie, "Pretty Boy Floyd," 1958, https://www.woodyguthrie.org/Lyrics/Pretty_Boy_Floyd.htm. Thanks to Jim Morone for this song.

12. Marcus Rediker, *Villains of All Nations: Atlantic Pirates in the Golden Age* (Boston: Beacon Press, 2005); Colin Woodard, *The Republic of Pirates: Being the True and Surprising Story of the Caribbean Pirates and the Man Who Brought Them Down* (Orlando: Harcourt, 2007).

13. Jacques Rancière, *Hatred of Democracy*, trans. Steve Corcoran (New York: Verso, 2006); Thaddeus Russell, *A Renegade History of the United States* (New York: Free Press, 2010), viiii.

14. Russell, *A Renegade History of the United States*, xii.

15. Vachel Lindsay, "Honor among Scamps," in *Selected Poems of Vachel Lindsay*, ed. Mark Harris (New York: Macmillan, 1963), 107.

16. "The demos is thus never very far away when one speaks of a *voyou*. Nor is democracy far from *voyoucratie*." Jacques Derrida, *Rogues: Two Essays on Reason*, trans. Michael Naas and Pascale-Anne Brault (Stanford, CA: Stanford University Press, 2005), 64. I discuss Derrida's position in more detail in the chapter "Democracy" in *On the Muslim Question* (Princeton, NJ: Princeton University Press, 2013), 118–137.

17. Robert Burns, "A Man's a Man for a' That," 1795, http://www.robertburns.org/works/496.shtml.

18. Sheldon Wolin, "Violence and the Western Political Tradition," *American Journal of Orthopsychiatry* 33, no. 1 (January 1963): 15–28. This rather obscure article is clear and prescient.

19. G. W. F. Hegel, *The Philosophy of History*, trans. J. Sibree (New York: Dover, 1956), 91.

20. Hegel, *The Philosophy of History*, 86–87.

21. This thesis echoes an essay I wrote to honor Sheldon Wolin. I hope that it carries within it my enduring respect and affection for that great democrat and brings something of his clear-sightedness to those who read it. Anne Norton, "Eveningland," in *Democracy and Vision: Sheldon Wolin and the Vicissitudes of the Political*, ed. Aryeh Botwinick and William Connolly (Princeton, NJ: Princeton University Press, 2001), 161–170.

II

1. In addition to his effort to make Washington king, an offer Washington refused, Hamilton made no secret of his ambition to make the new United States an empire "to rival Europe." Jay was a rich merchant who shared

Hamilton's interest in fostering the growth of a wealthy elite and national capital. Madison, whose ambitions were more moderate than Hamilton's, and who distrusted capital, was an early advocate of the American Colonization Society, which sought to send African Americans back to Africa.

2. Patrick Henry, quoted in Storing, *The Antifederalist*, 305.

3. Patrick Henry, quoted in Storing, *The Antifederalist*, 305.

4. Charles Tilly, "War-Making and State-making as Organized Crime," in *Bringing the State Back In*, ed. Peter Evans, Dietrich Rueschemeyer, and Theda Skocpol (Cambridge: Cambridge University Press, 1985), 171..

5. Constitution of the United States of America, Article 1, section 8.

6. Washington's Farewell Address is included in the collection of presidential speeches available from the Miller Center at the University of Virginia, https://millercenter.org/the-presidency/presidential-speeches/september-19-1796-farewell-address.

7. The literatures on the indigenous and on settler colonialism are astonishingly rich, and growing. I am especially indebted to the work of Kevin Bruyneel, Glenn Coulthard, Pekka Hämäläinen, Robert Nichols, K-Sue Park, and Patrick Wolfe and to conversations with the Pueblo and Navajo Diné.

8. On the history of the Lakota, see Pekka Hämäläinen, *Lakota America: A New History of Indigenous Power* (New Haven, CT: Yale University Press, 2019). On Standing Rock, see their website: https://standwithstandingrock.net/oceti-sakowin/.

9. Theodore Roosevelt, *The Strenuous Life* (Bedford, MA: Applewood Books, 1991).Note the entanglement of the desire for glory with the subjection of women in Roosevelt's account, 13, 22, 24, 16.

10. *Congressional Record: Senate*, January 9, 1900, 704–712.

11. *Congressional Record: Senate*, March 7, 1900, 2620. See also 2616–2630.

12. *Congressional Record: Senate,* January 9, 1900, 712. Recognition of the legacy of settler colonialism should not erase the work of those who opposed it.

13. "Bryan's Address on Imperialism," in *William Jennings Bryan: Selections*, ed. Ray Ginger (Indianapolis: Bobbs-Merrill 1967), 66–67. See also Ho Chi Minh, "Declaration of Independence of the Democratic Republic of Vietnam," September 2, 1945, https://shafr.org/sites/default/files/Ho%20Chi%20Minh-Declaration%20of%20Independence.pdf. It could have been otherwise.

14. Friedrich Nietzsche, "Prelude in Rhymes," in *The Gay Science*, trans. Walter Kaufmann (New York: Vintage Random House, 1974), 53.

15. Rudyard Kipling, "The Cat That Walked by Himself," in *Just-So Stories*, n.d., http://www.boop.org/jan/justso/cat.htm. Kipling's story is a version of the myth of the social contract, particularly the version Carole Pateman called "the sexual contract." Carole Pateman, *The Sexual Contract* (Stanford, CA: Stanford University Press, 1988). This appears in its clearest form in Rousseau's "Discourse on Political Economy." Jean-Jacques Rousseau, *The Social Contract, with the Geneva Manuscript and Political Economy*, trans. Judith R. Master, ed. Roger Masters (New York: Bedford, St. Martin's Press, 1978). Freud (himself a contractarian of sorts) called these "just-so stories." Kipling's version follows Rousseau's very closely but deserves more attention for its treatment of the ambiguities of consent and for its recognition of the possibility of the preservation of individual freedom.

16. Niccoló Machiavelli, *The Prince*, trans. and ed. Mark Musa (New York: St. Martin's Press, 1964), 37–39.

17. Rousseau, *The Social Contract*, 56.

18. Walt Whitman, "Song of Myself," in Murphy, *Walt Whitman*, 68.

19. Bob Marley, "Cornerstone," on *In Memoriam*, 1974.

III

1. *Summa Theologica*, Article 7, Reply to objection 2 and passim.

2. Thomas Rainsborough, quoted in *The Putney Debates* (New York: Verso), 69.

3. Malik el Shabazz (Malcolm X), "Message to the Grassroots," December 10, 1963, Black Past, https://www.blackpast.org/african-american-hist ory/speeches-african-american-history/1963-malcolm-x-message-gra ssroots/.

4. Sternchenproductions, "Solidarity with the People of Egypt," YouTube, January 29, 2011, https://www.youtube.com/watch?v=7hBV0ApIh_4.

5. Victor Turner, *The Ritual Process: Structure and Antistructure* (Ithaca, NY: Cornell University Press, 1977).

6. Simone Weil, *The Need for Roots: Prelude to a Declaration of Duties towards Mankind*, trans. Arthur Wills (London: Routledge, 2002), 43, 44, 4, 52.

7. Weil, *The Need for Roots*, 43, 44, 4, 52. Weil is astute in her recognition of the destructive effects dependence on money has on individuals, and imperialism has on nations. Her preference for settler colonialism is less discerning. ("There is a minimum of uprootedness when the conquerors are migrants who settle down in the conquered country" [44].)

8. Frederick Douglass, "My Bondage and My Freedom," in *Frederick Douglass: Autobiographies*, ed. Henry Louis Gates (New York: Library of America, 1994). See also David Owen, *What We Owe to Refugees* (Cambridge, UK: Polity Press, 2020) and Joseph Carens, *Culture, Citizenship, and Community: A Contextual Exploration of Justice as Evenhandedness* (New York: Oxford University Press, 2000).

9. Rogers Smith, "Living in a Promiseland?: Mexican Immigration and American Obligations," *Perspectives on Politics* 9, no. 3 (September 2011): 545–557.

10. Thomas Paine, *Common Sense*, in *Common Sense, Rights of Man, and Other Essential Writings* (New York: Penguin, 2003), 90.

11. I am grateful to Danielle Hanley for sharing this piece of Talmudic wisdom.

IV

1. Legal Information Institute, Dred Scott, Plaintiff in Error, v. John F. A. Sandford, 60 U.S. 393 (1865), https://www.law.cornell.edu/supremecourt/text/60/393.

2. Buck v. Bell, 274 U.S. 200 (1927), https://www.oyez.org/cases/1900-1940/274us200. Oyez.com, "a free law project from Cornell's Legal Information Institute (LII), Justia, and Chicago-Kent College of Law—is a multimedia archive devoted to making the Supreme Court of the United States accessible to everyone."

3. See Kim Scheppele, "Facing Facts in Legal Interpretation," *Representations* 30 (Spring 1990): 41–77.

4. Korematsu v. United States, 323 U.S. 214 (1944), https://www.law.cornell.edu/supremecourt/text/323/214.

5. James Baldwin, "In Occupied Territory," *The Nation*, July 11, 1966, https://www.thenation.com/article/archive/report-occupied-territory-2/.

6. John Locke, *Two Treatises of Government*, ed. Peter Laslett (Cambridge: Cambridge University Press, 1988),Second Treatise, II: 240, p. 427.

7. "Freedom's Plow," in *Collected Poems of Langston Hughes*, ed. Arnold Rampersand (New York: Knopf 1994), 265–266. If you have not read this poem, read the whole.

8. Didier Fassin, *The Will to Punish* (New York: Oxford University Press, 2018), esp. 120–125; Marie Gottschalk, *The Prison and the Gallows: The*

Politics of Mass Incarceration in America (New York: Cambridge University Press, 2006).

9. I am grateful to Asher Wycoff for reminding me that people make laws not only to achieve justice and the fullness of their rights but to make themselves. Alien laws do not command.

10. Marcuse, "Repressive Tolerance," 82, 81.

11. George Washington, "Letter to the Hebrew Congregation in Newport, Rhode Island, 18 August 1790," Founders Online, https://founders.archi ves.gov/documents/Washington/05-06-02-0135.

12. ibid.

13. Carl Schmitt, *Political Theology*, trans. George Schwab (Chicago: University of Chicago Press, 2005), 3.

14. Aristotle, *The Politics*, trans. Carnes Lord (Chicago: University of Chicago Press, 1984), book 3, chapter 11, 100–101. I thank Ashley Gorham for reminding me of this passage. The attentive reader may find, as I have, that this passage, echoed in Al-Farabi, can be read with a more democratic inflection. Aristotle anticipates objections to his arguments and notes his own doubts about whether the excellence of the multitude might equal (or surpass) that of excellent men, and whether there might be some multitudes who are no better than beasts.

15. Al Farabi, *Alfarabi: The Political Writings*, trans. and annotated by Charles E. Butterworth (Ithaca, NY: Cornell University Press, 2001), Aphorism 57.

16. Al Farabi, *Alfarabi*, Aphorism 10.

17. Cade Metz, "Oh, the Monotony of Shifting the Tedium to A.I.," *New York Times*, August 18, 2019, Business sec., 1.

18. Metz, "Oh, the Monotony," 5. For a fuller and quite different approach to this question, see Hélène Landemore, *Democratic Reason: Politics, Collective Intelligence, and the Rule of the Many* (Princeton, NJ: Princeton University Press, 2012).

19. William Jennings Bryan, or so the poet says that he said. I cannot find this phrase in Bryan, so I credit Vachel Lindsay, in his poem "Bryan, Bryan, Bryan."

20. I am grateful to James Morone for pointing this fact out to me.

21. This thesis and the one that follows were prompted by Sophie Rosenfeld's *Democracy and Truth: A Short History* (Philadelphia: University of Pennsylvania Press, 2018).

22. Bob Drogin, "'The Great Successor' Paints a Macabre Portrait of Kim Jong Un," *Baltimore Sun*, August 24, 2019, www.baltimoresun.com/great-succes

sor-kim-jong-un-anna-fifield-review-story.html; See also Anna Fifield, *The Great Successor* (New York: Hachette, 2019); Julian Ryall, "The Incredible Kim Jong-il and His Amazing Achievements," *The Telegraph*, January 31, 2011, https://www.telegraph.co.uk/news/worldnews/asia/nor thkorea/8292848/The-Incredible-Kim-Jong-il-and-his-Amazing-Achie vements.html.

V

1. Plato, *The Republic of Plato*, trans. Allan Bloom (New York: Basic Books, 1968), 557a.
2. Plato, *The Republic*, 557c. Those translations, including Bloom's, that give the Greek as "fair" undermine the condemnation of surface beauty by acknowledging the presence of justice.
3. It is Thrasymachus, an aristocrat with an aggressive, even tyrannical disposition, who objects to the simple life initially proposed in the *Republic*. His objection moves the dialogue from the never rejected but much disdained "city of pigs" to the elaborate, hierarchical, and rigid constructions of the later Republic.
4. The democratic possibilities of revealed religion are visible in Michel Walzer, *Revolution of the Saints: A Study in the Origins of Radical Politics* (Cambridge, MA: Harvard University Press, 1982) and *Exodus and Revolution* (New York: Basic Books, 1986), in the writings of Thomas Müntzer, in the Putney Debates, and in liberation theology, among many other places.
5. Al Farabi, "The Political Regime," trans. Fauzi Najjar, in *Medieval Political Philosophy*, ed. Ralph Lerner and Muhsin Mahdi (New York: Collier Macmillan, 1963), 51.
6. Nietzsche, *Genealogy of Morals*, Second Essay: 10.
7. Walt Whitman, "Song of Myself," in Murphy, *Walt Whitman*, 123.
8. *Twelve Articles of the Swabian Peasantry*, in *The Revolution of 1525: The German Peasants' War from a New Perspective*, ed. Peter Bickle, Thomas A. Brady Jr., and H. C. Eric Midelfort (Baltimore, MD: Johns Hopkins University Press, 1982).
9. Judith Butler, *Precarious Life: The Powers of Mourning and Violence* (New York: Verso, 2006).
10. Philip Baker, ed., *The Putney Debates* (New York: Verso, 2007), 69.

11. Ireton was clear. It was only those "who had a permanent and fixed interest in this kingdom," that is to say, those with property, wealth, or title, who should have any "interest or share" in governance. *The Levellers and The Putney Debates*, ed. Philip Baker (New York: Verso, 2007), 69–70.

12. Plato, *Republic*, 557a.

13. Ibn Khaldun, *Muqaddimah*, trans. Franz Rosenthal (Princeton, NJ: Princeton University Press, 2005).

14. W. E. B. DuBois, *Souls of Black Folk*. See also Anne Norton, "Law Breaker," in *A Political Companion to Frederick Douglass*, ed. Neil Roberts (Lexington: University of Kentucky Press, 2018), for an account of the role of precarity in Douglass's reconception of the democratic subject.

15. Uday Mehta, "Liberal Strategies of Exclusion," *Politics & Society* 18, no. 4 (December 1990): 427–454. See also Uday Mehta, *Liberalism and Empire* (Chicago: University of Chicago Press, 1999).

16. David Graeber, *Fragments of an Anarchist Anthropology* (Chicago: Prickly Paradigm Press, University of Chicago Press, 2004), 26.

17. The autocrat, Xenophon and Arendt variously remind us, breeds fear. See Xenophon's "Hiero" in Leo Strauss, *On Tyranny* (Chicago: University of Chicago Press, 2000); Hannah Arendt, *Origins of Totalitarianism* (New York: Harcourt, Brace Jovanovich, 1973).

18. Plato, *Republic*, 463a.

VI

1. Deborah Harrold provided this clear and succinct description.

2. Langston Hughes, "Freedom's Plow," in *The Collected Poems of Langston Hughes*, ed. Arnold Rampersad (New York: Alfred A. Knopf, 1994), 264.

3. Thomas Paine, "The Necessity of Taxation," April 4, 1782, Thomas Paine National Historical Association, https://thomaspaine.org/recently-dis covered/the-necessity-of-taxation.html.

4. This is an ideal and imperative I was taught by the Diné, also called the Navajo.

5. Anand Giridharadas discusses this with ruthless and revealing clarity in *Winners Take All: The Elite Charade of Changing the World* (New York: Alfred A. Knopf, 2018).

VII

1. Al Farabi, "The Political Regime," 51.
2. Hughes, "Freedom's Plow," 267.
3. The first reference is to the principle of *ijma*, an endorsement of popular sovereignty and the capacity for judgment in the Muslim tradition. It is echoed in the second reference, which comes from the Christian tradition.
4. For an account of this in the United States, see Sanford Levinson, *Our Undemocratic Constitution: Where the Constitution Goes Wrong (and How We the People Can Correct It)* (New York: Oxford University Press, 2006).
5. See Wendy Brown's brilliant critique of best practices in *Undoing the Demos: Neoliberalism's Stealth Revolution* (New York: Zone Books, 2015). This is a profoundly practical and democratic book.
6. Jacques Derrida, *On Grammatology,* trans. Gayatri Chakravorty Spivak (Baltimore, MD: Johns Hopkins University Press, 1976).
7. These processes have been usefully described by a number of theorists, notably Michel Foucault. Deleuze and Guattari's account of the rhizomatic takes on a darker and less emancipatory form in this context. Gilles Deleuze and Felix Guattari, *A Thousand Plateaus,* trans. Brian Massumi (Minneapolis: University of Minnesota Press, 2002).
8. https://www.thelocal.es/20190221/spains-king-felipe-speaks-out-dur ing-catalan-separatists-trial.
9. John Rawls, *The Law of Peoples* (Cambridge, MA: Harvard University Press, 1993), 64–68.
10. One of the few who calls himself a populist and maintains the policies and memory—and intellectual genealogy—of the People's Party is Jim Hightower of Texas (jimhightower.com). Hightower's popularity in Texas, along with that of the late Molly Ivins, should prompt people to reconsider their view of Texas as a conservative state.
11. See, for example, Jan-Werner Mueller, *What Is Populism?* (Philadelphia: University of Pennsylvania Press, 2016).
12. Sheldon Wolin, *Democracy, Inc: Managed Democracy and the Specter of Inverted Totalitarianism* (Princeton, NJ: Princeton University Press, 2008).
13. Sheldon Wolin, "Violence and the Western Political Tradition," *American Journal of Orthopsychiatry* 33, no. 1 (January 1963): 15–28.
14. Levinson provides an example of how to do this in his book *Our Undemocratic Constitution.*
15. Scott, *Weapons of the Weak.*
16. Scott, *The Art of Not Being Governed,* 9.

17. Massimiliano Tomba, *Insurgent Universality*, 10.
18. Thanks to Tariq Thachil, who showed this handwritten set of electoral rules to me.

VIII

1. Sanford Levinson, "The Embarrassing Second Amendment," *Yale Law Journal* 99 (1989): 637–659.
2. Weil, *The Need for Roots*, 296.
3. Weil, *The Need for Roots*, 296.

IX

1. Jacques Rancière, *Hatred of Democracy*, trans. Steve Corcoran (New York: Verso, 2006), 73–74. As Rancière writes, our freedoms "were won through democratic action and are only ever guaranteed through such action."
2. Kathleen Davis, *Periodization and Sovereignty* (Philadelphia: University of Pennsylvania Press, 2008), 7. I take "feudalism," as Davis does, as a recursive political category and concur in her judgment that the term "feudal" has functioned as a strategy of denial in a proud modernity, fixing disavowed hierarchies in the past as it veiled their presence in the present.
3. Karen Orren, *Belated Feudalism: Labor, the Law, and Liberal Development in the United States* (New York: Cambridge University Press, 1991), 2. Michael Hanchard suggests the term "feudality" to describe the enduring laws, institutions, practices, and dispositions that carry feudal servitude through the centuries into the present.
4. Orren, *Belated Feudalism*.
5. Anne Norton, *Bloodrites of the Poststructuralists: Word, Flesh and Revolution* (London: Routledge, 2002).
6. The present moment is seeing an efflorescence of work on the genealogies of race. Gabriel Salgado is giving a genealogy of race in Latin America, charting how the blood purity laws of the Inquisition were transformed into the racial regimes of colonial and postcolonial rule.
7. There is a large and powerful literature on race and science. I particularly commend the work of Dorothy Roberts and Adolph Reed.

8. Max Weber, "Politics as a Vocation," in *From Max Weber: Essays in Sociology*, ed. Hans Gerth and C. Wright Mills (New York: Oxford University Press, 1946), 128.

9. Hughes, "Freedom's Plow," 267.

10. Tzvetan Todorov, *The Conquest of America*, trans. Richard Howard (New York: Harper & Row, 1982), v.

X

1. I am grateful to the Ghanaian student who pointed this out to his astonished classmates in my seminar some years ago. I am ashamed to say I have forgotten his last name. His first name is Justice.

2. For a fuller and more scholarly discussion, see Demetra Kasimis, *The Perpetual Immigrant: Athenian Democracy* (Cambridge: Cambridge University Press, 2018).

3. David Graeber and David Wengrow, *The Dawn of Everything: A New History of Humanity* (New York: Farrar, Strauss Giroux, 2021).

4. Massimiliano Tomba, *Insurgent Universalities: An Alternative Legacy of Modernity* (New York: Oxford University Press, 2019). This book gives us hope and reason for hope. It teaches what has been built and how it might be built again.

5. John Locke, Second Treatise on Government.

6. Locke, Second Treatise on Government.

7. Famous correctives were offered by Carole Pateman in *The Sexual Contract* (Stanford, CA: Stanford University Press, 1988) and Charles Mills in *The Racial Contract* (Ithaca, NY: Cornell University Press, 1999).

8. Tomba, *Insurgent Universality*, 154–159 on the *mir*, 71–119 on the Commune.

XI

1. Quoted in Aristide Zolberg, "Moments of Madness," *Politics and Society* 2, no. 2 (1972): 183–207.

2. Zolberg, "Moments of Madness," 185.

3. Henri Lefèbvre, *La Proclamation de la Commune 26 mars 1871* (Paris: Gallimard, 1965), 11.

4. Lefebvre, *Proclamation*, 389.
5. Lefebvre, *Proclamation*, 390, 389.
6. Quoted in Zolberg, "Moments of Madness," 195.
7. Henry, speech in the Virginia Ratifying Convention, June 5, 1788, 305.
8. I am grateful to Michael Lamb for his work on Augustine, and what it taught me.
9. AFSCME, " 'I've Been to the Mountaintop' by Dr. Martin Luther King, Jr.," April 3, 1968, 6. https://www.afscme.org/union/history/mlk/ive-been-to-the-mountaintop-by-dr-martin-luther-king-jr. That which makes you part of a people gives you a future beyond your life and opens the possibility of political transcendence.

XII

1. Thomas Paine, *Common Sense, The Rights of Man, and Other Essential Writings of Thomas Paine* (New York: Penguin, 1984), 142. Paine was referring to Matthew 3:10.
2. Wendell Berry, *The Art of the Commonplace: The Agrarian Essays of Wendell Berry* (Berkeley, CA: Counterpoint, 2003), 58.
3. The project was the thought and work of Gunter Demnig. It is one of the most brilliant and thoughtful artistic works I have ever seen. This is democratic art: speaking of the many to the many, calling each passerby to judge.
4. Honor the stories and visions of the flying African. See Henry Louis Gates and Maria Tatar, eds., *The Annotated African American Folktales* (New York: W. W. Norton, 2018), 73–83; Rhiannon Giddens, "We Could Fly," on *Freedom Highway*, 2017.
5. Walt Whitman, "Song of Myself," in Murphy, *Walt Whitman*, 86.
6. Martin Luther King Jr., "I Have a Dream," speech at the Lincoln Memorial, August 28, 1963. https://www.archives.gov/files/social-media/transcripts/transcript-march-pt3-of-3-2602934.pdf. King is quoting scripture. Amos 5:24.

XIII

1. Thomas Müntzer, "Sermon to the Princes," in *Wu Ming Presents Thomas Müntzer* (New York: Verso, 2010), 4–5. As Müntzer noted, it is not always the religious who are given this gift. Like Müntzer, I have heard many

claim to speak to God, or claim that God has spoken to them, or that they have knowledge open only to believers, and watched as their conduct convicted them.

2. For an excellent discussion of the boss, see Elizabeth Anderson, *How Employers Rule Our Lives (and Why We Don't Talk About It)* (Princeton: Princeton University Press 2017).

3. Council of Europe, Commissioner for Human Rights, "Child Labour in Europe: A Persisting Challenge," August 20, 2013, https://www.coe.int/en/web/commissioner/-/child-labour-in-europe-a-persisting-challen-1.

4. Rancière refuses Arendt's distinction between political life and what Agamben has called "bare life" in Jacques Rancière, "Who Is the Subject of the Rights of Man?," *South Atlantic Quarterly* 103, nos. 2–3 (2004): 297–310.

5. Wendy Brown, *In the Ruins of Neoliberalism*, 47.

XIV

1. Brown, *In the Ruins of Neoliberalism*, 23.

2. Philip Baker, ed, *The Putney Debates* (New York: Verso, 2007), 69.

3. George Cruikshank and (probably) William Hone, *Political Alphabet*, a pamphlet published anonymously in 1820. Available from the British Library. Quoted in Eric Partridge, *Comic Alphabets* (New York: Routledge Revivals 2015), 35.

4. Friedrich Nietzsche, *The Gay Science,* trans. Walter Kaufmann (New York: Random House Vintage, 1974), section 61. I discuss friendship more extensively in Anne Norton, *Reflections on Political Identity* (Baltimore, MD: Johns Hopkins University Press, 1988), 35–37. It is telling that Jacques Derrida punctuates *The Politics of Friendship* with the apocryphal "Oh, friends, there is no friend!" *Politics of Friendship* (New York: Verso 2005), 1 and passim.

5. Havamal, http://www.publiclibrary.uk/ebooks/43/74.pdf, 5, 6. The Norse account, like that of Aristotle, acknowledges a hierarchy of friendships. I have changed the text slightly.

6. Aristotle, *Nichomachaean Ethics*, books 8 and 9.

7. Aristotle, *The Politics*, trans. Carnes Lord (Chicago: University of Chicago Press, 1984), 36.

8. Paine, *The Rights of Man*, 183–184, 185.

9. Paine, *The Rights of Man*, 233.

10. Karen Orren, *Belated Feudalism: Labor, the Law and Liberal Development* (New York: Cambridge University Press, 1992).

XV

1. Alexis de Tocqueville, *Democracy in America*, trans. George Lawrence, ed. J. P. Mayer (New York: Harper, 1988), 704.

2. e. e. cummings, "I sing of Olaf glad and big," in *e. e. cummings: Complete Poems 1904–1962*, ed. George J. Firmage (New York: Liveright, W. W. Norton, 2015), 362.

3. Albert Hourani, *Arabic Thought in the Liberal Age* (London: Oxford University Press 1962), 229–230. See also Nigel Coulson, *Conflicts and Tensions in Islamic Jurisprudence* (Chicago: University of Chicago Press 1969), 20–39.

4. Rousseau, *On the Social Contract*, ed. Roger Masters, Book 2, chapter 7 (New York: St. Martin's Press 1978), 68.

5. Rousseau, *Du contrat social*, book 1, chapter 8 (Oxford: Oxford University Press 1972), 119.

6. Schmitt, *Political Theology*, 49.

7. I learned this from Colin Zelicoff, whose work on music in politics taught me the power of singing in the civil rights movement. When he spoke to the late Congressman John Lewis about this, Lewis told him, "Without music, the civil rights movement was a bird without wings."

8. Reinhardt Koselleck, *Futures Past: The Semantics of Historical Time* (New York: Columbia University Press, 2004). This, perhaps, is the connection of the rule of the people to modernity. If, as Koselleck declared, modernity is the epoch that opens itself to the new then it is, at least at that one point, allied to the democratic.

Index

For the benefit of digital users, indexed terms that span two pages (e.g., 52–53) may, on occasion, appear on only one of those pages.